Epica Book 22
Europe's
Best Advertising

DIRECTOR
Andrew Rawlins

EDITOR
Patrick Taschler

ART DIRECTOR
Patrick Taschler

SYNOPSES
Mark Tungate

EDITORIAL ASSISTANT
Francelina Pacarić

COVER IMAGE
Tim Flach

PUBLISHER
AVA Publishing S.A.
enquiries@avabooks.ch

DISTRIBUTION
North America
Ingram Publisher Services
www.ingrampublisherservices.com
All other countries
Thames & Hudson Ltd.
www.thameshudson.co.uk

PRODUCTION
AVA Book Production Pte Ltd.
production@avabooks.com.sg

Printed in Singapore

EPICA S.A.

65 rue J.J. Rousseau,

92150 Suresnes, France

Tel: 33 (0) 1 42 04 04 32

Fax: 33 (0) 1 45 06 02 88

www.epica-awards.com
info@epica-awards.com

Epica S.A. has made every effort to publish full
and correct credits for each work included in this
volume based on the information provided on the
Epica entry forms. Epica S.A. and Applied Visual
Arts Publishing S.A. (AVA) regret any omissions
that may have occurred, but hereby disclaim
liability.

D

Contents

INTRODUCTION
Foreword by Amir Kassaei   5
2008 Winners   6
The Jury   8
Annual Report   10

GRAND PRIX 2008
Volkswagen Polo "Dog"   12
Marmite Snacks "LoveHate"   14
John Lewis "Shadows"   16
Absolut Vodka "Absolut Machines"   18
Turkcell Mobile Award "AMF Pension"   20

FOOD & DRINK
Food   22
Confectionery & Snacks   34
Dairy Products   40
Alcoholic Drinks   44
Non-Alcoholic Drinks   54

CONSUMER SERVICES
Communication Services   64
Transport & Tourism   74
Retail Services   84
Financial Services   98
Public Interest   106

THE HOME
Audiovisual Equipment & Accessories   132
Homes, Furnishings & Appliances   142
Household Maintenance   152

HEALTH & BEAUTY
Beauty Products & Services   164
Toiletries & Health Care   172

FASHION
Clothing & Fabrics   182
Footwear & Personal Accessories   194

AUTOMOTIVE
Automobiles   200
Automotive & Accessories   218

MEDIA & ENTERTAINMENT
Media   228
Recreation & Leisure   244

BUSINESS TO BUSINESS
Industrial & Agricultural Products   256
Professional Equipment & Services   260
Prescription Products   274

DIRECT MARKETING
Consumer Direct   278
Business to Business Direct   284

USE OF MEDIA
Media Innovation - Traditional Media   292
Media Innovation - Alternative Media   300

TECHNIQUES
Promotions & Incentives   314
Radio Advertising   322
Advertising Photography   326
Illustration & Graphics   334
Publications   346
Packaging Design   352

INTERACTIVE
Consumer Websites - Durables   362
Consumer Websites - Non-Durables   366
Business to Business Websites   372
Online Ads   374
Online Films   378
Integrated Campaigns   382

Amir Kassaei (Photographer: Oliver Helbig)

Foreword

by Amir Kassaei

At present we are living through one of the most radical but exciting periods in recent history.

It is not only the financial and economical crisis that is keeping the world in suspense. It is the speed with which it is undermining old structures and forcing new thinking.

We have reached the end of an era that has been driven by a policy of short-term gain and profit maximization. Now we are experiencing the beginning of a new era that spotlights innovation, creativity and sustainability.

Therefore, it is more important than ever to reward ideas that set standards beyond media and categories – standards for new thinking, for intelligent problem solving and for refreshing insights that affect people and markets.

The Epica Awards recognise exactly these sorts of ideas. And you can get an impression of their power and potential by leafing through this book.

Enjoy!

Amir Kassaei,
Chief Creative Officer, DDB Group, Germany

Epica d'Or (Film)

Epica d'Or (Press)

Epica d'Or (Outdoor)

Epica d'Or (Interactive)

EPICA D'OR (FILM)	DDB LONDON	VOLKSWAGEN POLO "DOG"
EPICA D'OR (PRESS)	DDB LONDON	MARMITE SNACKS "LOVEHATE" CAMPAIGN
EPICA D'OR (OUTDOOR)	LOWE LONDON	JOHN LEWIS "SHADOWS" CAMPAIGN
EPICA D'OR (INTERACTIVE)	GREAT WORKS, STOCKHOLM	ABSOLUT VODKA "ABSOLUT MACHINES"

FILM WINNERS

FOOD	LEO BURNETT, MILAN	KELLOGG'S COCO POPS "ANY GIVEN BREAKFAST"
CONFECTIONARY & SNACKS	JWT, PARIS	KITKAT "ULTIMATE BREAK"
DAIRY PRODUCTS	TRY ADVERTISING AGENCY, OSLO	TINE MILK "NO MILK TODAY"
ALCOHOLIC DRINKS	SELMORE, AMSTERDAM	BAVARIA BEER "LIFE"
NON-ALCOHOLIC DRINKS	WIEDEN+KENNEDY, AMSTERDAM	COCA COLA ZERO "TONGUES & EYEBALL LIAR"
COMMUNICATION SERVICES	PUBLICIS CONSEIL, PARIS	ORANGE "REWIND TV"
TRANSPORT & TOURISM	UPSET, ATHENS	AEGEAN AIRLINES "MORE GREEKS IN LONDON"
RETAIL SERVICES	DEMNER, MERLICEK & BERGMANN, VIENNA	MÖMAX "THROW THE SWEDES OUT"
FINANCIAL SERVICES	VELOCITY FILMS, CAPE TOWN	ALLAN GRAY FINANCIAL SERVICES "BEAUTIFUL"
PUBLIC INTEREST	MEDIA CONSULTA TV FILMPRODUKTION, BERLIN	EU & MARIE CURIE ACTIONS "CHEMICAL PARTY"
AUDIOVISUAL EQUIPMENT & ACCESSORIES	FALLON LONDON	SONY BRAVIA "PLAY DOH"
HOMES, FURNISHINGS & APPLIANCES	LA CHOSE, PARIS	IKEA "THE PENCIL"
HOUSEHOLD MAINTENANCE	SERVICEPLAN GROUP, MUNICH & HAMBURG	UHU "ONE-SECOND COMMERCIALS" CAMPAIGN
BEAUTY PRODUCTS & SERVICES	DDB LONDON	PHILIPS SATINELLE ICE EPILATOR "KARIS"
TOILETRIES & HEALTH CARE	SPECSAVERS CREATIVE, GUERNSEY	SPECSAVERS OPTICIANS "COLLIE WOBBLE"
CLOTHING & FABRICS	WIEDEN+KENNEDY, AMSTERDAM	NIKE WOMEN "SANDERS"
FOOTWEAR & PERSONAL ACCESSORIES	NEXUS PRODUCTIONS, LONDON	NOMIS FOOTBALL BOOTS "DAMN BOOTS"
AUTOMOBILES	DDB LONDON	VOLKSWAGEN POLO "DOG"
AUTOMOTIVE & ACCESSORIES	DDB LONDON	KWIK FIT GARAGES "BOY"
MEDIA (2 WINNERS)	LEO BURNETT, CAIRO	MELODY TUNES CHANNEL "MADONNA" & "PUSSYCAT DOLLS"
	DDB PARIS	GQ MAGAZINE "THE IDEAL MAN"
RECREATION & LEISURE	PUBLICIS YORUM, ISTANBUL	AKBANK JAZZ FESTIVAL "THE JAZZ OF THE CITY"
INDUSTRIAL & AGRICULTURAL PRODUCTS	VELOCITY FILMS, CAPE TOWN	SASOL CHEMICALS "QUESTIONS"
PROFESSIONAL EQUIPMENT & SERVICES	JWT, MOSCOW	SALVADOR-D PUBLIC RELATIONS "MICE vs HAMSTERS"

PRINT WINNERS

FOOD	DDB LONDON	MARMITE SNACKS "LOVEHATE" CAMPAIGN
CONFECTIONARY & SNACKS	FHV BBDO, AMSTELVEEN	M&Ms "KEYBOARD"
DAIRY PRODUCTS	THE SYNDICATE, ATHENS	DODONI ICE CREAM "DELICIOUS FLAGS" CAMPAIGN
ALCOHOLIC DRINKS	McCANN ERICKSON, TEL-AVIV	GOLDSTAR BEER "FLOW CHART"
NON-ALCOHOLIC DRINKS	EURO RSCG, LONDON	EVIAN "THE OTHER WATER" CAMPAIGN
COMMUNICATION SERVICES	GREY WORLDWIDE, DUBAI	YELLOW PAGES CAMPAIGN
TRANSPORT & TOURISM	LEG, PARIS	EUROSTAR "LONDON AT A HALLUCINATING PRICE"
RETAIL SERVICES	LOWE LONDON	JOHN LEWIS "SHADOWS" CAMPAIGN
FINANCIAL SERVICES	FORSMAN & BODENFORS, GOTHENBURG	AMF PENSION "MMS" CAMPAIGN
PUBLIC INTEREST	UNCLE GREY, AARHUS	WWF "TARZAN"
AUDIOVISUAL EQUIPMENT & ACCESSORIES	ADVICO YOUNG & RUBICAM, ZURICH	ROWEN SPEAKERS "MUSICAL INSTRUMENTS" CAMPAIGN
HOMES, FURNISHINGS & APPLIANCES	JUNG VON MATT, HAMBURG	BOSCH CORDLESS SCREWDRIVER "FLY"
HOUSEHOLD MAINTENANCE	GREY, ISTANBUL	ACE HOUSEHOLD BLEACH "WHITE WINS"
BEAUTY PRODUCTS & SERVICES	SAATCHI & SAATCHI, MOSCOW	OLAY CREAM "CORRECT YOUR AGE" CAMPAIGN
TOILETRIES & HEALTH CARE	SAATCHI & SAATCHI, GENEVA & MILAN	OTRIVIN NASAL SPRAY "HOUNDS" CAMPAIGN
CLOTHING & FABRICS	PUBLICIS CONSEIL, PARIS	WONDERBRA "FATHERS & SONS" CAMPAIGN
FOOTWEAR & PERSONAL ACCESSORIES	NEW MOMENT NEW IDEAS CO. Y&R, BELGRADE	STRADA SHOES "LITTLE BLACK DRESS"
AUTOMOBILES	BBDO, DÜSSELDORF	MERCEDES-BENZ "READ THE STREET" CAMPAIGN
AUTOMOTIVE & ACCESSORIES	DDB GERMANY, BERLIN	VOLKSWAGEN NAVIGATION SYSTEM "THAT WAY" CAMPAIGN
MEDIA	DDB GERMANY, DÜSSELDORF	PREMIERE PAY TV "MOVIE QUOTES" CAMPAIGN
RECREATION & LEISURE	LEAGAS DELANEY, ROME	BLOODBUSTER MOVIE STORE CAMPAIGN
INDUSTRIAL & AGRICULTURAL PRODUCTS	WÄCHTER & WÄCHTER, BREMEN	HEINEN FREEZING SYSTEMS "LIGHTER" & "MATCH"
PROFESSIONAL EQUIPMENT & SERVICES	RUF LANZ WERBEAGENTUR, ZURICH	McKINSEY & COMPANY "RECRUITING ENGINEERS"
PRESCRIPTION PRODUCTS	SENTRIX GLOBAL HEALTH COM., MILAN	NYCOMED INSTANYL "CANCER PAIN" CAMPAIGN

TECHNIQUE WINNERS

CONSUMER DIRECT	JUNG VON MATT, HAMBURG	IKEA "3D COVER"
BUSINESS TO BUSINESS DIRECT	DUVAL GUILLAUME, ANTWERP	SCOTTEX "THE STRENGTH OF SCOTTEX" MAILING
MEDIA INNOVATION - TRADITIONAL MEDIA	BETC EURO RSCG, PARIS	E-BAY "THE AD AUCTION"
MEDIA INNOVATION - ALTERNATIVE MEDIA	MORTIERBRIGADE, BRUSSELS	STUDIO BRUSSEL MUSIC FOR LIFE "THIRSTY BLACK BOY"
PROMOTIONS & INCENTIVES	UNCLE GREY, AARHUS	FAKTA "STAY LONGER" IN-STORE OPERATIONS
RADIO ADVERTISING	DDB GERMANY, BERLIN	IKEA "PRICES" CAMPAIGN
ADVERTISING PHOTOGRAPHY	OGILVY & MATHER, PARIS	LOUIS VUITTON "VOYAGE" CAMPAIGN
ILLUSTRATION & GRAPHICS	YOUNG & RUBICAM, PARIS	RADIO NOVA "LE GRAND MIX" CAMPAIGN
PUBLICATION DESIGN	YURKO GUTSULYAK GRAPHIC DESIGN, KIEV	VS ENERGY INTERNATIONAL "ENERGY CALENDAR"
PACKAGING DESIGN	LOVE, MANCHESTER	SILVER CROSS PACKAGING "BIG BOXES, SMALL KIDS"

INTERACTIVE WINNERS

CONSUMER WEBSITES - DURABLES	FORSMAN & BODENFORS, GOTHENBURG	IKEA "COME INTO THE CLOSET. LET'S DANCE"
CONSUMER WEBSITES - NON-DURABLES	GREAT WORKS, STOCKHOLM	ABSOLUT VODKA "ABSOLUT MACHINES"
BUSINESS TO BUSINESS WEBSITES	BLACKBELTMONKEY, HAMBURG	BLACKBELTMONKEY WEBSITE
ONLINE ADS	SERVICEPLAN GROUP, MUNICH & HAMBURG	YAQU PACHA NGO "SAVE THE OCEAN" SCREENSAVER
ONLINE FILMS	ABSTRACT GROOVE, MILAN	DIESEL KID "EXPLORERS OF THE PAST AND FUTURE"
INTEGRATED CAMPAIGNS	TBWA\GERMANY, BERLIN	ABSOLUT VODKA "IN AN ABSOLUT WORLD 08" CAMPAIGN

The jury

The Epica jury is made up of journalists from leading advertising magazines in Europe and the EMEA region. A total of 34 publications from 27 countries were represented on the jury in 2008.

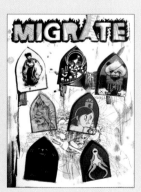

AUSTRIA
Extra Dienst

BELGIUM
Pub

CZECH REPUBLIC
Strategie

DENMARK
Markedsføring

ESTONIA
Best Marketing

FINLAND
Markkinointi & Mainonta

FRANCE
CB News

GERMANY
Lürzer's International Archive
Werben und Verkaufen

GREAT BRITAIN
Creative Review
Marketing Week
The Drum

GREECE
+ Design
Marketing Week

HUNGARY
Kreatív

IRELAND
IMJ

ITALY
ADV Strategie di Comunicazione
Pubblicitá Italia
Pubblico

LEBANON
ArabAd

THE NETHERLANDS
Marketing Tribune

NORWAY
Kampanje

POLAND
Media & Marketing Polska

PORTUGAL
Briefing

RUSSIA
Advertising Ideas

SERBIA
New Moment

SLOVAKIA
Stratégie

SLOVENIA
MM

SOUTH AFRICA
Migrate

SPAIN
El Publicista

SWEDEN
Resumé

SWITZERLAND
Persönlich
Werbe Woche

TURKEY
Marketing Türkiye

Photos: +design/Epica

Annual report

The awards ceremony took place in the Megaron Concert Hall, Athens, on January 23rd, 2009. The event was hosted by +design, Greece's leading bimonthly magazine devoted to advertising, graphic, web and industrial design.

In 2008 Epica received 4,945 entries from 664 companies in 51 countries.

DDB London won the film Epica d'Or with their Volkswagen Polo 'Dog' commercial, produced by Independent and directed by Noam Murro.

DDB London also won the press Epica d'Or with the Marmite Snacks 'LoveHate' campaign. This marked the first time that the same agency won two of Epica's top awards.

The outdoor Epica d'Or went to Lowe London for the John Lewis 'Shadows' campaign, shot by Nadav Kander.

Great Works, Stockholm, took the interactive grand prix with the Absolut vodka 'Absolut Machines' website.

The new Turkcell Mobile Award went to Forsman & Bodenfors, Gothenburg, for their AMF Pension campaign.

Germany was the most successful country in 2008, as it was the in the two previous years, with 12 winners. The UK moved back into second position, ahead of Sweden and France, while Ukraine and Egypt were both first-time winners.

DDB London was the only agency with 4 winners, 2 of which also won grand prix. DDB Germany had 3 winners, 7 silver and 3 bronze, making it the most successful agency in terms of total awards. These results, and a winner from France, helped DDB to remain the most successful network in the awards for the fourth year in a row with a total of 8 winners, ahead of Y&R and Grey with 4 each.

	Entrants	Entries	Winners	Silver	Bronze
Austria	16	102	1	1	1
Azerbaijan	1	2	-	-	-
Belgium	18	97	2	3	6
Bosnia-Herzegovina	1	1	-	-	-
Bulgaria	8	34	-	-	2
Croatia	9	27	-	-	1
Cyprus	1	4	-	-	-
Czech Republic	7	62	-	1	1
Denmark	17	78	2	4	5
Egypt	2	15	1	-	-
Estonia	1	1	-	-	-
Finland	20	153	-	-	4
France	33	491	9	20	17
Germany	98	1230	12	49	36
Greece	22	80	2	1	2
Hungary	10	33	-	-	-
Iceland	4	6	-	-	-
Ireland	9	31	-	2	2
Israel	10	86	1	1	2
Italy	40	212	5	2	6
Kazakhstan	1	6	-	-	-
Kosovo	1	2	-	-	-
Kuwait	1	3	-	-	-
Latvia	1	1	-	-	-
Lebanon	4	29	-	2	1
Lithuania	2	3	-	-	1
Luxembourg	1	4	-	-	-
Macedonia	2	10	-	1	-
Morocco	1	8	-	-	-
Netherlands	26	171	4	8	10
Norway	12	63	1	3	2
Oman	2	6	-	-	-
Poland	8	40	-	1	-
Portugal	9	67	-	1	2
Qatar	1	30	-	2	-
Romania	16	84	-	1	-
Russia	31	113	2	1	1
Saudi Arabia	1	3	-	-	-
Serbia	6	23	1	1	-
Slovakia	6	32	-	3	-
Slovenia	7	12	-	-	-
South Africa	9	35	2	2	2
Spain	24	134	-	6	10
Sweden	72	589	3	21	24
Switzerland	14	122	3	5	6
Tunisia	1	1	-	1	-
Turkey	17	98	2	-	1
Ukraine	12	40	1	2	1
United Arab Emirates	9	111	1	3	2
United Kingdom	39	358	10	22	23
USA	1	2	-	-	1
Total	664	4945	65	170	172

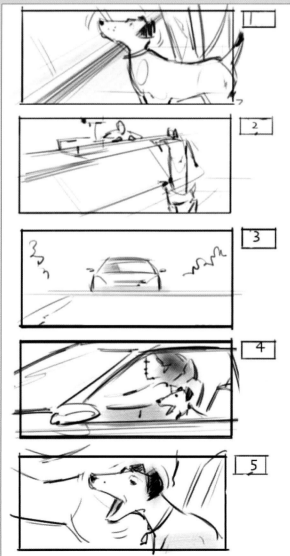

It's a dog's life

by Lewis Blackwell

We all know that it is the emotional connection that makes for great – and successful – advertising. An ad has to make you feel inclined to believe it's message, it cannot wrestle you into submission with logical argument. And belief is not entirely, or even at all, rational. Yet most of the ads out there all too literally try to tell us things, persuade us with logic even though we are not so logical, but highly emotional.

And then along comes an ad like 'Dog' for VW Polo out of DDB London. It wins the Epica d'Or for film because it entirely gets the need to connect at an emotional level. It does this so brilliantly that I for one could not even see the brief, but could only feel the force of its appeal. I was won over, ready to buy, by the sheer charm of the film.

So what is it about a small dog sitting in a small car alongside his owner, driving through Los Angeles, seeming to sing along to the classic song 'I'm a Man' (think Spencer Davis Group and Steve Winwood, 1960s), that makes this commercial so appealing? And just what is it saying about the product?

These questions were quickly answered by Dylan Harrison, the copywriter at DDB London who dreamt up the spot with art director Feargal Balance. "We wanted to move the Polo message on having previously established the association with the car being small and well-made, giving you protection. Now the agency knew that we needed to dig into that to get across the benefits of protection. We realized that the benefit is that it gives you confidence."

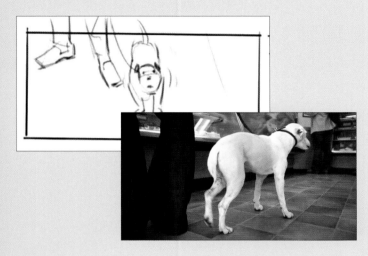

And that's it. That is the message of the commercial, that is the explanation of the crazy little scenario of a Jack Russell dog apparently singing along happily to an ancient pop song while being driven around in a small car. You watch this spot and without being able to put words to it, you get the feeling that this little dog is nervous out of the car but oozing confidence when he sits in the passenger seat and appears to know the words to 'I'm a Man'.

"The Polo is a small car you can feel confident in," says Harrison. "We wanted somehow to capture that confidence you have when you are singing in the shower, the complete confidence and sense of abandon that you have."

Through the thought processes that only a confident creative team working on one of the all-time great accounts can have, Harrison and Balance took this idea and transformed it into the scenario of 'Dog'. Their creative juices somehow flowed and settled on creating a highly cinematic experience in which a nervous little dog is clearly transformed by the confidence-inducing properties of the Polo. Out of the car he trembles and looks worried; inside he is cocky and sure of himself.

A Jack Russell was the breed chosen because of actually having similar characteristics – at times nervous, at other times full of life and confidence. Cody and Bear are the twin dogs that were cast in the role (of course, you only ever see one but two are needed to get through the shoot day without totally exhausting the star) and they carry off their Jack Russell-nature perfectly. They are method actors because they wouldn't know how to be anything else.

But why Los Angeles? "It needs to be in a sunny climate – you don't want to think the dog shivers because he is cold, but because he is nervous," explains Harrison. "And the slight fantasy element of LA also helps with the cinematic appeal." OK… although I suspect many creatives might just admire the chutzpah of getting to sell a small European car by shooting in California.

Director Noam Murro of Independent was chosen to shoot the spot. "Not only is he an all-round great director, but he is fantastic at blending in special effects and he is great with comedy timing," adds Harrison. The effects were particularly needed for the sense of the dog singing along to the song, which is done lightly enough so that the mouth movements look fairly natural, while also clearly signalling singing.

"He got straight away that this was all about the dog's world and he made that look real." And that is quite an achievement – we suspend disbelief and we go along with the ride, enjoying and feeling the confidence of the dog.

All this makes sense, emotionally speaking. As with most great commercials, retelling the idea or story in words doesn't do much to really capture why it works. If it did, you would write an article for an ad rather than make a film. But it absolutely needs to be the little film that it is – the dog, the music, the location and, of course, the car all fit together as if this is how they must be. And that's why VW Polo 'Dog' will probably do a good job at selling one small car with a strange emotional advantage over its competitors.

13

Lewis Blackwell is a creative director, writer and strategic consultant. He is the former editor/publisher of Creative Review and worldwide creative head of Getty Images. His new book Photowisdom is a collaboration with many of the world's leading photographers.

OR YOU'LL **HATE THEM** / **LOVE THEM** / YOU'LL EITHER

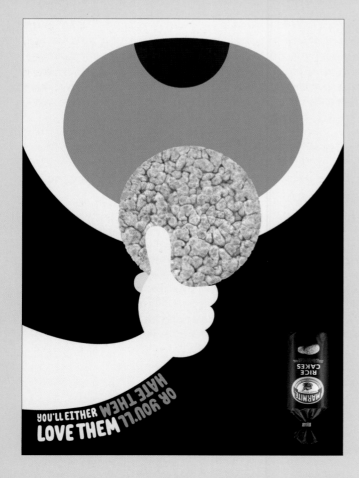

Love, hate, eat

by Jan Burney

As this is Europe's leading advertising award, with participants from the Baltic to the Black Sea and beyond, many of you may struggle to understand the culture behind the winner of the press Epica d'Or. The strengths of this innovative campaign from DDB London for the launch of Marmite Snacking products could be lost on you just where it matters most.

Yes, you might get that as a print campaign Marmite 'LoveHate' has a highly desirable graphic punch to it. You might appreciate the cool lines, bright colours and the short copy. You might admire how both a packshot and a product shot has been smoothly incorporated into every ad. And, most of all, the simple but tricky genius of creating a visual that says two different things when turned around will delight creatives everywhere.

But there is no getting around the fact that unless you have a little schooling in the meaning of Marmite, which requires years of exposure to the British Way of Life, then the charm of this campaign may pass you by.

"It's a very British brand and a very British tone of voice," says Graeme Hall, who with Noah Regan made up the creative team

behind the award-winning work. "It's a bold thing for a brand to not take itself too seriously and Marmite does this with a very particular tone. It knows people either love it or hate it and working with those big concepts is both wonderfully stimulating but also very demanding. You have to get the balance just right."

And in this case, it wasn't enough to just get across the love/hate mix that has made Marmite advertising so strong. The new campaign is not just for the core product but needs to promote a range of Marmite snacks. The salty, sticky yeast extract that is usually spread on toast, has now been imbued into various hand-held foodstuffs (rice cakes, breadsticks and similar fare) and this rash of new products is the spur for the campaign. It was important that customers appreciated the new products on offer while also responding to the uniqueness of the Marmite flavouring. "We couldn't allow ourselves to get carried away with having fun on the love-hate thing while not really getting across the new products."

The chosen medium of press became highly influential in helping Hall and Regan arrive at their concept. "We were looking for something that could help us get across the two ways of seeing the product, and this lead us to play with the medium. We got to the idea of turning the page physically as a trick to really get this across," explains Hall. "The finished ads are really quite close to what we drew up when we developed the approach."

"Bog Mouth was the first execution that really worked and once we got that, with the flat 2D style working, we were away. Other treatments followed quite quickly. We probably came up with about 30 different executions of varying success. At times the idea was stimulating, at times a bit of a straitjacket, but it certainly gave us a strong framework."

'Bog Mouth' is Hall's way of referring to the one where a rice cake is being put into a simple graphic mouth. Or, other way up, it is being dropped into a lavatory bowl.

"It was challenging to convince the client that people would get it, would turn the page and appreciate the two meanings," adds Hall. "But in fact it is not really that essential. The branding and message comes across anyway and if it takes a while to fully appreciate how the image works then that can add something to enjoy later. We had a lot of conversations about how much we should make it clear for the consumer but I am glad that we did not put any more signposts on the page about how to view it."

As you can see from the roughs on this page, the creatives had a close working relationship with illustrator Al Murphy, finessing their strong underlying ideas into graphic executions that have charm and simplicity.

Since the campaign Noah Regan has headed back to Australia, while Hall continues to enjoy the appreciative client base of DDB London. "We have some great brands here, with campaigns that are institutions in many ways and that give great opportunities for good advertising." He is even working on a couple of new Marmite Snacking treatments. So how does Hall feel about Marrmite? Love or hate?

"I hate the stuff. Of course, I had to eat some of the snacks in the course of my professional duties. All I can say in its favour is that the Marmite taste is quite light on the snacks. But I know just how much some people love the stuff."

Oh yes, they do, Graeme. Marmite – I for one can't live without it. Thanks for a great campaign, despite yourself.

Jan Burney is a writer and editor on the creative industries.

Selling illusions

by Lewis Blackwell

Take a look at these posters, winner of this year's Epica d'Or for outdoor, and you see not only a great idea and stunning execution – you also see a confident client who knows what they are and where they want to be. This is always the case when you look behind a great campaign.

John Lewis is a chain store with a difference: owned by its staff, able to pay bonuses even in heavy recession, known for its long-lasting slogan of 'never knowingly undersold'. It trades on quality while being reassuringly safe on delivering great value.

"Our challenge was to elevate John Lewis from being a place where you go to buy any old present to a place where you could find the perfect gift for somebody who you knew well," says copywriter George Prest of the campaign he created with his art director Johnny Leathers at Lowe London.

"There is the underlying fact that John Lewis doesn't sell any old rubbish, and they are a store that is very selective, careful about what they stock. But this back story is difficult to put across in words, let alone as a visual solution."

Inspiration came in the form of an image of shadow-play – a

motorbike depicted by the shadow of numerous forks - from the late, great Japanese designer/photographer Shigeo Fukuda, along with some other examples of illusions that Leathers and Prest had been toying with for a while. "We had been looking at shadow stuff and we even had this picture up on our wall for ages that we really liked," says Prest. "We realized if you could make the shadow of the person who could receive the gift through the range of gifts that they could receive, then that would be a lovely, elegant solution."

Leathers adds: "John Lewis has a certain restraint as a store – it's not a loud, brash retailer. Whatever we came up with had to reflect the qualities of the brand."

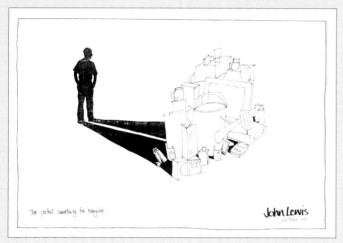

The next step was working out how it could be done. It's one thing to imagine the solution and quite another thing to deliver it for real. And it is for real – there is no photo-manipulation to fake the effect, but instead the objects really had to make the illusions being sought.

Numerous sketches were required, Leathers drawing intensively to try and visualize how the compositions might work, how to position objects in front of a light to create effects, and thinking of what silhouettes they wanted to make. And then a master photographer was needed to achieve the illusion. Fortunately, they had one in mind and he said 'yes' – Nadav Kander, an artist who is almost expected to deliver award-winning work.

"When he said he wanted to do the job it was a great moment," said Leathers. "These objects could have looked a bit dead on the page but he lit them brilliantly, really brought it to life. We also had an amazing stylist/art director, Rachel Thomas, somebody else I really wanted to work with, and we spent a lot of time working with her on getting the objects right."

Leathers did 'about a hundred drawings' roughing the ideas out and then there was a test shoot to show the client that it was possible. On the days before the proper shoot, they worked with Thomas to go through various options to settle on the ones they really wanted.

"This was the hardest thing we have ever done," says Prest. "Our whole thing, and Nadav felt exactly the same, was that this had to work in-camera. You couldn't retouch it heavily as that would ruin the magic. Pretty much what you see is what we did."

Finally three compositions were produced out of a week-long shoot. The client approval process was 'fluid' recalls Prest. "There were certain items they wanted to promote for Christmas but beyond that they were remarkably flexible as to what ended up in or out of the composition, which really helped. There was a great leap of faith from them in going with this idea."

Thousands of products were on tap, lined up in the studio to be used as potential elements in the construction, which indicates just how much creative space the team were given by the client in coming up with a successful composition. John Lewis had their eye clearly on the overall effect as much as thinking it was going to really push any one product.

As it happens, this highly successful work experience resulting in top award-winning work is the swansong of the Leathers and Prest team. After 10 years together they have taken up big new roles elsewhere. This interview was one of the last things the team did on their final day in the Lowe London office, before Leathers headed off to become head of art at Publicis and Prest took up the executive creative director spot at Delaney Lund. The team certainly went out in style.

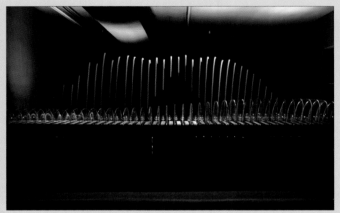

Absolut machines: artificial creativity

by Mark Tungate

Art is such a human endeavour that it seems unlikely that a robot would be very good at it. Nonetheless, a famous vodka brand, a Swedish digital agency and two teams of wildly talented designers got together to explore the virgin terrain of "artificial creativity."

Ted Persson, creative director of Stockholm agency Great Works, takes up the story. "Since the 1980s, Absolut vodka has supported creative professionals in the fields of art, music and fashion. It was almost the first brand to become seriously involved with the art world. And for Absolut this made perfect sense, because choosing the brand was a form of self-expression."

In parallel, Absolut ran a long and highly popular print campaign based on the unusual design of its bottles. Then, last year, Absolut bravely ditched this successful strategy in favour of a new slogan: "In an Absolut world…" The idea was simple: what if we lived in a world where everything was as perfect as Absolut?

Persson says, "We started thinking about how this might apply to

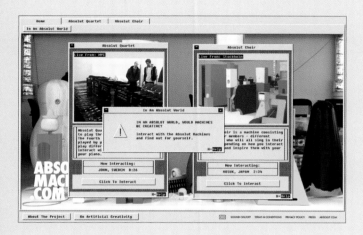

technology and the internet. In order to be true to the brand, we felt that it should involve art in some way, so we began looking for ways to blur the borders between art and technology."

After talking to dozens of design teams, Great Works narrowed its choice down to two. In Sweden, it decided to work with a collective called Teenage Engineering. In the United States, the agency turned to Dan Paluska and Jeff Lieberman, both from MIT in Boston. "We chose them essentially because we liked their initial ideas," explains Persson. "After that, it was a case of working together on the final concepts."

Teenage Engineering came up with Absolut Choir, a robotic choir of 22 endearing singing characters of various shapes and sizes. It relied on a complex fusion of sophisticated speech synthesizers and artificial intelligence. It was installed in the PUB department store in Stockholm.

Paluska and Lieberman responded with Absolut Quartet, an awesome "electro-mechanical" sculpture. On show at an event space in Orchard Street in New York, it consisted of a giant marimba played by balls shot from a robotic cannon, wine glasses caressed by robotic fingers and an array of robotic percussive instruments. The fourth member of the quartet was the internet user.

That was the ultimate challenge of the project: having collaborated on the construction of the machines, the agency and the designers had to make them interactive. The machines were exhibited between January 31 and April 27, 2008. While physical visitors could experience them live, online users could interact with them at absolutmachines.com, creating music in real time. The interaction was filmed and broadcast live on the internet.

Each machine worked in a different way. For Absolut Choir, users typed a phrase that could be a song title – for instance, "I Need Love". The choir would then harmonise a song using those words. The Absolut Quartet was marginally more complicated: users played a tune on their keyboards, which was then interpreted by the machine.

Says Persson: "Only one user could interact at a time. Each machine was filmed by four cameras and after your interaction, you received a video clip that you could send to friends or post on your website or blog."

The machines were at the core of a wider campaign aimed at raising awareness of Absolut's new positioning. Articles in the art and design press promoted the project. Print ads were run in media likely to appeal to opinion formers. The machines generated press coverage around the world and wide internet buzz. DJs took samples of the tunes played by the machines and remixed them.

Today, the interactive element of the project is over. But the machines are currently touring the world's art museums. And Ted Persson found the project personally fulfilling. "It was one of the most enjoyable campaigns I've ever worked on. It wasn't just about selling vodka or putting a picture of a product on a page. Scientists followed our efforts and we made genuine progress in the field of artificial creativity. We contributed something to the world."

Mark Tungate is a journalist and writer based in Paris. He is the author of Adland - A Global History of Advertising.

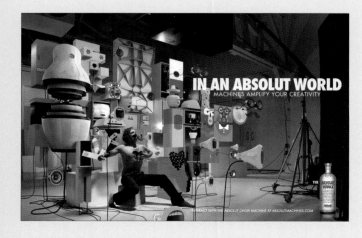

19

Turkcell
Mobile Award

The Turkcell Mobile Award honours the most creative advertising involving the use of mobile phones. Candidates for the award were identified across a variety of Epica categories including Direct Marketing, Media Innovation, Promotions, Interactive and Integrated Campaigns.

Forsman & Bodenfors, Gothenburg, won the first Turkcell Mobile Award with their campaign for AMF Pension.

The aim of the campaign was to encourage people to start thinking about their pensions while they were still relatively young. Outdoor advertising invited passers-by to take a picture of themselves with their mobile phones and to MMS it to the pension provider. A few minutes later AMF Pension sent back a picture showing how the person might look when they are 70 years old.

The AMF Pension campaign also won in Epica's Financial Services category (page 99).

21

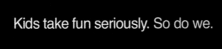
Kids take fun seriously. So do we.

Agency	Leo Burnett, Milan
Creative Directors	Sergio Rodriguez
	Enrico Dorizza
Copywriter	Paolo Guglielmoni
Art Director	Alessia Casini
Production	Bedeschi Film, Milan
Director	Andrea Cecchi
Producers	Manuela Murelli
	Ascanio Capparoni
Client	Kellogg's Coco Pops,
	"Any Given Breakfast"

"No football today," says a kid's mother, who would prefer him to do his homework. Undaunted, the boy steps down from the breakfast table, squares his shoulders and begins a speech. Every wasted minute is a chance missed, he explains. "And I'll fight for that minute – for every single minute of fun. Because when I add them all together, the sum will make the difference between a fulfilling existence or not. This is life. This is football." Kids take fun seriously. So does Kellogg's. The kid's mum still says no, though.

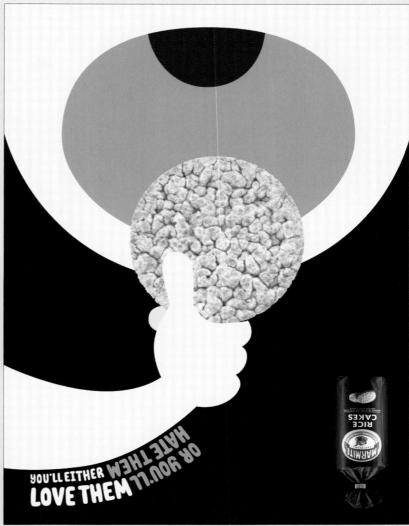

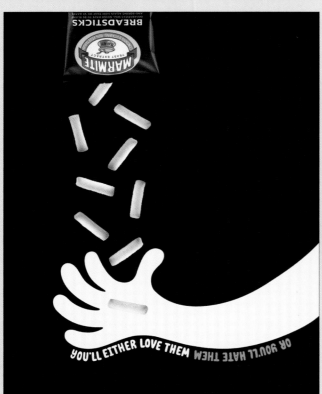

Agency	DDB London
Creative Director	Jeremy Craigen
Copywriters	Graeme Hall
	Noah Regan
Art Directors	Noah Regan
	Graeme Hall
Illustrator	Al Murphy
Client	Marmite Snacks

24 Food

Agency	TBWA\Paris
Creative Director	Erik Vervroegen
Copywriter	Benoit Leroux
Art Director	Philippe Taroux
Photographer	Joseph Ford
Client	Pedigree Dentastix

Agency.	.start, Munich	Agency	Dinamo Reklamebyrå,
Creative Directors	Marco Mehrwald		Oslo
	Thomas Pakull	**Creative Directors**	Henrik Sæther
	Shin Oh		Henrik Hagelsten
Copywriters	Gunnar Immisch	**Copywriter**	Henrik Hagelsten
	Bjoern Pfarr	**Art Director**	Henrik Sæther
Art Director	Felix Hennermann	**Photographer**	Ole Musken
Client	Burger King	**Illustrator**	Lis Lonning
		Client	Open Bakery

Agency	TBWA\Istanbul	Agency	Leo Burnett, Moscow
Creative Director	Ilkay Gurpinar	Creative Director	Mikhail Kudashkin
Copywriter	Volkan Karakasoglu	Copywriter	Arina Avdeeva
Art Director	Burak Kunduracioglu	Art Director	Vera Karpova
Client	Uno Light Bread	Photographer	Sergey Mart'yakhin
		Client	Doshirak Instant Noodles

Agency	Shalmor Avnon Amichay\
	Y&R Interactive, Tel Aviv
Creative Directors	Gideon Amichay
	Yoram Levi
	Nadav Pressman
Copywriter	Matan Yedidya
Art Director	Tani Zipper
Photographer	Yoram Aschheim
Client	Heinz Ketchup

Agency	Leo Burnett, Brussels
Creative Director	Jean-Paul Lefebvre
Copywriter	Wim Corremans
Art Director	Alex Gabriels
Photographer	Marc Paeps
Client	Heinz Hot Ketchup

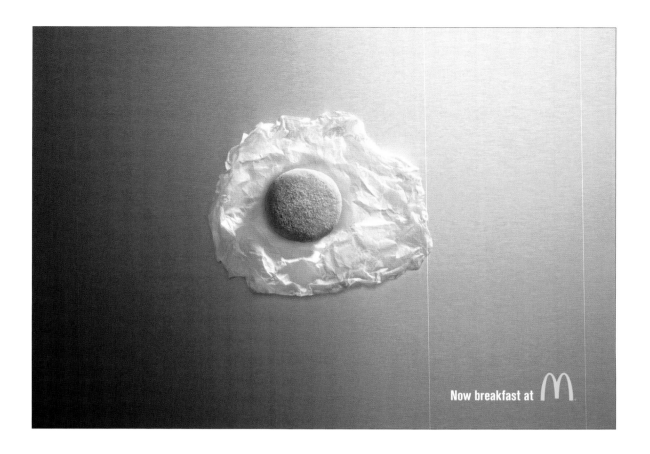

Now breakfast at M

All in one pack.

The pasta with omega-3, fiber and protein.

Agency	DDB Warsaw	Agency	Tank/Y&R,
Creative Director	Darek Zatorski		Stockholm
Copywriter	Michal Desowski	Creative Director	Hans Ahlgren
Art Director	Zuza Duchniewska	Copywriter	Daniel Rinaldo
Photographers	Giblin & James	Art Directors	Fredrik Forsling
Client	McDonald's		Magnus Uddenberg
		Photographer	Eric Satten
		Client	Barilla Plus Pasta

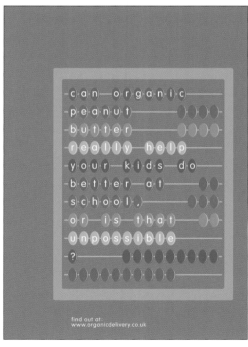

Agency	Abbott Mead Vickers BBDO, London
Creative Directors	Paul Brazier
	Mark Fairbanks
Copywriter	Mark Fairbanks
Art Director	Mark Fairbanks
Illustrator	Dingus Hussey
Client	Organic Delivery Company

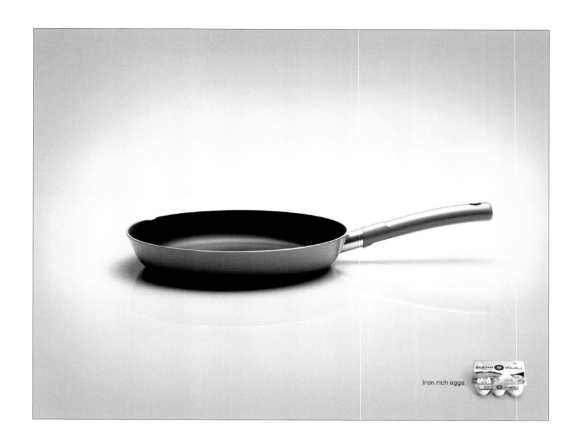

Iron rich eggs.

Agency	Brandcom Middle East, Dubai	Agency	Gitam BBDO, Tel-Aviv
		Executive CD	Guy Bar
Creative Director	Manoj Ammanath	Creative Director	Eran Bar-Yochai
Copywriter	Manoj Ammanath	Copywriter	Ariel Vitkon
Art Directors	Grant Linton	Art Director	Ariel Vitkon
	Javed Obaid	Client	Osem's Ketchup
Photographer	Khurram Khan		
Client	Bustan Eggs		

Agency	WatersWidgren\TBWA, Stockholm
Copywriter	Kalle Widgren
Art Director	Carl Dalin
Production	Camp David, Stockholm
Director	Christoffer von Reis
Producers	Anna Adamsson
	Peter Kydd
Client	Kelda Soup, "Struggle"

Not everyone is a talented cook. Here we see an absent-minded woman who puts a lasagne in her briefcase – and her laptop in the oven. A young man prepares a steak for his new girlfriend, who turns out to be vegetarian. A woman doesn't know what to make of an aubergine, typing "black + cucumber" into a search engine. A middle-aged man accidently cremates a piece of chicken. And a father juggles looking after his kids with feeding them. Luckily, for people who struggle with everyday dinner, there's always Kelda soup.

Agency	FP7 Doha
Creative Director	Fadi Yaish
Copywriter	Kalpesh Patankar
Art Directors	Fadi Yaish
	Kalpesh Patankar
Client	Friskies

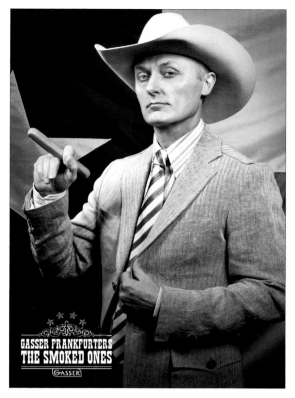

Agency	TBWA\Italia, Milan	Agency	Demner, Merlicek & Bergmann,
Creative Director	Fabrizio Russo		Vienna
Copywriter	Sara Ermoli	Creative Directors	Rosa Haider
Art Director	Cristina Baccelli		Tolga Büyükdoganay
Photographers	Winkler & Noah	Art Director	Tolga Büyükdoganay
Client	Gasser Frankfurters	Photographer	Robert Staudinger
		Graphic Design	Karin Wedl
		Client	Felix Hellfire Ketchup

THE QUEST FOR THE
ULTIMATE BREAK
BEGINS

34   **Confectionery & Snacks**

Agency	JWT Paris
Creative Directors	Ghislain de Villoutreys
	Olivier Courtemanche
	Xavier Beauregard
Copywriter	Hadi Hassan
Art Director	Xavier Beauregard
Production	Wanda, Paris
Director	Akama
Client	KitKat, "Ultimate Break"

In this animated film, lightly inspired by topical events, a young stock trader is faced with a screen of crashing share prices. He leaves his desk and slopes off to the KitKat dispenser, ignoring his more successful rivals and a sexy co-worker. As soon as he bites into the KitKat, he feels better. He feels better still when the entire building is transported into space. Stepping out of the elevator, he is confronted by a glowing white light. The quest for the ultimate break begins - and is continued on the KitKat website.

Communication just got Sweeter

Personalise your M&M's at mymms.nl

 Confectionery & Snacks **35**

Agency	FHV BBDO, Amstelveen
Creative Directors	Maarten van de Vijfeijken
	Joris van Elk
Copywriter	Stef Jongenelen
Art Director	Yona Hümmels
Photographer	Studio Beerling
Client	M&M's

Instant freshness.

36   **Confectionery & Snacks**

Agency	JWT London		
Executive CD	Russell Ramsey		
Creative Directors	Greg Martin		
	Mike McKenna		
Copywriters	Phillip Meyler		
	Darren Keff		
Art Directors	Phillip Meyler		
	Darren Keff		
Production	Partizan, London		
Director	Traktor		
Client	Trident Fresh, "Fresh"		

In a crowded elevator, a man pops some Trident chewing gum into his mouth. An attack of freshness begins. First, he's rained on. Then, he flies out of the bottom of the elevator on the end of a kite. Landing, he finds himself in the middle of a water pistol battle. A second later, he's transported into an icy landscape, where a polar bear shakes droplets of snow over him. Finally, he's back in the elevator, with a happily refreshed look on its face. Trident – it's fresh.

Agency	DDB España, Barcelona
Creative Directors	Bernat Sanroma
	David Perez
Copywriter	Joan Gallifa
Art Director	Marta Monsarro
Client	Smint

Have a break. Have a KitKat

Agency	JWT London	Agency	JWT Dubai
Executive CD	Russell Ramsey	Creative Director	Chafic Haddad
Creative Directors	Nick Bell	Copywriter	DV Hari Krishna
	Howard Willmott	Art Director	Kedar Damle
Copywriters	Mark Norcutt	Photographer	Tejal Patni
	Laurence Quinn	Illustrators	Milind Aglave
Art Directors	Mark Norcutt		Jomy Varghese
	Laurence Quinn	Client	KitKat
Photographer	Mike Russell		
Client	KitKat		

All the nuts in the world in finest chocolate.

Confectionery & Snacks

Agency	Serviceplan, Munich & Hamburg
Creative Director	Ilka Vogtmann
Copywriter	Petra Nachtigall
Art Director	Patrizia Marroni
Photographer	Felix Holzer
Graphic Design	Daniel Tomcic
	Miro Moric
Client	Seidl Chocolates

Agency	BBDO Düsseldorf		**Agency**	Callegari Berville Grey, Paris
Creative Directors	Marie-Theres Schwingeler		**Creative Director**	Andrea Stillacci
	Toygar Bazarkaya		**Copywriter**	Luissandro Del Gobbo
Copywriter	Michael Reinhardt		**Art Director**	Giovanni Settesoldi
Art Director	Lidia Pranjic		**Photographer**	Riccardo Bagnoli
Illustrators	Jan Bazing		**Illustrator**	Claudio Luparelli
	Lidia Pranjic		**Client**	Pringles Hot & Spicy
Client	Juicy Fruit Tropikiwi			

Your natural source of vitamins and minerals

TINE

Dairy Products

Agency	Try Advertising Agency, Oslo
Copywriters	Kjetil Try
	Jørgen Bøhle-Bakke
Art Director	Einar Fjøsne
Production	Monster Commercials, Oslo
Director	Ole Endresen
Producers	Helene Hovda Lunde
	Eivind Moe
	Cecilie Thue
Client	Tine Milk, "No Milk Today"

Genuine film clips show people slipping, stumbling and falling in embarrassing circumstances. A politician tumbles down the steps of an aeroplane. A catwalk model comes a cropper thanks to her high heels. A hurdler, an astronaut and a weight lifter – all of them end up flat on their (presumably red) faces. The tagline reads "Milk. For a stronger body." The last image shows a wedding. Inevitably, the best man keels over as the couple are saying their vows. Drink milk – from Tine.

Federation of Nirvana

Popular Republic of Lust

Emirate of Bliss

Dairy Products **41**

Agency	The Syndicate, Athens
Creative Director	Nicholas Koligiannis
Copywriters	Nikos Pechlivanidis
	Nicholas Koligiannis
Art Director	Despoina Agianoglou
Photographer	Kostas Kostopoulos
Digital Imaging	Thanassis Pozantzis
Client	Dodoni Ice Cream

42 **Dairy Products**

Agency	Geller Nessis Leo Burnett, Tel Aviv
Creative Director	Merav Koren
Copywriter	Judy Rotem
Art Director	Shiri Mann Zemmer
Client	Nok Out Ice Cream

Agency	Spillmann/Felser/Leo Burnett, Zurich	Agency	Wächter & Wächter Bremen
Creative Director	Martin Spillmann	Creative Director	Andreas Rüthemann
Copywriter	Maren Beck	Copywriter	Jan Portius
Art Director	Karin Estermann	Photographer	Nadine Elfenbein
Photographer	David Willen	Client	Ammerland Dairies
Client	PSL Swiss Milk Producers		

Life is a cosmic symphony.

This doesn't rock. We're *underground.*

Life is like a fire..

Right!

Life is..

..LIFE!

Bavaria PILSENER

44 **Alcoholic Drinks**

Agency	Selmore, Amsterdam
Creative Directors	Poppe van Pelt
	Diederick Hillenius
Copywriter	Poppe van Pelt
Art Director	Diederick Hillenius
Production	Bonkers, Amsterdam
Director	Jonathan Herman
Producers	Saskia Kok
	Violet van der Straaten
Client	Bavaria Beer, "Life"

This film reveals how the rock band Opus came up with the lyrics for one of the hits of the 1980s. The boys arrive at a recording studio in drizzly Graz, Austria. "Life," sings the lead vocalist, "is a rocky road." But he's told the lyrics are "too superficial". Lots of failed attempts follow. Is life like a cosmic symphony, a tunnel, a celebration, or a fire? Frustrated, the guys take a break to drink some Bavaria beer. It clearly does the trick, because we cut to the band's big debut. "Life," they sing, "is life." Bavaria beer: it's right.

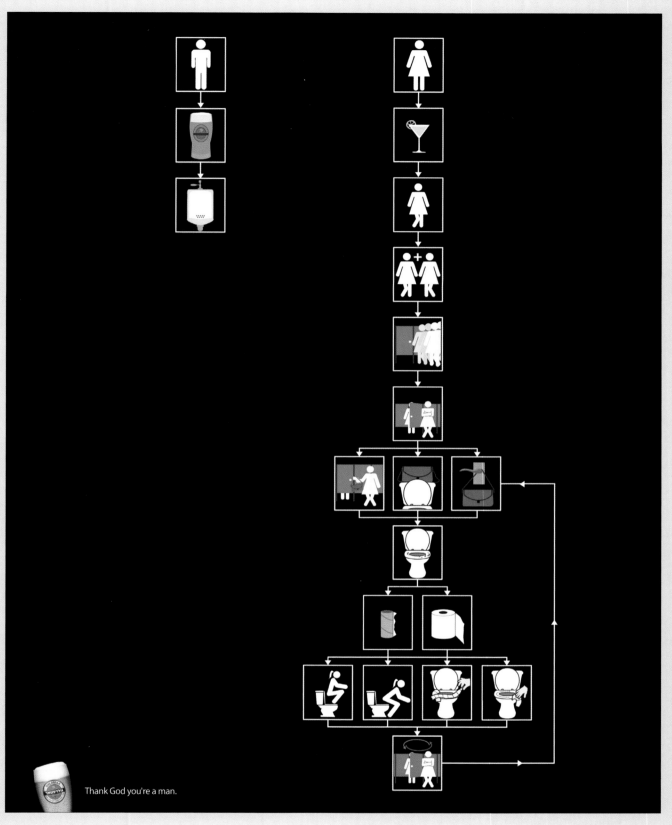

Thank God you're a man.

 Alcoholic Drinks 45

Agency	McCann Erickson Israel, Tel Aviv
Creative Director	Ido Ben Dor
Copywriters	Asaf Zelikovich
	Elad Gabison
Art Director	Geva Gershon
Client	Goldstar Beer

Agency	TBWA\Germany, Berlin
Creative Directors	Dirk Henkelmann
	Philip Borchardt
Copywriters	Martin Sulzbach
	Matthäus Frost
Art Directors	Martin Sulzbach
	Matthäus Frost
Production	Julian Schneiders
Director	Julian Schneiders
Producers	Julian Schneiders
	Johannes von Liebenstein
Project Manager	Tanja Kurr
Client	Absolut Vodka, "Washing Machine"

At a launderette, we see shirts churning around inside a washing machine. Round and round they go, faster and faster. The spin cycle commences, then the drier. The shirts are a blur. But when the machine stops, we see that the shirts are perfectly pressed and folded. In an Absolut World, all washing machines would work like this. We know the reality isn't quite as wonderful. Yet Absolut Vodka is perfect every time.

46   Alcoholic Drinks

Agency	Mother, London
Production	Sonny, London
Director	Fredrik Bond
Producers	Ran Holst
	Richard Firminger
Client	Stella 4%, "Smooth Outcome"

We're beside a pool on the French Riviera. A smoothie in trunks sees a blonde beauty and asks if he can apply her sunscreen. She accepts. Things are going nicely until the woman's husband shows up. Knocked off balance, the man falls from the terrace and plunges straight down. Luckily for him, he falls into a suit hanging on a clothesline. This enables him to stroll into a bar and ask for a glass of the new "smooth" Stella 4%. When the husband arrives, he fails to recognise the Romeo – despite the women's shoes that the man has fallen in to.

Agency	Irish International BBDO, Dublin
Creative Director	Mal Stevenson
Copywriters	Sophie Farquhar
	Jason Hynes
	Catherine Lennon
Art Director	Catherine Lennon
Production	Gorgeous Enterprises, London
Director	Peter Thwaites
Producers	Anna Hashmi
	Noel Byrne
Client	Guinness, "Light Show"

Hordes of office workers enter a deserted skyscraper at night. Taking their positions, they wait for a signal. Then, using a combination of switches and blinds, they put on a spectacular light display for anybody who happens to be looking at the building. Pedestrians stop and stare. At the end of the show, only a strip of lights at the top of the tall building remain, creating the impression of a pint of Guinness. It's the beer that's alive inside.

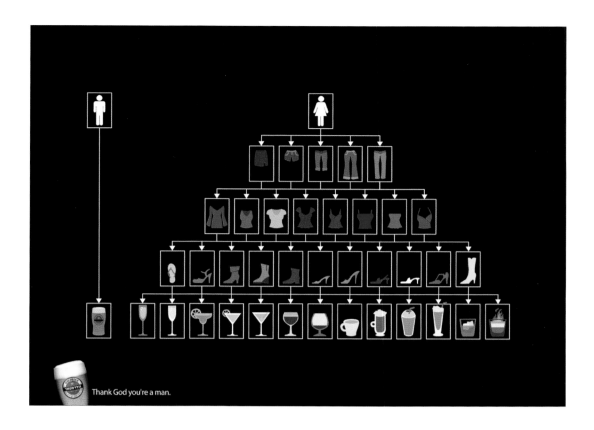

Thank God you're a man.

Agency	McCann Erickson Israel, Tel-Aviv	Agency	Lowe London
Creative Director	Ido Ben Dor	Creative Director	Ed Morris
Copywriters	Asaf Zelikovich	Copywriter	Patrick McClelland
	Elad Gabison	Art Director	Simon Morris
Art Director	Geva Gershon	Photographer	Lawrence Haskell
Client	Goldstar Beer	Illustrator	David Lawrence
		Client	Artois

Agency   DraftFCB Cape Town
Creative Directors   Francois de Villiers
    Schalk van der Merwe
Copywriters   Liora Friedland
    Themba Mthambo
Art Directors   Alessandro Betti
    Rafe-Jon Burchell
    Monde Lawrence Lobola
Production   Velocity Films,
    Cape Town
Director   Greg Gray
Producers   Helena Woodfine
    Caz Friedman
Client   Savanna,
    "With Compliments"

A young guy in a bar takes his first sip of Savanna. Suddenly, he overhears a woman saying, "Hi there, sexy." He looks around, but can only see a biker chick with her tough boyfriend. "Over here, handsome," beckons another voice. But the blonde at the other end of the bar ignores him. "We love what you've done with your hair," says a male voice. Finally, the barman clears up the mystery. "It's the peanuts," he explains, with a touch of dry humour. "They're complimentary." Savanna – it's dry, but you can drink it.

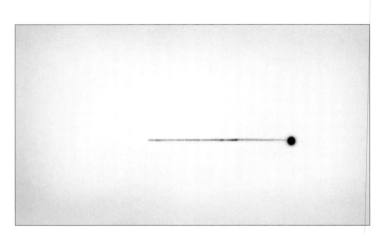

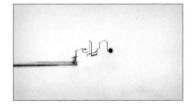

48   **Alcoholic Drinks**

Agency   Abbott Mead Vickers
    BBDO, London
Creative Director   Paul Brazier
Copywriter   Bern Hunter
Art Director   Mike Bond
Production   Studio Aka, London
Director   Marc Craste
Producers   Sharon Titmarsh
    Carol Powell
Client   Guinness, "Rugby"

Guinness was not an official sponsor of the Rugby World Cup, but it leant its tacit support to the event through this stunning animated commercial, directed by Marc Craste. Based on characters from one of his short films, it shows two teams of Manga-like characters (one dressed in black, the other in white) who play a dramatic game of rugby in a strange stadium that turns out to be a pint of Guinness. "Seconds from greatness," says the tagline, evoking the famous long pour of a pint of the black stuff.

Agency   Irish International
    BBDO, Dublin
Creative Director   Mal Stevenson
Copywriter   Rory Hamilton
Art Director   Jonathon Cullen
Production   Stink, London
    Psyop, New York
Director   Eben Mears
Producers   Sophie Kluman
    Jen Glabus
    Onagh Carolan
Client   Guinness, "Dot"

This charming animated tale features the career of a black dot. With an urge to travel, the dot first becomes a line. It crosses many landscapes, through jungles and under seas. Soon it multiplies, making many new friends. It even becomes the pupil of a human eye. Before long, the black dot realises that it can literally become anything. Finally, it makes a choice. It becomes a pint of Guinness.

Agency	Fallon London
Copywriter	John Allison
Art Director	Chris Bovill
Production	2 AM, London
Director	Harmony Korine
Producers	Candice Chubb
	Jo Charlesworth
Client	Budweiser,
	"True Dedication"

More likely lads use beer to unusual ends. This time we meet an alternative country rock group who use empty Budweiser bottles as drumsticks, cowbells and part of a slide guitar – among other things. We see them rehearsing as their cowboy-style manager urges them to play an increasingly fast version of the tune "Popcorn". When they're finally playing it at an almost supersonic pace, he declares the version "rockin'". Budweiser: sheer dedication.

Agency	JWT Italia, Milan
Creative Director	Pietro Maestri
Deputy CD	Bruno Bertelli
Copywriter	Bruno Bertelli
Art Director	Cristiana Boccassini
Production	Filmmaster, Milan
Directors	Dom & Nic
Producers	Lilli Auteri
	Ada Bonvini
Client	Heineken Italia,
	"Concert"

Empty beer bottles are all the rage this year. Here, a gang of lads on a rooftop entertain the city with a rendition of the Dépêche Mode hit "I Just Can't Get Enough" created by blowing on beer bottles. The bottle choir gets toes tapping and captures everyone's attention – especially that of the cute chicks in bikinis on the roof opposite. Heineken was made to entertain.

Agency	& Co., Copenhagen
Creative Director	Thomas Hoffmann
Art Directors	Thomas Hoffmann
	Martin Storgaard
Production	Bacon, Copenhagen
Director	Adam Hashemi
Producer	Christian Zethner
Client	Carlsberg, "Pong"

A group of mates develop numerous ways of bouncing ping-pong balls into glasses of lager. Their first attempt is merely a single bounce across the kitchen table and – "plop!" – into the glass. Then they get more ambitious. The quadruple bounce from wooden stools, for example. That's followed by a single golf putt into a glass. Three balls thrown into three glasses? No problem. Or how about standing the glass on your head? Beer pong could catch on. Carlsberg: our beer, our projects.

Agency	TBWA\Germany, Berlin
Creative Director	Stefan Schmidt
Copywriters	Frederick Kober
	Djamila Rabenstein
Art Directors	Djamila Rabenstein
	Frederick Kober
Illustrator	Jue Zhang
Client	Absolut Vodka

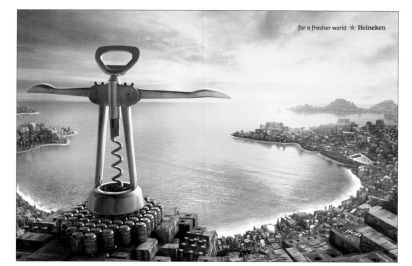

Agency   Publicis Conseil, Paris
Creative Director   Olivier Altmann
Copywriter   Nicolas Schmitt
Art Director   Pierre Penicaud
Illustrators   Denis Assor
                Christophe Schmitt
Client   Heineken

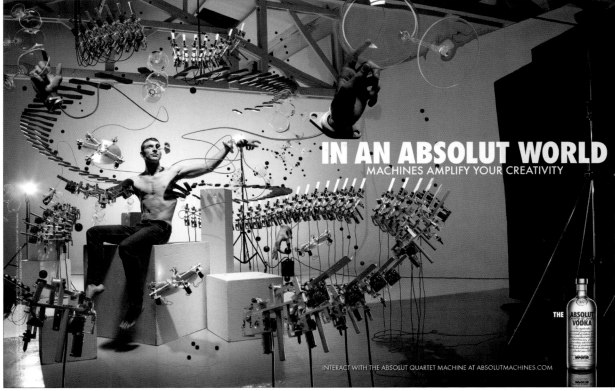

52 **Alcoholic Drinks**

Agency	Irish International BBDO, Dublin
Creative Director	Mal Stevenson
Copywriter	Ted Barry
Art Director	Catherine Lennon
Photographer	Muiris Moynihan
Client	Guinness, "April 1st" Ad

Agency	TBWA\MAP, Paris
Creative Directors	Manoëlle van der Vaeren
	Sébastien Vacherot
Copywriters	Julien Boissinot
	Nicolas Pontacq
Art Directors	Nicolas Pontacq
	Julien Boissinot
Photographer	Laurent Seroussi
Client	Absolut Vodka

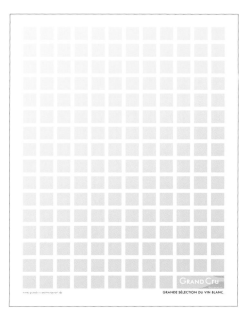
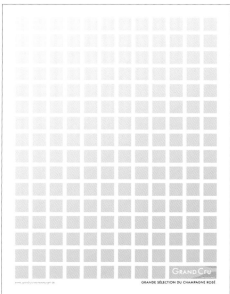
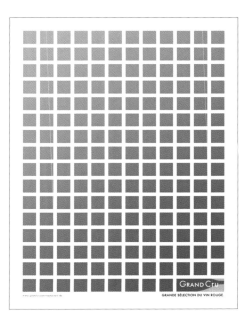

Agency	Cheil Communications Germany, Schwalbach im Taunus
Creative Director	Patrick Thiede
Copywriter	Berend Enslin-Lohmann
Art Director	Kathrin Marseille
Client	Grand Cru Wine Restaurant

Agency	Ogilvy & Mather, Copenhagen
Copywriter	Mikkel Elung-Jensen
Art Director	Claus Collstrup
Client	Fernet Branca

Agency	Wieden+Kennedy Amsterdam
Executive CDs	John Norman Al Moseley
Copywriter	Patrick Almaguer
Art Director	Blake Kidder
Production	Against All Odds, Sausalito Passion Pictures, London
Producers	Lottie Hope Orlando Wood
Client	Coca Cola Zero, "Tongues & Eyeball Liar"

Two animated tongues are clumsily trying to sip from a Coke bottle. An animated eyeball – with a suave French accent – wanders up and asks them what they're doing. They tell him they're drinking Coca-Cola. "It says Coca-Cola Zero on the bottle," the eye points out. One of the tongues accuses him of being a "big, fat liar". Somewhat vainly, the eye protests "I am not fat!" Coca-Cola Zero. Coke taste – zero sugar.

THE OTHER OFFICIAL WATER OF
THE CHAMPIONSHIPS, WIMBLEDON

THE OTHER OFFICIAL WATER OF
THE CHAMPIONSHIPS, WIMBLEDON

IN THE EVENT OF RAIN
SPECTATORS ARE REQUESTED
NOT TO RAISE UMBRELLAS
UNTIL PLAY HAS BEEN STOPPED

THE OTHER OFFICIAL WATER OF
THE CHAMPIONSHIPS, WIMBLEDON

Non-Alcoholic Drinks   55

Agency	Euro RSCG London
Creative Director	Mark Hunter
Copywriter	Samantha Richards
Art Director	Phil Beaumont
Typographers	Matt Palmer
	Christian Williams
Client	Evian

Agency	Fred & Farid, Paris	Plunging into a strange animated world, we meet humanoid animals enacting a musical routine. The action centres on a muscular bear with a fixation on a curvaceous deer. After initially rejecting his attentions, she leads him into a nightclub-style environment where they begin a flirtatious dance to a Latin beat, surrounded by suggestively cavorting animals. Of course, they get together at the end over a shared bottle of Orangina. It's naturally juicy.
Creative Directors	Fred & Farid	
Copywriters & ADs	Alphée Ballester	
	Baptiste Clinet	
	Mathieu Colloud	
	Joseph Dubruque	
	Emmanuelle Durand	
	Nicolas Lauthier	
	Juliette Lavoix	
	Olivia Meyer	
	Pauline de Montferrand	
	Thomas Raillard	
	Michael Zonnen	
Production	Stink, London	
Director	Psyop, New York	
Producers	Daniel Bergman	
	Richard Fenton	
	Sylvaine Mella	
Client	Orangina, "Naturally Juicy"	

56 **Non-Alcoholic Drinks**

Agency	McCann Erickson, Madrid
Chief Creative Officer	Leandro Raposo
Executive CDs	Monica Moro
	Pablo Colonnese
	Pablo Stricker
Copywriter	Ander Mendivil
Art Director	Eduardo Hernandez
Production	Indio Films, Madrid
Director	Fran Torres
Producers	Dani Boyero
	Luis Felipe Moreno
Client	Nestea

A Nestea spokesman points out that these days, it's trendy to be yourself and accept imperfection as the rule. "But what about people who are perfect, isn't there a place in our society for them too?" A woman changes seats on a bus to avoid being next to a "perfect" man, while the presenter continues, "If you can't accept the perfection of others, isn't that a form of discrimination?" The Nestea Project for the Integration of Perfect People believes that if you embrace the perfection of Nestea, you should be able to accept perfect people too.

In the second spot, a mother recalls the time that her son came to her and admitted, "Mum – I'm perfect." Of course a mother knows these things, but the boy's father has trouble dealing with his offspring's "coming out". The perfect boy has to put up with self-doubt and strange looks on the street. Then the guru from the Nestea Project for the Integration of Perfect People arrives to comfort the family. He urges us all to embrace perfection – as we embrace Nestea, the perfect beverage.

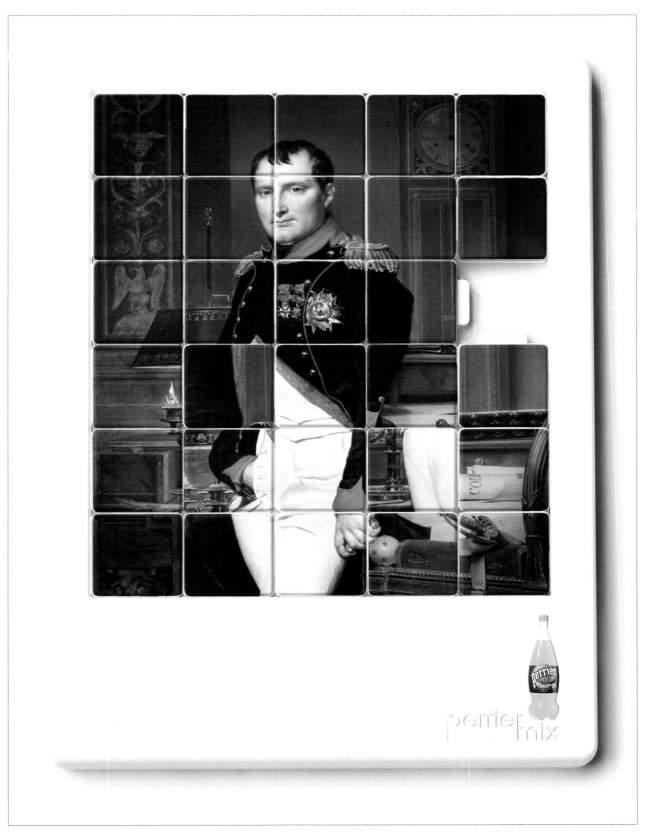

Agency Ogilvy & Mather, Paris
Creative Director Thierry Chiumino
Copywriter Maxence Garnier
Art Director Mathias Laurent
Client Perrier Mix

Don't look at me!

Café Noir

100% black

Agency	& Co., Copenhagen
Creative Director	Robert Cerkez
Copywriter	Thomas Fabricius
Art Director	Robert Cerkez
Production	Bacon, Copenhagen
Director	Martin Werner
Producer	Christian Zethner
Client	Café Noir, "Serge"

In Danish, black is not just a colour – it means anything weird or bizarre. In this black and white film, a woman is rowed across a lake to a mysterious island. A man in a cape stands before a doorway. "Do you really want him back – no matter what?" says the man. The woman says "I love him." She enters what appears to be a Parisian apartment. "Serge, is that you?" Serge appears, saying "Don't look at me." He has been transformed into an anteater. If you think that's black, try Café Noir.

Carlsberg SPORT
SPORT INSIDE

Live Olympic on the Coke side of life

Non-Alcoholic Drinks

58

Agency	& Co., Copenhagen
Creative Director	Thomas Hoffmann
Art Directors	Thomas Hoffman
	Martin Storgaard
Production	Bacon, Copenhagen
Director	Adam Hashemi
Producer	Christian Zethner
Client	Carlsberg Sport, "Squirrel"

In a park, a couple of pranksters fill the plastic lid from a bottle of Carlsberg Sport with the new drink. Then they retire to a safe distance and wait. Sure enough, a squirrel hops from the bushes and sips the Carlsberg Sport. Seconds later, he picks up a nut, throws it in the air, and begins performing soccer tricks with it – much to the amusement of his audience. Carlsberg Sport: it's got sport inside.

Agency	W+K Amsterdam
Executive CDs	John Norman
	Al Moseley
Copywriter	Dave Smith
Art Director	Pierre Janneau
Production	Partizan, London
Directors	Eric Lerner
	Thomas Hilland
Producers	Isabella Parish
	Julie Crosbie
	Neil Henry
	Wendy Carpenter
Client	Coca-Cola, "Bird's Nest"

A little cartoon bird reads the headline "Bird's Nest Stadium Ready" in a newspaper, referring to the Olympic stadium in Beijing. He grabs a drinking straw and gets moving, carrying it like an Olympic torch. All around the world, other little birds grab discarded drinking straws. They converge on Beijing, where we see they've used the straws to build a smaller "bird's nest". The original bird arrives with the last straw. It's all to let us know that Coca-Cola is supporting the Beijing Olympics.

Agency	BBDO Düsseldorf
Creative Directors	Toygar Bazarkaya
	Sebastian Hardieck
Copywriter	Christopher Neumann
Art Directors	Michael Plueckhahn
	Fabian Krueger
Production	Stefan Kranefeld Imaging,
	Düsseldorf
Client	Pepsi

SOME TABLE WATERS HAVE
ARTIFICIALLY INJECTED BUBBLES...

...NOT THIS ONE.

NATURAL. SPARKLING.
REFRESHING.

THE QUEEN OF TABLE WATERS

Agency	BPG, Kuwait City		**Agency**	Impact/BBDO, Riyadh
Creative Director	Souheil Arabi		**Creative Director**	Ahmad Beck
Copywriter	Aaron Arthur		**Copywriter**	Ahmad Beck
Art Director	Mazen Daou		**Art Director**	Ahmad Beck
Client	Apollinaris		**Client**	Aroma Coffee

Agency	Abbott Mead Vickers BBDO, London
Creative Director	Paul Brazier
Copywriter	Diane Leaver
Art Director	Simon Rice
Photographer	Nadav Kander
Client	Pepsi

62   **Non-Alcoholic Drinks**

Agency	FHV BBDO, Amstelveen
Creative Director	Robbert Jansen (Laboratorivm)
Photographer	Trabbor
Typographer	Jeroen Bijl
Client	Dampkring Coffee House

Agency	McCann Erickson, Bucharest
Creative Directors	Adrian Botan
	Alexandru Dumitrescu
Copywriter	Adela Dan
Art Director	Ela Ciorita
Client	Nescafé Decaffeinated

En de rest van de appel zit in Tropicana!

Tropicana
pure premium
APPLE

100% puur
geperst fruitsap

Tout le reste de l'orange est dans Tropicana.

Tropicana
pure premium
ORIGINAL
ORANGE

100% pur
jus de fruit pressé

THE MOST

MAJESTIC

ESPRESSO EXPERIENCE

LAVAZZA
ESPRESS YOURSELF

www.lavazza2008.com

Agency	DDB Brussels
Creative Director	Peter Aerts
Copywriter	Tom Berth
Art Director	Geert De Rocker
Photographer	Kris Van Beeck
Client	Tropicana

All the rest of the apple/orange is in Tropicana.

Agency	Armando Testa, Turin
Creative Directors	Michele Mariani German Silva, Ekhi Mendibil Haitz Mendibil
Copywriter	Cristiano Nardò
Art Director	Andrea Lantelme
Photographer	Finlay Mackay
Graphic Design	Laura Sironi
Client	Lavazza

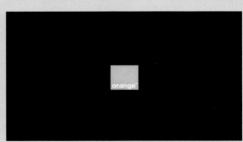

Communication Services

Agency	Publicis Conseil, Paris	
Executive CD	Olivier Altmann	
Copywriter	Olivier Camensuli	
Art Director	Frédéric Royer	
Production	Rattlingstick, London	
	Wanda, Paris	
Director	Ringan Ledwidge	
Producers	Patrick Barbier	
	Nancy Gabriel	
	Pierre Marcus	
	Muriel Allegrini	
Client	Orange, "Rewind TV"	

In a crowded Indian street, a taxi driver spots a foreign young woman in tears. Getting an idea, he signals the people around her to walk backwards. Then he puts his car into reverse. Miraculously, everyone joins in: pedestrians, vehicles and workmen all pretend to have gone into reverse. The girl is baffled. Then a bus reverses down the street. The passengers file out backwards – including the girl's boyfriend, who now gets to kiss her hello instead of goodbye. What if you could live the best moments again? With Orange TV, you can rewind television.

Weddings   Pages

Funerals   Pages

Roses   Pages

Grocers   Pages

 Communication Services   **65**

Agency   Grey Worldwide, Dubai
Creative Director Alisdair Miller
Copywriter   Jay Furby
Art Director   Alisdair Miller
Client   Yellow Pages

Agency	Ogilvy Group Ukraine, Kiev
Creative Director	Bartek Rams
Copywriter	Sergey Kolos
Art Director	Taras Dzendrovskii
Production	Tantrum Productions, London
Director	Mikko Lehtinen
Client	System International, "Elevator"

A group of grey-suited men are in an elevator. Suddenly, there is a farting sound. The men glance suspiciously at one another, but nobody is taking responsibility. After a couple of seconds, another fart rents the air. Again, all the men exchange disapproving looks. Finally, at the sound of the third fart, one of them realises that it's his mobile phone. New ringtones are now available. As he's chatting, however, there's another, even louder farting sound. And this time, it's not a phone.

Agency	Kitchen Leo Burnett, Oslo
Copywriters	Thomas Askim
	Christian Hygen
Art Directors	Per Erik Jarl
	Eirik Stensrud
Production	Paradox, Oslo
Directors	Andreas Riiser
	Kristoffer Carlin
Producers	Gry Sætre
	Caroline Werring Otnes
Client	Djuice, "Strange Voices"

In this campaign, people with "strange voices" explain the benefits of SMS. In the first spot, a thuggish-looking man explains that he was never taken seriously as a gang leader because he talks like a child. We see him "menacing" a blindfolded prisoner, who starts giggling. A woman chorister has the voice of a truck driver and a "party organiser" speaks like an old woman, which makes him sound desperately unhip. Now they all use SMS instead. Djuice is the network for heavy SMS users.

Agency	DDB, Paris
Creative Directors	Alexandre Hervé
	Sylvain Thirache
Copywriter	Olivier Henry
Art Director	Mathieu Nevians
Production	Tokib, Paris
Director	Baker Smith
Producer	Agathe Michaux Terrier
Client	Bouygues Telecom, "Creation of the List"

A group of people meet in a field under a sign saying "Matthew's Phone Book". They are the physical embodiments of all the numbers Matthew has stored on his phone. "I'm Matthew's father," says a man in a suit. "And I'm Matthew's father at home," says the man's double, carrying a watering can. Gym instructors, dentists, bank managers and "the number of somebody Matthew can't remember" are all here. It just shows you how cheap it is to make calls with Bouygues Telecom.

Agency	DDB Germany, Hamburg
Executive CD	Hans Albers
Creative Directors	Marcus Kaspar
	Ulrike Schmiege
Copywriter	Nikolai Baradoy
Art Director	Marjorieth Alzen-Sanmartin
Production	Erste Liebe Filmproduktion, Hamburg
Director	Cadmo Quintero
Producers	Fabian Heinel
	Sascha Driesang
Client	T-Mobile, "Memorable Moments"

A plain, overweight man takes the stage during a TV talent show. He tells the impassive jury that he is going to "sing opera". They look unimpressed. Until, that is, he opens his mouth. We see people all around the country riveted to communications devices – TVs, laptops and mobile phones – as the amateur belts out an incredibly moving version of Nessun Dorma. The jury and most of the country are reduced to tears by mobile phone salesman Paul Potts, the real-life winner of the show. T-Mobile helps you catch those memorable moments.

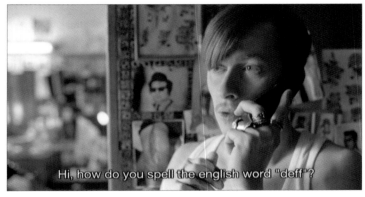

Communication Services   **67**

Agency	New Moment New Ideas Company Y&R, Skopje
Creative Director	Dusan Drakalski
Copywriters	Dusan Drakalski
	Filip Dimitrov
Production	Mainframe Production, Zagreb
Directors	Dusan Drakalski
	Marko Gjokovik
Client	Cosmofon, "Nuns"

A silent order of nuns is sitting around the communal dining table in the refectory. One of them whips out a mobile phone and begins texting. Another nun receives the message: "Pass the salt, please." She obliges. But yet another nun, also by SMS, points out: "That's not the salt, it's the pepper." The original nun sneezes. Phones bleep all over the place as everyone texts: "Bless you!" Now that Cosmofon offers free SMS every weekend, being silent isn't so restricting.

Agency	Hei Reklamebyrå, Oslo
Copywriter	Thomas Mittun-Kjos
Art Director	Nico Wahl
Production	Paradox, Oslo
Directors	Andreas Riser
	Kristoffer Carlin
Producer	Jarle Tangen
Client	Opplysningen 1881, "Tattoo"

A young man is on the phone to the 1881 information service. "How do you spell 'death'?" he asks. The girl at the call centre says: "Like in 'deaf' or 'death'?" The young man tells her: "Like in death metal." The girl spells out D-E-A-T-H. "No 'f' then?" asks the man hopefully. As the camera pans across the room we see that it is a tattoo parlour. A client is sitting there with a half-completed tattoo that reads: "Deaf Metal". 1881 can help you with anything. Almost.

Agency	Forsman & Bodenfors, Gothenburg
Production	Bacon, Copenhagen
Director	Kasper Wedendahl
Producer	Christian Zethner
Client	Tele2, "Cheaper Internet" Campaign

We see kids watching a series of inane and extremely amateurish films on the Internet. One features an overweight woman attempting to breakdance. Another shows a teenager who can make his tongue ripple as if he's some kind of alien. It's exactly the kind of trash you can see on YouTube. Sure enough, we cut to another young man watching the "Alien Tongue" performance and half-heartedly trying to copy it. "So," says the caption, addressing the parents, "how much are you paying for this?" Internet is cheaper with Tele2.

- God damn, thats good!

68   **Communication Services**

Agency	Forsman & Bodenfors, Gothenburg
Production	FLX, Stockholm
Director	Felix Herngren
Producer	Ylva Axell
Client	Comviq, "Amigos" Campaign

Two spots warn young people about the dangers of leaving their parents at home unsupervised. In the first, the oldsters have gotten hold of their kid's moped and are taking it for a tyre-shredding spin around the living room, much to the amusement of their party guests. Just because the Comviq Prepaid card means you can call free from 21 countries, it doesn't mean that going away is a good idea.

In the second spot, we see a middle-aged man climbing out of a swimming pool with a bicycle. We then discover that the parents and their friends are practising "extreme sports" by leaping from the roof of the house into the pool on their kids' bikes and skateboards. When you're travelling, you can call free from 21 countries using the Comviq Prepaid card. Check up on your parents.

Agency	Publicis Conseil, Paris
Executive CD	Olivier Altmann
Copywriter	Fabrice Dubois
Art Director	Pascale Gayraud
Production	Les Télécréateurs, Paris
Director	Didier Barcelo
Producers	Hélène Daubert
	Pierre Marcus
	Muriel Allegrini
Client	Orange Football Channel, "Piano"

Two scruffy men amble into a musical instrument shop filled with gleaming grand pianos. A salesman approaches them. One of the men says: "I've got a problem with my horn." "Your what?" The friend butts in: "With his horn." The man produces an air horn of the type used at soccer matches. "I think it's out of tune," he says. He sounds the horn, making the salesman jump. "See? It's not the same sound. If you could adjust it just a tone, or a maybe a half-tone." Orange is now broadcasting football. Get ready to support your team.

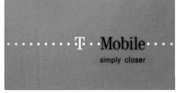

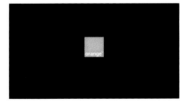

Agencies	Publicis Group Austria, Vienna
	Saatchi Europe
Creative Director	Jason Romeyko
Copywriter	Andreas Eisenwagen
Art Director	Jason Romeyko
Production	Pioneer, Budapest
Director	Fredrik Callingaard
Producers	Melinda Szepesi
	Mads Marstrand
	Laszlo Bederna
Client	T-Mobile, "Hugging"

A young man walks down a snowy, empty city street. He takes out his mobile phone and dials a number. Then he holds out his arms, as if waiting for an embrace. Magically, a young woman appears and he hugs her close. Then more people appear out of thin air – friends, family members – all taking part in a big, warm, group hug. Finally, they melt away. But the man is smiling as he walks on, suddenly happy on this bitter winter's day. T-Mobile brings people closer.

Agency	Publicis Conseil, Paris
Executive CD	Olivier Altmann
Copywriter	Olivier Camensuli
Art Director	Frédéric Royer
Production	Wanda, Paris
Director	Philippe André
Producers	Pierre Marcus
	Muriel Allegrini
Client	Orange, "Christmas for Grown-Ups"

We are all kids at heart, this ad suggests. A group of builders are playing with a giant plastic crane. A woman tenderly grooms a My Little Pony. Another lives in a doll's house. A cashier plays with an oversized plastic till. And a pilot gazes admiringly from the terminal building at a full size space fighter from Star Wars. It's not only kids who dream of toys. This Christmas, the toys for adults are at Orange.

Communication Services

Agency	Storåkers McCann, Stockholm
Copywriters	Hanna Belander
	Martin Johansen
Art Director	Henric Almquist
Photographer	Andreas Ackerup
Production	Adamsky, Stockholm
Client	Telia

Agency	Ogilvy & Mather, Copenhagen
Copywriter	Mikkel Elung-Jensen
Art Director	Claus Collstrup
Photographer	Søren Hald
Client	Telia

SOMEWHERE OUT THERE
SOMEONE IS WAITING TO
HEAR FROM YOU.

We just want to prepare you for the ad from Tele2 later in this newspaper. Well, there are still quite a few pages left until you reach it, but it's good to know in advance.

Alright, now it's almost time for the Tele-2 ad. You've probably never seen it before, but it's not dangerous in any way. A totally normal ad then, in just a few pages.

There's still a bit left until you reach the Tele-2 ad we just talked about. Maybe we should mention that it's black-and-yellow and has a special offer. Okay then, don't worry.

Good news for people that don't like surprises:
FIXED PRICE ON EVERYTHING!

Agency — Jung von Matt, Berlin
Creative Directors — Mathias Stiller
Wolfgang Schneider
Jan Harbeck
David Mously
Copywriter — Jessica Hoppe
Art Director — Julien von Seherr-Thoß
Client — Deutsche Post

Agency — Forsman & Bodenfors, Gothenburg
Client — Tele2

passez d'une musique à l'autre sans limite.
musique max. 1,3 millions de titres à télécharger.

passez d'une musique à l'autre sans limite.
musique max. 1,3 millions de titres à télécharger.

Agency	Shalmor Avnon Amichay\ Y&R Interactive, Tel Aviv	**Agency**	Publicis Conseil, Paris	Move from one kind of music to another without limits. Music Max - 1.3 million titles to download.		
Creative Directors	Gideon Amichay Tzur Golan Yariv Twig	**Executive CD** **Copywriter** **Art Director**	Olivier Altmann Patrice Lucet Charles Guillemant			
Copywriter	Geva Kochba	**Photographer**	Geoffroy de Boismenu			
Art Director	Asaf Covo	**Client**	Orange			
Client	Orange					

Communication Services 73

Agency	Saatchi & Saatchi, London
Creative Directors	Paul Silburn
	Kate Stanners
Copywriters	Paul Silburn
	Howard Green
	Suzanne Hails
Art Directors	Dennis Willison
	Pablo Videla
Photographer	Nick Meek
Typographer	Tim Quest
Client	T-Mobile

Come on you slow-coach. Move it.

Who are you calling a slow-coach?

Move on, I'll run you over!

They put the steering wheel on the opposite side
and you got your nickers in a knot. Idiot!

www.aegeanair.com   Θέλω να πετάξω τώρα.

74   **Transport & Tourism**

Agency	Upset, Athens
Creative Director	Yola Gyftoula
Copywriter	Manos Moschonas
Art Director	Kallina Kyratsouli
Production	Boo Productions, Athens
Director	Giorgos Lanthimos
Producers	Aris Dayios
	Stelios Lykouresis
Client	Aegean Airlines, "More Greeks in London"

A normal-looking woman walks across a zebra crossing in London. A taxi stops to let her past – but a speeding Mini almost crashes into the back of it, screeching to a halt. The Mini's driver hits the horn and leans out, shouting in Greek: "Get a move on, slowcoach!" The woman explodes with rage, also in Greek. "Chimpanzee, caveman! They put the wheel on the other side and you get your knickers in a knot, idiot!" Ah, those hot-blooded Greeks. Thanks to cheap flights with Aegean Airlines, there are more of them in London these days.

LONDON AT A HALLUCINATING PRICE: €66 RETURN

 Transport & Tourism **75**

Agency	Leg, Paris
Creative Director	Gabriel Gaultier
Copywriter	Gabriel Gaultier
Art Director	Christophe Dru
Illustrator	Christophe Dru
Client	Eurostar

Agency	Goss, Gothenburg
Copywriters	Micke Schultz
	Ulrika Good
	Elisabeth Berlander
Art Directors	Mattias Frendberg
	Mimmi Andersson
	Jan Eneroth
	Albin Larsson
	Gunnar Skarland
Client	Langley Travel

Agency	Ogilvy & Mather, Frankfurt
Creative Directors	Christian Mommertz
	Dr. Stephan Vogel
Copywriter	Alexander Haase
Art Directors	Kirsten Rosenberger
	Marco Weber
Production	Telemaz, Hamburg
Director	Eugen Stemmle
Producer	Petra Felten-Geisinger
DOP	Michael Krauter
Client	Deutsche Bahn, "Silent Night"

A caption reads: "Silent Night in Germany." But instead of scenes of Christmas peace on December 24, we see a series of stalled cars. Their engines rasp and splutter as their owners try to start them in the extreme cold. The irony becomes as bitter as the weather when we realise that the desperate noises form the tune of the Christmas carol "Silent Night". It's going to be exactly that for these frozen motors. None of the drivers are going anywhere. They should have relied on German Rail.

Agency	McCann Erickson, Madrid
Chief Creative Officer	Leandro Raposo
Executive CD's	Monica Moro
	Pablo Colonnese
	Pablo Stricker
Creative Director	Raquel Martinez
Copywriter	Isidro Casanova
Art Director	Pablo Stricker
Production	Indio Films, Madrid
Director	Fran Torres
Producer	Diego Mañas
Client	Metro de Madrid

Returning to a tiny village called "Madrid" in the Philippines, a young man recounts his adventures in the "big" Madrid. The Prado museum was not bad, the ham was even better – but the best thing about Madrid was its metro system. Inspired, villagers decide to build their own version. When it's completed, it looks exactly like the original – except that it has just one stop. Its passengers include a bemused goat. Madrid metro is the metro system every city would like to have when it grows up.

Agency	Euro RSCG Spain, Madrid	Agency	King, Helsinki
Creative Directors	German Silva	Creative Director	Jouko Laune
	Eva Conesa	Copywriters	Timo Koskinen
	Felipe Crespo		Olli Hietalahti
Copywriter	Elena Cubells	Art Director	Jouko Laune
Art Directors	Clara Vilaseca	Photographer	Kari Ylitalo
	German Silva	Illustrators	Vesa Sammalisto
			Pasi Pitkänen
Client	Air France	Client	Carpark

THE PLACE: RISKY DISCO
THE PRICE: 77€ A/R

The best House, Cosmic and Electro-boogie DJ's in London play every third Saturday of the month at the Risky Disco@The Prince parties. Unique and inimitable. Risky Disco@The Prince, 467-469 Brixton Road, London SW9. Tube station: Brixton.

THE PLACE: SH! WOMEN'S EROTIC EMPORIUM
THE PRICE: 77€ A/R

Here men can only enter if accompanied. Sh! is the ultimate, chic, English temple dedicated to the service of sensuality. 57 Hoxton Square, London N1. Tube station: Old Street. www.sh-womenstore.com.

THE PLACE: THE ELECTRIC BIRDCAGE
THE PRICE: 77€ A/R

It's in this new baroque West End address that extravaganza now meets for a drink with her old friend decadence. 11 Haymarket - London SW1. Tube station: Piccadilly Circus. www.electricbirdcage.com.

THE PLACE: CYBERDOG
THE PRICE: 77€ A/R

This futuristic clothes and accessories shop, where fluo and decibels rule, will deafen you, but ensure you are perfectly dressed to travel through time. The Stables Market, Chalk Farm Road, London NW1. Tube station: Camden Town. www.cyberdog.net.

78 Transport & Tourism

Agency	Leg, Paris
Creative Director	Gabriel Gaultier
Copywriter	Gabriel Gaultier
Art Director	Stéphane Richard
Photographers	Francis Azemard
	Ola Bergengren
Client	Eurostar

Agency   Leg, Paris
Creative Director   Gabriel Gaultier
Copywriter   Bernard Naville
Art Director   Cédric Moutaud
Photographer   Cédric Delsaux
Client   Eurostar

Playa de Strömstad

SEK **95**

SJ

Costa de Stockholm

SEK **95**

SJ

Göteborg-sur-Mer

SEK **95**

SJ

Playa de Malmö

SEK **95**

SJ

Lago di Östersund

SEK **95**

SJ

Playa de Karlstad

SEK **95**

SJ

Costa de Halmstad

SEK **95**

SJ

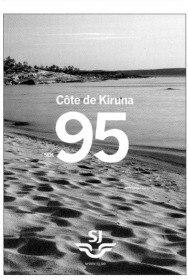

Côte de Kiruna

SEK **95**

SJ

Luleå al mare

SEK **95**

SJ

80   **Transport & Tourism**

Agency	King, Stockholm
Creative Director	Frank Hollingworth
Copywriter	Niclas Carlsson
Art Director	Josephine Wallin
Client	Swedish Railways

Agency	King, Stockholm
Creative Director	Frank Hollingworth
Copywriter	Niclas Carlsson
Art Director	Josephine Wallin
Photographers	Petrus Olsson
	Adamsky
Client	Swedish Railways

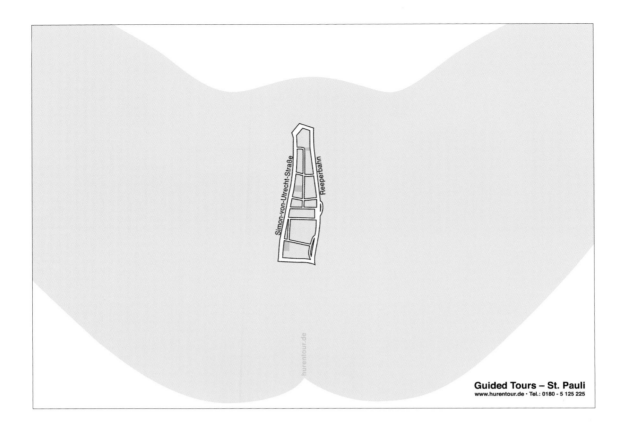

Guided Tours – St. Pauli
www.hurentour.de · Tel.: 0180 - 5 125 225

82 Transport & Tourism

Agency	Weigertpirouzwolf, Hamburg		Agency	Scholz & Friends, Hamburg
Creative Director	Kay Eichner		Creative Director	Timm Weber
Copywriter	Anna Wilhelmi		Copywriter	Mathias Brueckner
Art Director	Joana Haars		Art Director	Sebastian Kaufmann
Client	Hurentours		Photographer	Clemens Ascher
			Illustrator	Torsten Lass
			Client	Queer-Travel.de

You've looked at their brochure and finally found your paradise.

Now, you're in your room with hundreds of angels flying around.

∞
Exclusive Escapes
TRAVEL AGENCY
"Best places, no surprises"

www.exclusiveescapes.co.uk

TRY IT ONCE AND FORGET THE ROAD.

corail Téoz | SNCF

Agency	Markom Leo Burnett, Istanbul	Agency	TBWA\Paris
Creative Directors	Yasar Akbas Idil Akoglu Ergulen	Creative Director	Erik Vervroegen
Copywriter	Ilker Dagli	Copywriter	Ghislaine de Germon
Art Directors	Guven Haktanir Erkan Kaya	Art Director	Marianne Fonferrier
Photographer	Suleyman Kacar	Photographer	David Harriman
Client	Exclusive Escapes	Client	SNCF Teoz Trains

Throw the Swedes out.

mömax
finally a new furniture store
www.moemax.at

84   Retail Services

Agency	Demner, Merlicek & Bergmann, Vienna	A man and a woman walk into their bedroom. On their way, they are forced to pass a group of lurking, silent, fair-haired men dressed in strangely familiar blue and yellow outfits. The men watch the couple menacingly. Pulling the bedcovers back, the couple discover two more blue-clad men in their own bed. A caption reads "Throw the Swedes out." Mömax – finally, there's a new furniture store.
Creative Directors	Sebastian Kainz Marc Wientzek	
Copywriter	Nina Havlicek	
Art Director	Mark Hinckley	
Production	Demner, Merlicek & Bergmann, Vienna	
Director	Albert Waaijenberg	
Producer	Eva Hessler	
Client	Mömax, "Throw the Swedes Out"	

WHOEVER YOU'RE LOOKING FOR THIS CHRISTMAS **John Lewis**

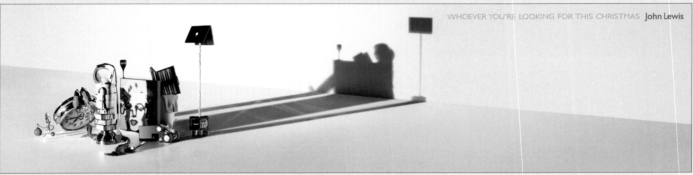

WHOEVER YOU'RE LOOKING FOR THIS CHRISTMAS **John Lewis**

WHOEVER YOU'RE LOOKING FOR THIS CHRISTMAS **John Lewis**

Agency	Lowe London
Creative Director	Ed Morris
Copywriter	George Prest
Art Director	Johnny Leathers
Photographer	Nadav Kander
Typographer	Dave Towers
Client	John Lewis
	Department Store

Agency	Heye & Partner, Unterhaching
Creative Director	Thomas Winklbauer
Copywriter	Thomas Winklbauer
Art Director	Wolfgang Biebach
Production	GAP Films, Munich
Director	Charley Stadler
Producers	Andreas Simon
	Natalie Bitnar
	Cordula Schrenk
Client	McDonald's, "Prison Visit"

A woman visits her husband in prison. Carrying a big bag over her arm, she looks nervous. She sits down in front of the glass screen. "Did you bring it?" he says, eagerly. The woman hesitates. "Go on," the man urges, "put it on!" The woman unenthusiastically takes her top off. She puts on the clothes in the bag. Suddenly, she's transformed into a McDonald's staff member. "A Big Mac please," orders the man. The woman goes along with the game. "And would you like that to stay or to go?" Abruptly, a prison guard hauls the man off – to stay.

86   Retail Services

Agency	Ruf Lanz Werbeagentur, Zurich
Creative Directors	Markus Ruf
	Danielle Lanz
Copywriter	Markus Ruf
Production	OnFilm, Zurich
Director	Serge Hoeltschi
Producer	Daniela Berther
Client	Hiltl Vegetarian Restaurant, "Sound-Designer"

Hiltl is a caterer providing fresh vegetarian snacks to Swiss cinemas. And here we see a sound designer using fresh vegetables to provide the smacks and thumps for a fight scene in a Quentin Tarantino movie. A snapped celery stick stands in for a broken arm, a crunched carrot is a punch in the jaw and a pummelled melon is a killer blow to the head. Movies just wouldn't be the same without Hiltl snacks.

Agency	Lowe London
Creative Director	Ed Morris
Copywriter	George Prest
Art Director	Johnny Leathers
Production	Partizan, London
Director	Michael Gracey
Producers	Ella Sanderson
	Hannah Boase
Client	John Lewis Department Store, "Shadows"

Echoing the award-winning print campaign, this ad shows what happens when a collection of gifts is arranged in a certain way and their shadow is projected onto a blank wall. As workers add each new gift to the selection, the shadow takes shape. Finally we see that it has become the outline of a woman walking her dog. Find the right gift for the right person this Christmas, at John Lewis department store.

AS CLOSE TO A GOOD CINEMA AS YOU CAN GET.

FIND THE BEST* SEATS HERE:

Not everyone gets to experience their films via a Pause audiovisual system. But with a little care, the closest you can get is actually pretty good. Try out a good audiovisual system this weekend with the help of this practical seat guide.

And if that whets your appetite for a home cinema system of your very own, do come and see us at Pause.

PAUSE ♥ MOVIE

TAILOR-MADE HI-FI AND HOME THEATRE SYSTEMS. WWW.PAUSELJUDBILD.COM

DECEMBER 2, 2007, SOUTHERN ÄNGBY BEACH BLACKEBERG

UNUSUALLY BIG FILM EXPERIENCES.

Saving Private Ryan is one of five unusually powerful film experiences included in the Pause DVD Collection Vol 1. Drop by our shop and find out which equipment will do them justice.

Pause
Home Entertainment

Agency	Åkestam Holst, Stockholm
Copywriter	Mark Ardelius
Art Director	Andreas Ullenius
Illustrator	Torbjörn Krantz
Client	Pause Ljud & Bild

Not everyone can enjoy films with a Pause home entertainment system, so the advertiser visited 45 Stockholm cinemas to identify the seats that offer the best audiovisual experiences. Comfort and leg-room were also taken into account. Those who used one of these selected seats were invited to save their theatre tickets and exchange them for generous discount vouchers on Pause's home cinema equipment.

Agency	Åkestam Holst, Stockholm
Copywriter	Mark Ardelius
Art Directors	Andreas Ullenius Johan Landin
Photographer	Sven Prim
Illustrator	Torbjörn Krantz
Producers	Lotta Linde Helena Holmberg
Client	Pause Ljud & Bild

To prove that the people at Pause home entertainment stores are true film specialists, the CEO and staff re-enacted key scenes from blockbuster movies. The copy provides a detailed description of the scene. In addition to "Saving Private Ryan", other executions included scenes from "A Clockwork Orange", "The Matrix" and "Titanic" (page 331).

Agency	DDB Stockholm
Creative Director	Andreas Dahlqvist
Copywriters	Simon Higby
	Viktor Arve
	Felix Söderlind
	Tove Eriksen Hillblom
Art Directors	Simon Higby
	Viktor Arve
	Felix Söderlind
	Tove Eriksen Hillblom
Client	McDonald's &
	Coca-Cola

88   Retail Services

Agency	TBWA\Paris
Creative Director	Erik Vervroegen
Copywriters	Pierre-Louis Messager
	Ghyslaine de Germon
Art Director	Marianne Fonferrier
Production	La Pac, Paris
Director	Lieven van Baelen
Client	La Redoute,
	"Styling Contest"
	Campaign

These two ads show how easy it is to change your look thanks to the catalogue La Redoute. In the first spot, two women on either side of the street notice that they're wearing the same dress. They magically transform their outfits, one after another, flinging clothes on and off as they walk in a style duel. When it starts to rain, ironically, they end up in the same red raincoat.

In the second ad, a woman decorating her apartment notices that the lady across the street has bought the same lampshade. By changing one object in the room, she instantly changes its entire look. But the woman in the window opposite does the same thing, redesigning her apartment at light speed to show how trendy she is. The duel commences, until one woman turns out to have the one thing the other does not – a boyfriend. With its low prices, La Redoute makes fashion fun.

Agency	DDB Stockholm	Agency	Ruf Lanz Werbeagentur, Zurich
Creative Director	Andreas Dahlqvist		
Copywriter	Martin Lundgren	Creative Directors	Markus Ruf
Art Directors	Simon Higby		Danielle Lanz
	Ted Harry Mellström	Copywriters	Markus Ruf
	Viktor Arve		Torsten Maas
Photographer	Alexander Pihl	Art Director	Grit Wolany
Illustrator	Simon Higby	Photographer	Stefan Minder
Client	McDonald's	Client	Fashion Outlet Zurich

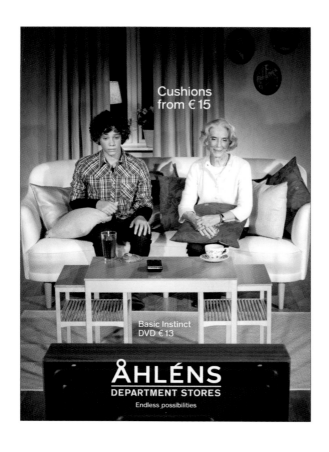

Agency	King, Stockholm		**Agency**	Callegari Berville Grey, Paris
Creative Director	Frank Hollingworth		**Creative Director**	Andrea Stillacci
Copywriters	Hedvig Hagwall Bruckner		**Copywriters**	Mathieu Grichois
	Pontus Ekström			Lessly Chmil
Art Directors	Alexander Elers		**Art Director**	Cedric Auzannet
	Graziela Lages		**Photographer**	Romain Laurent
Photographer	Bisse Bengtsson		**Illustrators**	David Martin
Client	Åhléns Department Store			Benoit Monceau
			Client	123fleur.com

Agency	King, Stockholm	Agency	Lowe Brindfors, Stockholm
Creative Director	Frank Hollingworth	Creative Director	Håkan Engler
Copywriters	Hedvig Hagwall Bruckner	Copywriter	Aron Levander
	Pontus Ekström	Art Directors	Tove Langseth
Art Directors	Alexander Elers		Pia-Maria Falk
	Axel Isberg	Photographer	Anders Sjödin
	Graziela Lages	Client	Nordiska Kompaniet
Photographer	Henrik Halvarsson		Department Store
Final Art	King studio		
Client	Åhléns Department Store		

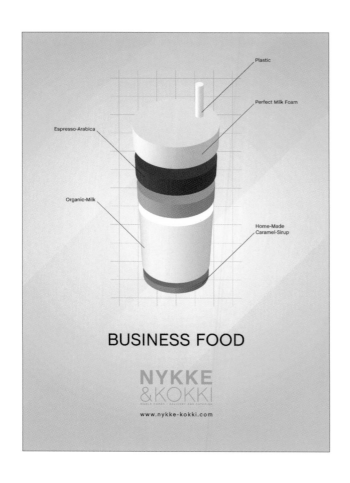

BUSINESS FOOD

NYKKE
&KOKKI

www.nykke-kokki.com

THERE'S A VEGETARIAN IN EVERY FOOTBALL PLAYER.
Hiltl. The Vegetarian Caterer at Euro 2008.

HILTL

THERE'S A VEGETARIAN IN EVERY FOOTBALL PLAYER.
Hiltl. The Vegetarian Caterer at Euro 2008.

HILTL

92 **Retail Services**

Agency	Scholz & Friends, Hamburg
Creative Directors	Stefan Setzkorn
	Matthias Schmidt,
	Gunnar Loeser
	Heiko Schmidt
Copywriter	Lena Krumkamp
Art Director	Sascha Mauson
Client	Nykke & Kokki Catering

Agency	Ruf Lanz Werbeagentur, Zurich
Creative Directors	Markus Ruf
	Danielle Lanz
Copywriter	Torsten Maas
Art Director	Marcel Schlaefle
Client	Hiltl Vegetarian Restaurant

סיפורה של מדינה

חוגגים 60 לישראל

If you can imagine it
you can build it.

HORNBACH
Home Improvement Superstores

Agency	Shalmor Avnon Amichay\ Y&R Interactive, Tel Aviv	The titles of well-known Israeli literary works are arranged in an order that recounts the history of the State of Israel. The names of more than 500 books are used to this end, without a single word being added.	**Agency** Heimat, Berlin
Creative Directors	Gideon Amichay Tzur Golan Amit Gal		**Creative Directors** Guido Heffels Matthias Storat
Copywriter	Geva Kochba		**Copywriters** Matthias Storath Susanne Düber
Art Director	Ran Cory		**Art Directors** Kai Gerken Danny Baarz
Photographer	Yoram Aschheim		**Photographer** Markus Müller
Client	Steimatzky Book Stores		**Illustrator** Jennifer Schumacher
			Client Hornbach Home Improvement Superstores

94 **Retail Services**

Agency	DDB London
Creative Director	Jeremy Craigen
Copywriters	Graeme Hall
	Noah Regan
Art Directors	Graeme Hall
	Noah Regan
Photographer	Jonathan De Villiers
Client	Harvey Nichols

Agency	DDB London
Creative Director	Jeremy Craigen
Copywriter	Grant Parker
Art Director	Grant Parker
Photographer	Giles Revell
Client	Harvey Nichols, Bristol

Retail Services

Agency	DDB London
Creative Director	Jeremy Craigen
Copywriter	Dave Henderson
Art Director	Richard Denney
Photographer	Karena Perronet-Miller
Client	Harvey Nichols

THE
HARVEY NICHOLS
SALE
DOORS OPEN 27 DECEMBER 10AM

UP TO 50% OFF
KNIGHTSBRIDGE · LONDON

THE
HARVEY NICHOLS
SALE
DOORS OPEN 27 DECEMBER 10AM

UP TO 50% OFF
KNIGHTSBRIDGE · LONDON

THE
HARVEY NICHOLS
SALE
DOORS OPEN 27 DECEMBER 10AM

UP TO 50% OFF
KNIGHTSBRIDGE · LONDON

Retail Services   **97**

Agency   DDB London
Creative Director   Jeremy Craigen
Copywriter   Thierry Albert
Art Director   Damien Albert
Photographer   Ben Hassett
Client   Harvey Nichols

98   **Financial Services**

<table>
<tr><td>Agency</td><td>King James,
Cape Town</td></tr>
<tr><td>Creative Director</td><td>Devin Kennedy</td></tr>
<tr><td>Art Director</td><td>Damian Bonse</td></tr>
<tr><td>Production</td><td>Velocity Films,
Cape Town</td></tr>
<tr><td>Co-Production</td><td>Pioneer Productions,
Buenos Aires</td></tr>
<tr><td>Director</td><td>Keith Rose</td></tr>
<tr><td>Producers</td><td>Karen Kloppers
Caz Friedman</td></tr>
<tr><td>Client</td><td>Allan Gray Investment
Management, "Beautiful"</td></tr>
</table>

A small boy will do almost anything for a rather plain little girl. He buys her candyfloss, accompanies her to ballet class – where he watches her intently – and protects her from the taunts of other pupils, even getting himself badly beaten up in the process. What's so special about the girl? "My papa told me two things," explains the boy. "Always look for potential…" We see him waving to the little girl's mother, a raven-haired Latin beauty. "Then, have the patience to wait for it." Financial consultancy Allan Gray has the same policy.

GO AHEAD.
TURN 70
YEARS OLD
TODAY.

Take a picture of yourself with your phone and then MMS it
to 712 12. In just a few minutes we'll send you back a picture
of how you might look when you are 70 years old.

AMF PENSION

More to live for

JCDecaux

GREY HAIR
AND WRINKLES
IN JUST
3 MINUTES!

Take a picture of yourself with your phone and then MMS it
to 712 12. In just a few minutes we'll send you back a picture
of how you might look when you are 70 years old.

AMF PENSION

More to live for

JCDecaux

NOW!
GET 40 YEARS
OLDER IN JUST
3 MINUTES.

Take a picture of yourself with your phone and then MMS it
to 712 12. In just a few minutes we'll send you back a picture
of how you might look when you are 70 years old.

AMF PENSION

More to live for

Take a picture of yourself with your phone and then MMS
it to 712 12. In just a few minutes we'll send you back a
picture of how you might look when you are 70 years old.

AMF PENSION

More to live for

Take a picture of yourself with your phone and then MMS
it to 712 12. In just a few minutes we'll send you back a
picture of how you might look when you are 70 years old.

AMF PENSION

More to live for

Take a picture of yourself with your phone and then MMS
it to 712 12. In just a few minutes we'll send you back a
picture of how you might look when you are 70 years old.

AMF PENSION

More to live for

 Financial Services 99

Agency — Forsman & Bodenfors, Gothenburg
Photographer — Erik Undéhn
Client — AMF Pension

Agency	Forsman & Bodenfors, Gothenburg
Production	Flodell Film, Stockholm
Director	Tomas Jonsgården
Producer	Magnus Åkerstedt
DOP	Henrik Stenberg
Client	AMF Pension, "Good Old Days"

"Some people talk about the good old days," says the narrator, as we see scenes from the recent past. A boy sits in the back of a smoke-filled car. A man struggles through the rain to a phone box. A computer is a glorified calculator. There are only two TV channels. A father is not responsible for changing his baby's nappy. And pizza has not yet been invented, so kids eat semolina. "Were the good old days really so good?" wonders the narrator. "Or do things get better and better all the time?" AMF Pension: funds for the future.

Agency	Forsman & Bodenfors, Gothenburg
Production	Social Club, Stockholm
Director	Jesper Ericstam
Producer	Magnus Theroin
DOP	Pär M Ekberg
Client	AMF Pension, "Wakening"

It's 7am. An alarm goes off and a young man is jolted awake. Then the scene repeats itself: same man, slightly older. We then follow our hero through his life as he wakes up in a variety of different circumstances – in the army, on a sofa, with a girl, with a wife and kids, on a plane – and always by the 7am alarm. In the final scene, we see the man, much older now, sleeping on when 7am comes silently around. The future – a pretty good reason for a pension plan.

Agency	Forsman & Bodenfors, Gothenburg
Production	Social Club, Stockholm
Director	Jesper Ericstam
Producer	Magnus Theroin
DOP	Carl Sundberg
Client	AMF Pension, "Sports Fan"

A supporter of Malmö soccer team is in for a lifetime of disappointment. The ad follows him from match to match and year to year as his team consistently fails to bring home a trophy. Admirably, though, he remains unwaveringly loyal. Years later, his hair and moustache grey, we see him watching the match in the local pub. And – what's this? – Malmö have won! Our hero enjoys an emotional celebratory pint with his fellow fans. The future: not a bad reason to have a pension plan.

Agency	MUW/Saatchi &Saatchi, Bratislava
Creative Director	Rasto Ulicny
Copywriters	Jozef Chmel
	Rasto Michalik
	Matus Svirloch
	Katarina Kureckova
Art Director	Radim Blaho
Production	AVI Studio, Bratislava
Director	Vladislav Struhar
Producer	Vlasto Paulik
Client	Kooperativa Car Insurance, "Truck"

A long-distance lorry driver is beginning to nod off at the wheel. He wakes his colleague who emerges from the rear to take over. In the next scene, though, we see that both men are falling asleep. A loud blast on a horn wakes them up. But where did the sound come from? Another truck overtakes them, with its driver asleep at the wheel – his head resting on the horn. You share the road with guys like this. Wake up, and get decent car insurance.

Centraal Beheer

The insurance company
in Apeldoorn. (055) 579 8000

Agency	DDB Amsterdam
Creative Director	Martin Cornelissen
Copywriters	Ruben Sonneveld
	Daniel Snelders
Art Directors	Robert van der Lans
	Niels de Wit
Production	Stink, London
Director	Stylewar
Producers	Mungo Maclagan
	Yuka Kambayashi
Client	Centraal Beheer Insurance, "UFO"

A spaceship filled with gruesome aliens approaches earth. The invasion is imminent and the creatures are sure of victory. The ship plunges through the earth's atmosphere and prepares to crash land. Meanwhile, on a tranquil campsite, a couple sit outside their caravan. Surely they're about to be crushed by the UFO? Not quite: there's a problem of scale, and the miniscule space ship lands on a dangling strip of flypaper. Most of the time, you don't need to make an insurance claim. But when you do, call Centraal Beheer.

Agencies	JWT London
	JWT New York
Global CD	Axel Chaldecott
Art Director	Michael Ashley
Copywriter	Dinesh Kapoor
Production	Gorgeous Enterprises, London
Director	Vince Squibb
Producers	Spencer Dodd
	Dean Baker
Client	HSBC, "Lumberjack"

Police arrive at a construction site in the forest, where environmental activists are preventing trees from being knocked down. As one of the tree huggers is dragged away by the cops, she says to a chainsaw-wielding lumberjack: "Happy now, are you?" Later, we see the same woman in prison. The lumberjack is there to bail her out – and it slowly dawns on us that they are a couple. People value some things differently. HSBC treats customers as individuals.

Agency	Jung von Matt, Berlin
Creative Directors	Mathias Stiller
	Wolfgang Schneider
	David Mously
	Jan Harbeck
Copywriter	Teja Fischer
Art Director	Florian Pack
Client	Sparkasse

Invest cleverly with investment products by Sparkasse.

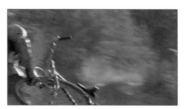

Agency	Duval Guillaume, Antwerp
Creative Directors	Geoffrey Hantson
	Dirk Domen
Copywriter	Kristof Snels
Art Director	Sebastien De Valck
Production	Caviar, Brussels
Director	Kurt Deleier
Client	Mercator Insurance, "Never Trust a Man"

A beautiful blonde walks through a crowded shopping centre, showing her considerable charms a little too obviously in a short skirt and a tight top. Every man she passes turns to look at her, momentarily forgetting the wife or girlfriend on his arm. It's a sad demonstration of what a pretty face and a nice body can do to a man. Ladies, you better rely on yourselves for the future. Save for your pension with Mercator.

Agency	Grabarz & Partner, Hamburg
Creative Directors	Ralf Heuel
	Dirk Siebenhaar
Copywriter	Martin Grass
Art Director	Djik Ouchiian
Production	Big Fish Filmproduktion, Berlin
Director	Andreas Hoffmann
Producer	Patrick Cahill
DOP	Pascal Walder
Client	DEVK Insurance, "Bicycle"

A man is cycling down a quiet country track. Suddenly a bizarre figure dressed in armour bursts out of the bushes, grunting savagely. Astonished, the cyclist struggles briefly as the 'knight' grabs the bike, wrenches it out of his grasp and drags it off into the forest, still grunting. A caption reads: 'How do you explain this to your insurance?' Luckily, there is always DEVK, an understanding insurer.

Agency	Caldas Naya, Barcelona	So many privileges may go to your head.	Agency	Ogilvy Amsterdam
Creative Director	Gustavo Caldas		Creative Directors	Darre van Dijk
				Piebe Piebenga
Copywriter	Gustavo Caldas		Copywriter	Piebe Piebenga
Art Director	Mireia Puig		Art Director	Darre van Dijk
Photographers	Mike Diver		Photographer	Arno Bosma
	Pedro Aguilar		Client	Funeral.eu
Client	LKXA Youth Bank			

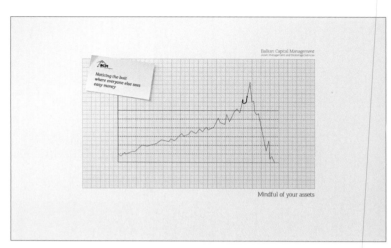

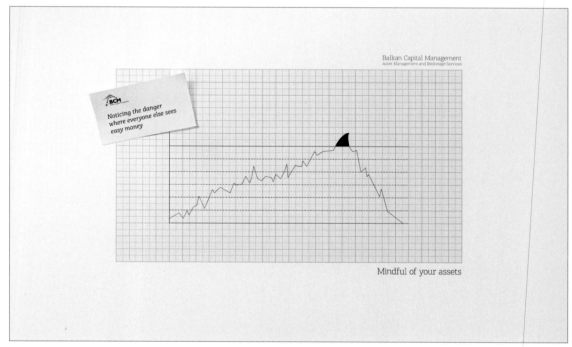

Agency	Saatchi & Saatchi Beirut		**Agency**	Reforma Advertising, Sofia
Creative Director	Samer Younes		**Creative Director**	Martin Dimitrov
Art Director	Marwan Kanaan		**Copywriter**	Tsanka Krusheva
Client	Libano-Française Bank		**Art Director**	Boris Bratkov
			Photographer	Vasil Enchev
			Client	Balkan Capital Management

Agency	Ruf Lanz Werbeagentur, Zurich	Save the beauty of nature: invest in our ecological financial products.
Creative Directors	Markus Ruf	
	Danielle Lanz	We let you know about the opportunities
Copywriter	Thomas Schoeb	on the stockmarket. And about the risks
Art Director	Lorenz Clormann	as well.
Photographers	Felix Streuli	
	Felix Schregenberger	To make sure that your pension won't give
Origami-Artist	Armin Täubner	you headaches, just contact us.
Client	Coop Bank	

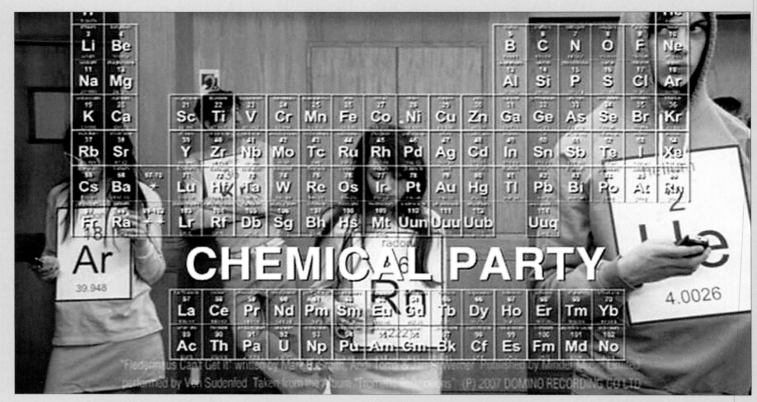

CHEMICAL PARTY

CARBON

+

ATTRACTION

CARBON CAN ATTRACT

EXPLOSIVE REACTION

EU SUPPORTS
RESEARCH CAREERS

Public Interest

Production	Media Consulta, Berlin
	Hungry Man, London
Director	Roderick Fenske
Producers	Camilla Wilson
	Till Dreier
Clients	EU & Marie Curie Actions,
	"Chemical Party"

Party guests wear signs identifying themselves as chemicals. We learn a thing or two about how chemicals behave. For instance, neon and hydrogen dance without much interest in one another – but hydrogen is highly attracted to carbon. Electricity ends a beautiful relationship between sodium and chloride. Oxygen bonds with itself, until hydrogen intervenes. And water and potassium are an explosive mixture! It's all to show how the European Union supports research careers.

15km² of rain forest disappears every minute

Agency	Uncle Grey, Aarhus
Creative Director	Per Pedersen
Copywriter	Michael Paterson
Art Directors	Jesper Hansen
	Rasmus Gottliebsen
Client	WWF

Agency	Scholz & Friends, Berlin
Creative Directors	Oliver Handlos
	Wolf Schneider
	Matthias Spaetgens
Copywriter	Edgar Linscheid
Art Director	Sara Viera
Production	Markenfilm, Berlin
Director	Benjamin Wolff
Producers	Nina Heyn
	Nele Juergens
	Daniel Klessig
Client	Amnesty International, "Crazy-Leader-Commercial"

Have all these leaders got a screw loose? A series of rapid cuts show us George Bush making an origami bird, Vladimir Putin playing with balloon animals and Iranian president Mahmoud Ahmadinejad demonstrating his rapid knitting skills for a thrilled audience. Leaders can often seem insane. But we can change what they do, by supporting Amnesty International.

108   **Public Interest**

Agency	McCann Erickson, Lisbon
Creative Directors	Diogo Anahory
	José Bomtempo
Copywriter	Diogo Anahory
Art Director	José Bomtempo
Production	Seagulls Fly
	Rio de Janeiro
Director	Flávio Mac
Producer	Nuno Calado
Client	Quercus, "Animals"

To a soundtrack of Peter Gabriel singing "Don't Give Up", we see animals in extreme circumstances. A chimpanzee sits in a bare tree in a blighted forest. A polar bear contemplates the melting ice cap. And a kangaroo is stranded in an industrial wasteland. One by one, they commit suicide. The monkey hangs itself with a vine. The polar bear tumbles from a cliff. And the kangaroo throws itself in front of a train. If you give up, they give up. Stop global warming.

Agency	DraftFCB, Stockholm
Creative Director	Anders Dalenius
Copywriter	Jesper Eronn
Art Director	Andreas Englund
Production	Colony, Stockholm
	Mister Krister, Stockholm
Directors	Jens Sjögren
	Henning Mark
Producers	Josefine Rosengren
	Marcus Sundqvist
Client	Swedish TV Licence Fee, "Thank you!" Campaign

A man is about to enter the water in a public swimming pool when a stranger, seated on the diving board, asks him: "Excuse me, is your name Torkel Jörgensen?" "Yes," replies the man. Abruptly, the stranger breaks into song, praising Torkel for having paid the TV licence fee and thanking all the other Swedes who do the same. Other swimmers join in the chorus; only the lifeguard looks baffled. In a second spot librarian Katarina Tillberg is given the same treatment. Thanks to people like Torkel and Katarina there is a public TV service in Sweden.

Agency	TBWA\Paris
Creative Directors	Erik Vervroegen
	Franck Pralong
Art Director	Franck Pralong
Production	U-Man, Paris
Director	Olivier Dahan
Client	Amnesty International, "Domestic Violence"

A film recalling old silent movies shows a woman at a stove. Her husband enters, drunk. He takes a swing at her. The violence escalates as he throws a drink in her face and chases her around the dinner table. An audience gathers at the window. At first they find the scene amusing, but when the woman is punched and they realise she is in real danger. The husband proceeds to beat her to a pulp. The audience leaves, apart from one woman who shouts: "Stop!" But nobody hears – this is a silent movie. Domestic violence: speak up, if you can.

Agency	Walker, Zurich
Creative Director	Pius Walker
Art Directors	Serge Pennings
	Steven Clark
Production	Sonny, London
Director	Jeff Thomas
Client	Amnesty International, "Cattle Market."

Hundreds of bedraggled young women are herded into a bleak concrete space. They are confused and frightened. Above, men hold up numbers and make bids for them. The women are pushed and prodded, their jaws forced open so bidders can examine their teeth. It's literally a cattle market. 500,000 girls are sold into the sex industry every year. Slavery needs to be abolished – again.

Agency	TBWA\MAP, Paris
Creative Directors	Manoëlle
	van der Vaeren
	Sébastien Vacherot
Copywriter	Alban Penicaut
Art Director	Stéphane Lecoq
Production	Space Patrol, Paris
Directors	Philippe Gamer
	Fred Remuzat
Client	Douleurs Sans Frontières, "Stop Pain"

In an animated spot, we see a boy walking through a war-torn landscape with his mother. Strangely, the passing landscape and the path they are on move at different speeds. The boy's mother dies. He watches his town being destroyed by war. Then he passes the body of his mother again. Walking on, he is wounded by a flying bullet. Again, he comes across his mother's body. As the camera pans out, we see that he is on an endless treadmill. For some, the pain never stops. But you can help: give to Pain Without Borders.

Agency	Brainwaves, Munich
Creative Director	Andreas Grassl
Copywriters	Oliver Oelkers
	Andreas Grassl
Art Director	Christoph Göpner
Production	Darkofilms, Munich
Director	Andreas Grassl
Producers	Darko Lovrinic
	Hesham Khalifa
Client	Bavarian Ministry
	of Social Affairs,
	"Stop the Nonsense"

Addressing the board, the big boss says: "The salaries of our executives have to be cut by a quarter...But we can't fire people, nor can we make them work longer, and qualifications have to remain as high as they are now." One of the executives stands up and takes off his shirt. He then puts on a bra and a wig. The boss gets the idea – women earn up to 23% less for the same job. Isn't it time to stop this nonsense?

Agency	Grey London
Creative Director	Jon Williams
Copywriter	Joanna Perry
Art Director	Damon Troth
Production	RSA, London
Director	Brett Foraker
Producers	Rebecca Pople
	Suki Drane
Client	British Heart
	Foundation,
	"Watch Your Own
	Heart Attack"

We see through the eyes of a man who is getting an extremely tough lecture about what it's like to have a heart attack. For starters, the lecturer punches his "student" in the chest. The first symptom is chest pains. "Or it could just be a bit of tightness around the chest," the lecturer says, holding his victim in a vice-like grip. "What if it spreads to your neck, to your jaw?" The "lecturer" tortures his victim to simulate the different stages of a heart attack. If you experience any of the symptoms, call an ambulance, before it's too late.

Agency	WCRS, London
Production	Gorgeous Enterprises,
	London
Director	Chris Palmer
Producer	Rupert Smythe
Client	Transport for London -
	Cycle Safety,
	"Awareness Test"

We see a line-up of basketball players. The voiceover says: "How many passes does the team in white make?" We watch them play, intently counting the passes. "The answer is 13," the narrator tells us. Then he adds: "But – did you see the moon-walking bear?" The film rewinds and when we watch again, we spot a man dressed in a bear suit. He is, indeed, doing a moon-walk. This is not a trick – it's easy to miss things you're not looking for. Look out for cyclists when you're driving.

Agency	Forsman & Bodenfors, Gothenburg
Production	Camp David, Stockholm
Directors	Måns Mårlind
	Björn Stein
Producer	Therese Engberg
DOP	Victor Davidsson
Client	Unicef, "AIDS"

This ad takes us to an alternate Europe, in the form of a trailer for a bleak science fiction movie. A virus has spread across the land. One million children have lost their parents. We see a pair of them, struggling to survive in their ruined housing estate. They can't afford medicine. They are at the mercy of marauding gangs. And the few remaining degenerate adults only want them for sex. Science fiction? In Ethiopia, it's real. Please support unicef.

Agency	VCCP, London
Production	Gorgeous Enterprises, London
Director	Vince Squibb
Producer	Spencer Dodd
Client	Home Office, "Anti Binge Drinking" Campaign

Two humorous yet hard-hitting spots aim to convince young people that hard drinking is not clever. In the first execution, a young man gets ready to go out. He rips his shirt, pours curry down himself, pisses on his shoes, rips out his earring, tears his jacket, beats himself up and smashes his stereo. By the time he leaves the house, he's a wreck. You wouldn't start a night like this – so why end it that way?

In the second spot, a girl gets ready for her fabulous night out. She deliberately ladders her tights, rips her camisole, vomits – making sure some of it gets in her hair – smudges her make-up and wets her skirt. For the final touches, she chucks red wine over her coat and snaps a heel. Looking a right state, she's ready to leave. You wouldn't start a night like this – so why end it that way?

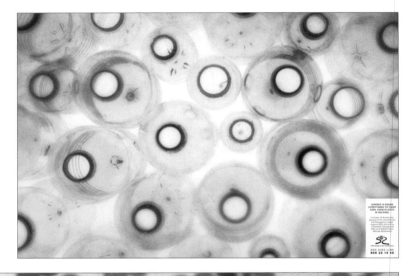

112   **Public Interest**

		Science is doing everything to fight against
Agency	Cream, Athens	AIDS, even plastic is helping. The copy
Creative Director	Fotis Georgiou	explains that the Portuguese League
Copywriter	Alex Esslin	Against AIDS will receive a donation for
Art Director	Filimonas Triantafyllou	every 20 plastic bottles placed in recycling
Photographer	Kostas Papatheodorou	bins.
Client	World AIDS Day	

Agency	McCann Erickson, Lisbon
Creative Directors	Diogo Anahory
	José Bomtempo
Copywriter	Emerson Braga
Art Director	André Lopes
Client	Portuguese League Against AIDS

Agency   TBWA\Paris
Creative Directors Erik Vervroegen
                    Michel De Lauw
Copywriter   Xander Smith
Art Director   Jonathan Santana
Illustrator   James Jean
Client   AIDES

Public Interest

Agency	DraftFCB Kobza, Vienna	**Agency**	DDB&Co., Istanbul
Creative Director	Joachim Glawion	**Creative Director**	Karpat Polat
Copywriter	Arno Reisenbüchler	**Copywriter**	Zeynep Karakasoglu
Art Director	Roman Steiner	**Art Director**	Caglar Eser
Photographer	Robert Striegl	**Client**	DHKD,
Client	Greenpeace		Association for
			Nature Preservation

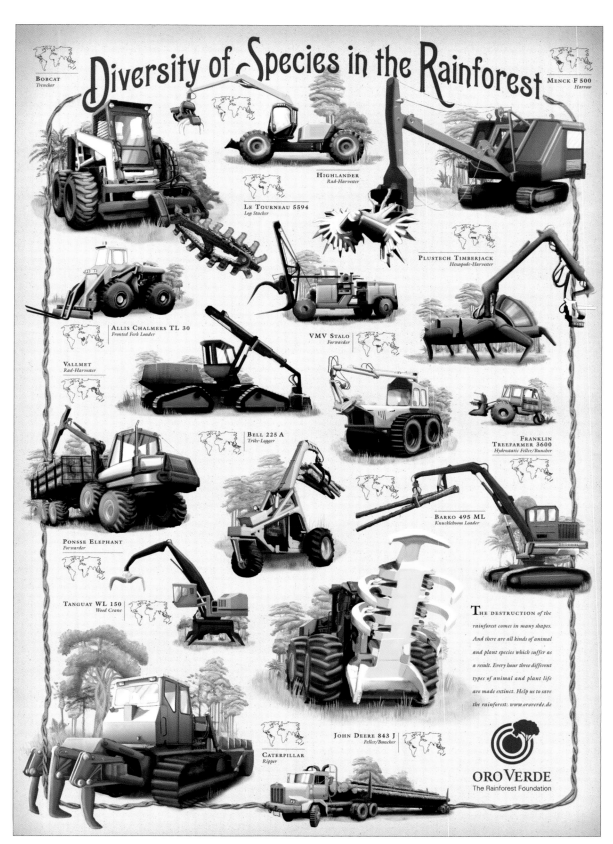

Diversity of Species in the Rainforest

BOBCAT
Trencher

MENCK F 500
Harrow

HIGHLANDER
Rad-Harvester

LE TOURNEAU 5594
Log Stacker

PLUSTECH TIMBERJACK
Hexapode-Harvester

ALLIS CHALMERS TL 30
Fronted Fork Loader

VMV STALO
Forwarder

VALLMET
Rad-Harvester

BELL 225 A
Trike-Logger

FRANKLIN TREEFARMER 3600
Hydrostatic Feller/Buncher

PONSSE ELEPHANT
Forwarder

BARKO 495 ML
Knuckleboom Loader

TANGUAY WL 150
Wood Crane

THE DESTRUCTION of the rainforest comes in many shapes. And there are all kinds of animal and plant species which suffer as a result. Every hour three different types of animal and plant life are made extinct. Help us to save the rainforest: www.oroverde.de

CATERPILLAR
Ripper

JOHN DEERE 843 J
Feller/Buncher

ORO VERDE
The Rainforest Foundation

Agency	Ogilvy Frankfurt
Creative Directors	Christian Mommertz
	Dr. Stephan Vogel
Copywriter	Stefan Lenz
Art Directors	Stefan Lenz
	Marco Weber
Illustrator	Anke Vera Zink
Graphic Design	Sonja Fritsch
Client	OroVerde
	Rainforest Foundation

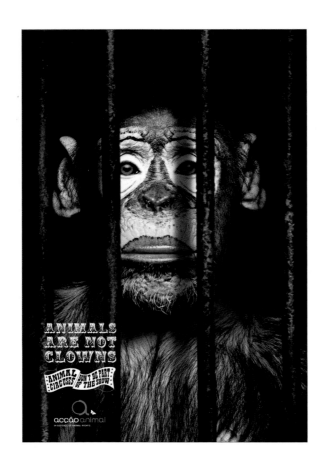

Agency	MSTF Partners, Lisbon	Agency	KNSK Werbeagentur
Creative Directors	Susana Sequeira		Hamburg
	Lourenço Thomaz	Creative Directors	Anke Winschewski
Copywriter	Pedro Lima		Tim Krink
Art Director	Ivo Purvis		Niels Holle
Client	Liga Direitos dos Animais,	Copywriters	Kurt Müller-Fleischer
	Acção Animal		Irina Schüller
		Art Directors	Bill Yom
			Nathalie Krüger
		Client	Federal Ministry
			for the Environment

Agency	Young & Rubicam, Paris
Creative Directors	Les Six
Copywriter	Pierre-Antoine Dupin
Art Director	Louis Carpentier
Client	Eco-Systèmes

THE WAVE OF BLOOD

GENUINE LYNX.
FOR THE PRIMITIVE WOMAN.

GENUINE SILVER FOX.
FOR THE PRIMITIVE WOMAN.

118   **Public Interest**

Agency	Ogilvy Frankfurt		**Agency**	Grabarz & Partner, Hamburg
Creative Directors	Simon Oppmann		**Executive CD**	Ralf Heuel
	Peter Roemmelt		**Creative Directors**	Ralf Nolting
Copywriters	Peter Roemmelt			Patricia Pätzold
	Taner Ercan		**Copywriter**	Constantin Sossidi
Art Director	Simon Oppmann		**Art Director**	Oliver Zboralski
Illustrator	Daniel Cojocaru		**Photographers**	Tina Luther
Client	Ocean Care			Birgit Stöver
			Graphic Design	Julia Elles
				Anna Hiemann
			Client	Die Tierfreunde

250 000 HECTARES OF RAINFOREST ARE MOWN DOWN EVERY WEEK.
Preserve forests by only buying wood that carries the FSC label. www.wwf.fr

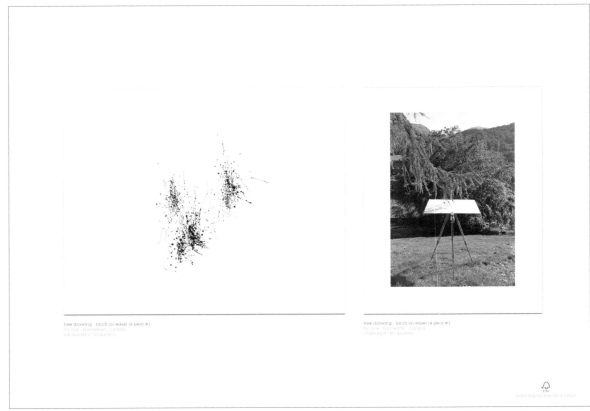

tree drawing - larch on easel (4 pen) #1

tree drawing - larch on easel (4 pen) #1

Agency	Publicis Conseil, Paris	Agency	Jung von Matt, Stuttgart
Executive CD	Olivier Altmann	Creative Directors	Joachim Silber
Copywriter	Reza Behnam		Michael Ohanian
Art Director	Reza Behnam		Tim Knowles
Photographer	Vincent Dixon	Copywriter	Lennart Frank
Client	WWF	Art Director	Tim Knowles
		Graphic Design	Thomas Lupo
		Client	Forest Stewardship Council

120   **Public Interest**

Agency	Young & Rubicam, Paris
Creative Directors	Les Six
Copywriter	Josselin Pacreau
Art Director	Sébastien Guinet
Photographer	Marc Gouby
Client	Surfrider Foundation

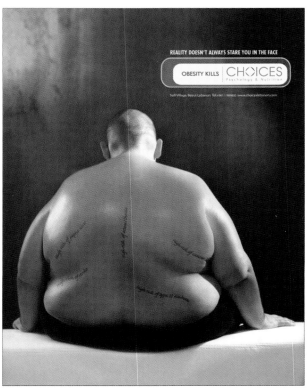

IF YOU DRIVE TOO FAST YOU WON'T SEE HIM

Agency	Memac Ogilvy & Mather, Beirut	The hand-written text on the two bodies	**Agency**	Saatchi & Saatchi, Brussels
Creative Director	Rami Traboulsi	describe the risks associated with anorexia	**Creative Director**	Jan Teulingkx
Copywriter	Dalia Menhall	(high risk of depression, osteoporosis,	**Copywriter**	Bouke Zoete
Art Director	Leslie Mourad	premature death, heart and kidney failure)	**Art Director**	Stijn Klaver
Photographer	Rodrigue Najarian	and obesity (high risk of cancer, diabetes,	**Photographer**	Guy Kokken
Client	Choices Clinic	strokes, osteoarthritis and peptic ulcers).	**Client**	BIVV, Road Safety

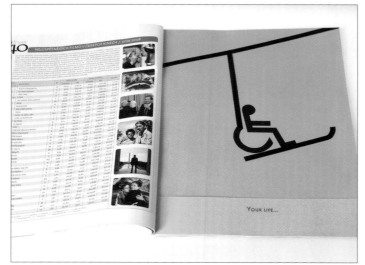
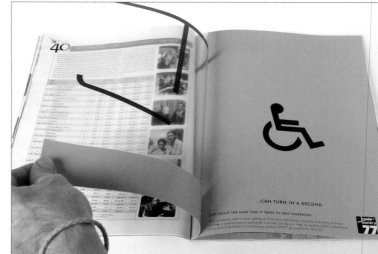

122 Public Interest

Agency	McCann Erickson, Prague
Creative Director	Lars Killi
Copywriter	Katerina Holubova
Art Director	Michal Kotulek
Client	Conto Barriers

If you use your
mobile whilst
crossing the road,
your kids
will copy you.

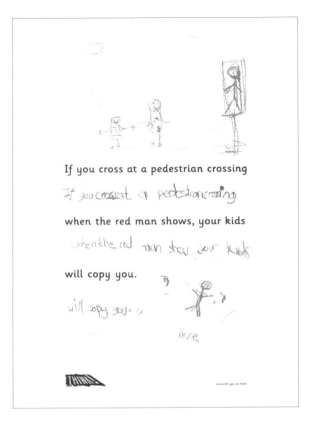

If you cross at a pedestrian crossing

when the red man shows, your kids

will copy you.

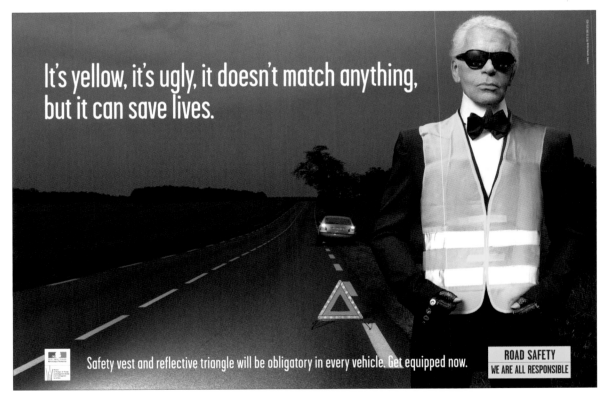

It's yellow, it's ugly, it doesn't match anything, but it can save lives.

Safety vest and reflective triangle will be obligatory in every vehicle. Get equipped now.

ROAD SAFETY
WE ARE ALL RESPONSIBLE

Agency	Leo Burnett, London
Executive CD	Jon Burley
Creative Directors	Tony Malcolm
	Guy Moore
Copywriters	Daniel Fisher
	Richard Brim
Art Directors	Daniel Fisher
	Richard Brim
Client	Department for Transport - Child Road Safety

Agency	Lowe Stratéus, Paris
Creative Director	Vincent Behaeghel
Copywriter	Philippe Lopez
Art Director	Jocelyn Berthat
Photographer	Dimitri Daniloff
Client	DSCR, Road Safety

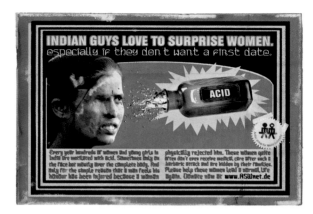

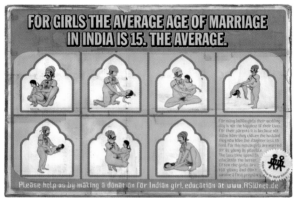

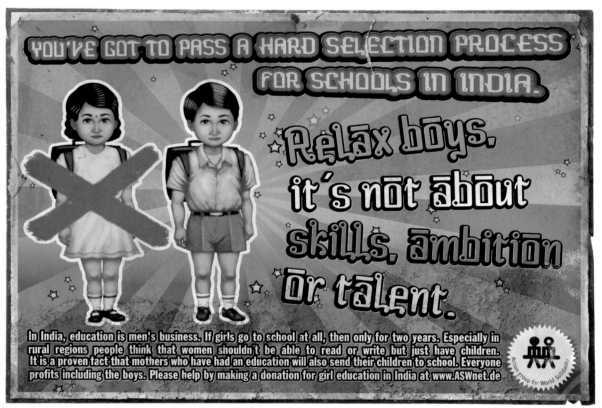

Agency	Ogilvy Frankfurt
Creative Director	Helmut Meyer
Copywriters	Dr. Stephan Vogel
	Alexander Haase
Art Directors	Ina Thedens
	Albert S. Chan
Illustrator	Martin Popp
Client	Action Group for
	World Solidarity

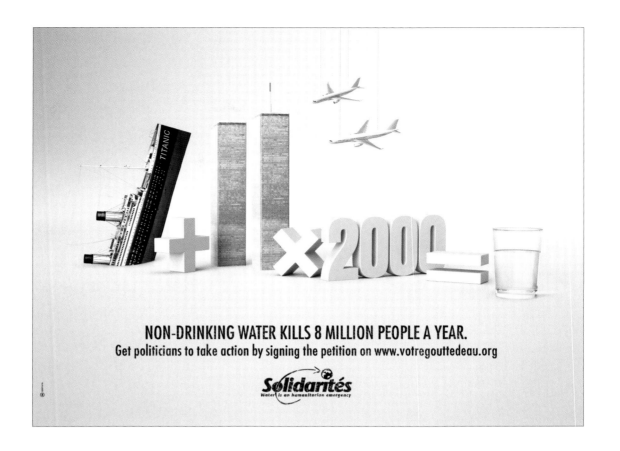

NON-DRINKING WATER KILLS 8 MILLION PEOPLE A YEAR.
Get politicians to take action by signing the petition on www.votregouttedeau.org

Agency	BDDP & Fils, Paris
Creative Director	Guillaume-Ulrich Chifflot
Copywriter	Fabien Duval
Art Director	Fabien Nunez
Illustrator	Cédric Houplain
Client	Solidarités

Agency	Lowe Brindfors, Stockholm
Creative Director	Rickard Villard
Copywriter	Aron Levander
Art Director	Pelle Lundquist
Photographer	Peter Alendahl
Client	Save the Children

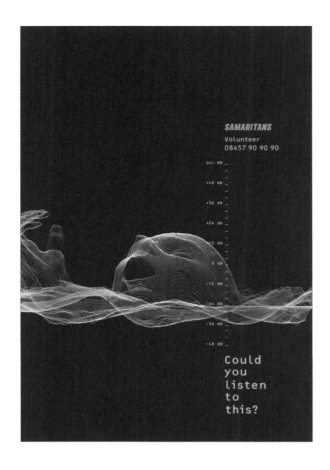

Public Interest

Agency	Lunar BBDO, London	Agency	TBWA\MAP, Paris	To put an end to endless pain. Make a donation: www.douleurs.org.
Creative Directors	Ben Kay	Creative Directors	Manoëlle van der Vaeren	
	Daryl Corps		Sébastien Vacherot	
Copywriter	Ben Kay	Copywriter	Alban Penicaut	
Art Director	Daryl Corps	Art Director	Stéphane Lecoq	
Client	Samaritans	Photographer	Platinum	
		Client	Douleurs Sans Frontières	

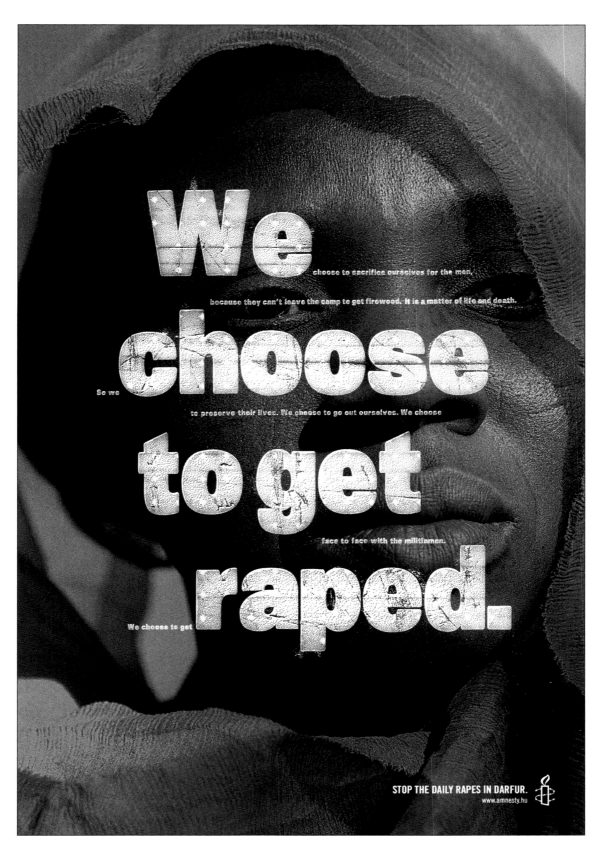

Agency	DDB, Budapest
Creative Director	Dezsö Nagy
Copywriters	Rodrigo Fernandes
	Giovanni Pintaude
	Holly Flemming
Art Director	Rodrigo Fernandes
Client	Amnesty International

Agency	Leo Burnett Ukraine, Kiev
Creative Director	Briana Bolger
Copywriter	Tatiana Fedorenko
Art Director	Pavel Klubnikin
Illustrator	Pavel Klubnikin
Client	International Organization for Migration

Agency	Publicis, Stockholm	Every year, two million girls suffer the pain of	**Agency**	BDDP & Fils, Paris
Copywriter	Malin Åkersten Triumf	genital mutilation - a clear violation of their	**Creative Director**	Guillaume-Ulrich Chifflot
Art Director	Yasin Lekorchi	human rights. Amnesty calls for donations	**Copywriter**	Eddy Wilmerts
Photographers	Niklas Alm	to help stop this violence against women.	**Art Director**	Antoine Mathon
	Mattias Nilsson		**Client**	Fondation Abbé Pierre
Client	Amnesty International			

Agencies	McCann Erickson, Prague
	Momentum, Prague
Creative Director	Jakub Mraz
Copywriter	Dusan Koutsky
Art Director	David Prochazka
Photographer	David Prochazka
Client	Amnesty International

No privacy? Amnesty International asks us to imagine what it's like to be locked inside a cell that's only twice the size of a toilet, in solitary confinement and under continuous surveillance. Sign Amnesty's online petition to end the human rights abuses at Guantanamo.

Agency	Kolle Rebbe Werbeagentur,
	Hamburg
Creative Directors	Sven Klohk
	Lorenz Ritter
Copywriter	Maik Beimdieck
Art Director	Maik Beimdieck
Illustrator	Eva Salzmann
Client	Misereor

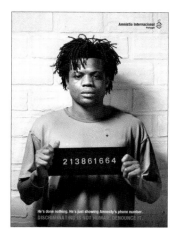

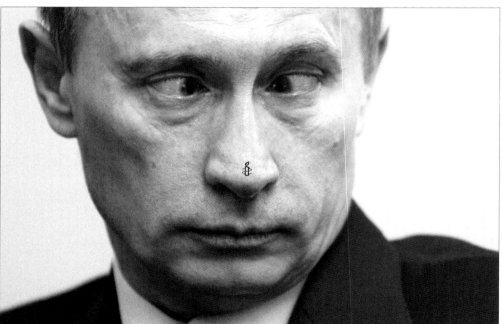

Agency	McCann Erickson, Lisbon	Agency	Contrapunto, Madrid
Creative Directors	Diogo Anahory	Creative Directors	Antonio Montero
	José Bomtempo		Carlos Jorge
Copywriter	Emerson Braga		Félix del Valle
Art Director	André Lopes	Copywriter	Félix del Valle
Photographer	Gonçalo Almeida	Art Director	Carlos Jorge
Client	Amnesty International	Client	Amnesty International

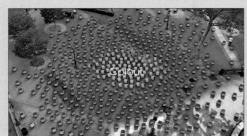

Audiovisual Equipment & Accessories

Agency	Fallon London
Executive CD	Richard Flintham
Creative Director	Juan Cabral
Copywriter	Juan Cabral
Art Director	Juan Cabral
Production	Gorgeous, London
Director	Frank Budgen
Producers	Rupert Smythe
	Nicky Barnes
Client	Sony Bravia,
	"Play Doh"

In this triumph of stop motion animation, a pink Play Doh bunny emerges from a drainpipe onto the streets of New York. Soon equally colourful rabbit friends have joined him – and they all begin leaping around the city to the sound of "She's a Rainbow" by the Rolling Stones. They converge on a central square, where they transform into a wave, a whale surfacing in icy waters, a giant scarlet rabbit – and finally a series of cubes that form beautiful swirling patterns. Sony Bravia. Colour, like no other.

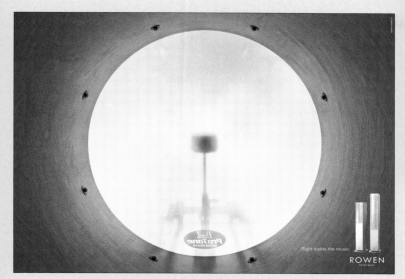

▲ **Audiovisual Equipment & Accessories**   **133**

Agency	Advico Young & Rubicam, Zurich
Creative Director	Urs Schrepfer
Copywriter	Florian Birkner
Art Director	Nicolas Vontobel
Photographer	Derron & Kuhn
Client	Rowen Speakers

Agency	Fallon London
Creative Director	Juan Cabral
Copywriters	Samuel Akesson
	Tomas Mankovsky
Art Directors	Samuel Akesson
	Tomas Mankovsky
Production	Academy Films, London
Director	Nick Gordon
Producers	Sally Campbell
	Lucy Gossage
	Jo Charlesworth
Client	Sony Walkman, "Music Pieces"

A single note on a horn begins a musical recital. We can't help noticing that the orchestra is huge, because each instrument is represented in multiple numbers. Drum kits and electric guitars are in the mix alongside miniature pianos and exotic instruments from around the world. As we watch, we realise that most members of the 128-piece orchestra play only a single note of music. But the recital works thanks to brilliant planning, timing and conducting. Sony Walkman: music, like no other.

Sunrise

is the atmospheric phenomena accompanying the daily appearance of the sun. It is the event or time when the sun is first seen above the eastern horizon. Because atmospheric refraction causes the sun to be seen while it is still below the horizon, from a particular point of view, sunrise is an optical illusion. And so is the sun appearing larger on the horizon. When it comes to changes in timing of sunrise, it is driven by the axial tilt of Earth and the planet's movement in its annual orbit around the sun. The Sun rises exactly East and sets exactly West on two days: March 21 and September 21 which are known as the two equinoxes. Due to the Earth's axial tilt, whenever and wherever sunrise occurs, it is always in the northeast quadrant from the March equinox to the September equinox and in the southeast quadrant from the September equinox to the March equinox. Now if this answers most of your queries, when do you think you actually see the sun rise? Is it when the middle of the Sun crosses the horizon, or the top edge, or the bottom edge? Also do you take the horizon to be sea level or do you take into account the topography of the location you are at? Though by definition, we cannot see the sun before it rises, we only see it when it's geometrically just below the horizon, during sunrise. This is because of the refraction of the light from the Sun by the Earth's atmosphere. Earth's atmosphere bends the path of the light so that we see the Sun in a position slightly different from where it really is. The magnitude of this effect varies with latitude, but it is strongest at the equator, where the sun rises two minutes earlier than it would if the Earth had no atmosphere.

Canon
Higher definition Cameras

134 **Audiovisual Equipment & Accessories**

Agency	Fallon London
Executive CD	Richard Flintham
Copywriters	Tomas Mankovsky
	Samuel Akesson
Art Directors	Tomas Mankovsky
	Samuel Akesson
Production	HLA, London
Director	Simon Rattigan
Producers	Mike Wells
	Emma Gooding
Client	Sony Cybershot, Handycam & Alpha, "Foam City"

It's another piece of creative fun for Sony. Or perhaps we should say "creative foam", as this time the city streets are filled with soap bubbles. Light as air, they float into the sky like snow and provide a white fluffy playground for people of all ages. Some record the event on their Sony cameras – the products being promoted here. Images like no other.

Agency	Grey Worldwide, Dubai
Creative Director	Alisdair Miller
Copywriter	Vidya Manmohan
Art Director	Prasad Pradhan
Client	Canon High Definition Cameras

Agency	FP7 Doha
Creative Director	Fadi Yaish
Copywriter	Kalpesh Patankar
Art Director	Kalpesh Patankar
Photographer	Jeremy Wong
Client	Medal of Honor

Kino means precise framing, thoroughly rehearsed action and dialogue.

K. i. N. C.
Четко. Ярко. Реалистично.

K. i. N. C.
глазами режиссера Алексея Германа-младшего
K.I.N.O. as seen by Alexei German, Jr.

Agency   Cheil Russia, Moscow
Creative Directors   Jean Shuldeshov
    Sergei Balabonin
Copywriter   Daria Artamonova
Art Director   Jean Shuldeshov
Production   Metra Films, Moscow
Director   Alexei German, Jr.
Producers   Artem Vassiliev
    Natalia Demidova
    Vassiliy Kisselev
Client   Samsung K.I.N.O.,
    "K.I.N.O.by
    Alexei German, Jr."

"For me, 'kino' means waiting." Film director Alexei German Jr. describes his interpretation of "kino" – or "cinema". As he talks, we see a desolate railway track. "Waiting for the moment when the world created in my imagination becomes reality." We pan across to a figure waiting by the tracks. "When characters appear…each with his own story and his own fate." The figure turns out to be a young woman. She has tears in her eyes. "But the most important thing is truth…That's how Kino is born." The new Samsung Kino TV.

the war of the gods has broken out

PSP.
PlayStation·Portable

PSP
PlayStation·Portable

Agency   TBWA\España, Madrid
Executive CDs   Juan Sánchez
    Guillermo Ginés,
Creative Directors   Montse Pastor
    Bernardo Hernández
    Vicente Rodríguez
Copywriter   Vicente Rodríguez
Art Director   Bernardo Hernández
Production   Pirámide, Madrid
Director   Fernando de France
Producer   Mariluz Chamizo
Client   Sony PSP,
    "Blood Rain"

A single drop of red falls onto a newspaper outside a kiosk. Another besmirches the nose of a statue. Rapidly, more red drops begin to fall into a swimming pool filled with elderly folk, onto the white dress of a bride, onto the windscreen of a bemused taxi driver and the clothes of passers by. Soon, the city is awash with red, bloody, rain. A caption reads: "The war of the gods has broken out." It's a trailer for God of War, the new game for Sony PlayStation.

Agency   TBWA\España, Madrid
Executive CDs   Juan Sánchez
    Guillermo Ginés
Creative Directors   Montse Pastor
    Vicente Rodríguez
    Bernardo Hernández
Copywriter   Vicente Rodríguez
Art Director   Bernardo Hernández
Photographer   Gonzalo Puertas
Client   Sony PSP

Audiovisual Equipment & Accessories **137**

Agency	TBWA\España, Madrid
Executive CDs	Juan Sánchez
	Guillermo Ginés
Creative Directors	Montse Pastor
	Vicente Rodríguez
	Bernardo Hernández
Copywriter	Esteban Tabares
Art Director	Carolina Rodríguez
Photographer	Julio Bárcena
Client	Sony PSP

Audiovisual Equipment & Accessories

Agency	Ogilvy & Mather, Copenhagen	**Agency**	Grey Worldwide, Dubai
Art Director	Thomas Boldsen	**Creative Director**	Alisdair Miller
Photographers	Morgan & Morell	**Copywriter**	Vidya Manmohan
Client	Duracell	**Art Director**	Alisdair Miller
		Client	Canon Cameras

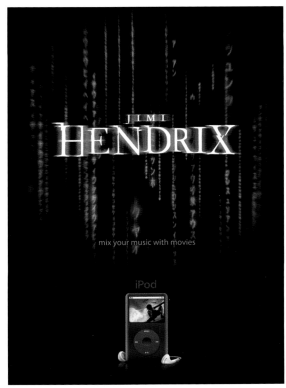

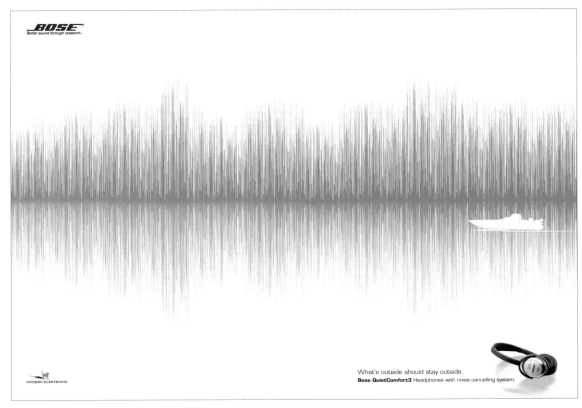

Agency	Wiktor Leo Burnett, Bratislava	Agency	Medina Turgul DDB, Istanbul
Creative Director	Peter Kacenka	Creative Director	Kurtcebe Turgul
Copywriter	Vlado Slivka	Copywriter	Gokhan Erol
Art Director	Jonas Karasek	Art Director	Asligul Akin
Client	iPod	Client	Bose Headphones

140   **Audiovisual Equipment & Accessories**

Agency	Fortune Promoseven, Dubai
Creative Director	Marc Lineveldt
Copywriters	Ali Ali
	Magad Nassar
Art Directors	Ali Ali
	Maged Nassar
Photographer	Jaime Mandelbaum
Client	Sony In-Car DVD Players

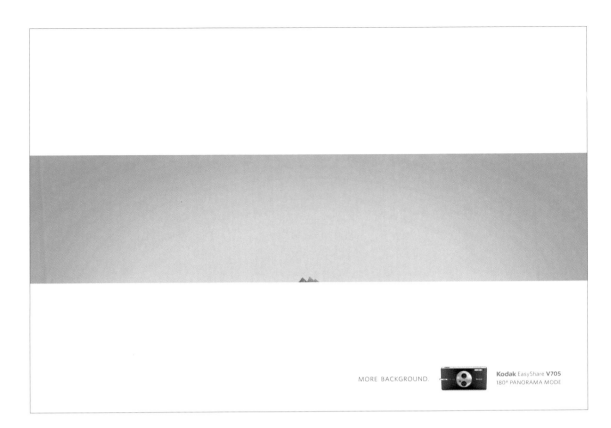

MORE BACKGROUND.

Kodak EasyShare **V705**
180° PANORAMA MODE

PLAYSTATION 3

Agency	Ogilvy & Mather, Frankfurt	Agency	TBWA\España, Madrid
		Executive CDs	Juan Sánchez
Creative Director	Lars Huvart		Guillermo Ginés
Copywriter	Lothar Mueller	Creative Directors	Montse Pastor
Art Director	Till Schaffarczyk		Peru Sáez y Fran López
Client	Kodak EasyShare	Copywriter	Peru Saiz
		Art Director	Fran Lopez
		Photographer	Gonzalo Puertas
		Client	Sony PlayStation

142   Homes, Furnishings & Appliances

Agency	La Chose, Paris	In a cosy French flat, a man is filling in the crossword puzzle when his wife confronts him. "Nicolas – what's this?" she says, holding up an object. "That? That's an old Ikea pencil." His wife points out that he is already using the old Ikea pencil. This is a brand new one. "You went to Ikea without me?" she demands. The man looks flustered. "Yeah, I went…I was just looking for some ideas for the kitchen." His wife is heartbroken. Ikea is more than a furniture store.
Creative Director	Pascal Gregoire	
Copywriters	Laurie Lacourt	
	Benjamin Parent	
	Guillaume Rebbot	
Art Directors	Laurie Lacourt	
	Benjamin Parent	
	Guillaume Rebbot	
Production	Les Télécréateurs, Paris	
Director	Tim Gotshal	
Producers	Arno Moria	
	Nicolas Buisset	
Client	Ikea, "The Pencil"	

It's faster than you think: the PSR 14,4 LI-2 cordless screwdriver.

BOSCH
Invented for life

Homes, Furnishings & Appliances 143

Agency	Jung von Matt, Hamburg
Executive CDs	Wolf Heumann
	Dirk Haeusermann
Creative Directors	Sascha Hanke
	Timm Hanebeck
Art Director	Kathrin Seupel
Photographers	Annika Rose
	Andreas Mock
Client	Bosch Cordless Screwdriver

Agency	Grabarz & Partner, Hamburg
Creative Directors	Ralf Heuel
	Dirk Siebenhaar
Art Director	Vanessa Iff
Photographers	Christian Kerber
	Waldmann Solar
Client	Ikea

You've come for the apartment to share ?

144   Homes, Furnishings & Appliances

Agency	DDB, Paris
Creative Directors	Alexandre Hervé
	Sylvain Thirache
Copywriter	Fabien Teichner
Art Director	Faustin Claverie
Production	Mister Hide, Paris
Director	Keith Bearden
Producers	Dominique Porte
	Florence Potthié
	Sperry
Client	Brandt, "Co-Rent"

A prospective flatmate arrives at an apartment he might end up sharing. Guided by one of the occupants, he quickly sees that the place is packed out. They have to crawl over a mass of bodies to get to the living room. The bathroom is no place for the prudish. The kitchen is also a sardine can. "And here's our washing machine," says the "guide", indicating a tiny Brandt top-loader. Fortunately, it is surprisingly efficient: 7kg of laundry in only 40 centimetres.

Agency	DDB, Johannesburg
Executive CD	Gareth Lessing
Copywriter	Claudi Potter
Art Director	Andre Vrdoljak
Production	Velocity Films, Johannesburg
Director	Anton Visser
Producer	Prenneven Govender
Client	Energizer ER Lamp, "Scary Things"

In her home at night, an elderly woman is reading a book in front of the telly. Her small dog lies in a basket nearby. Suddenly there's a power cut and they are plunged into darkness. The dog whimpers. We hear the woman reassuring the dog and kissing it. The lights abruptly go on and we see that the woman is kissing the dog's arse. She drops the mutt like a hot brick. Scary things happen in the dark. But the Energizer rechargeable lamp comes on when the lights go off.

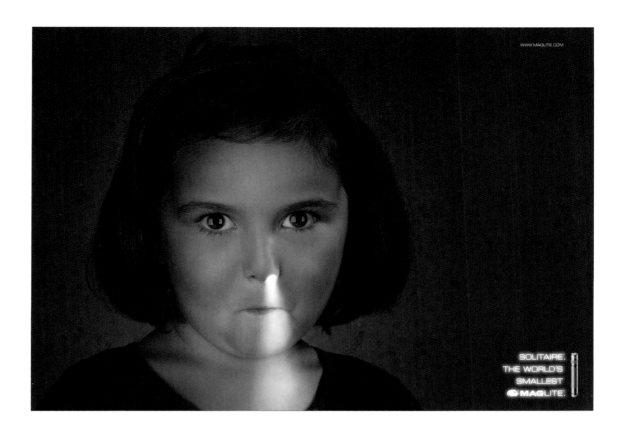

Agency	Leagas Delaney, Hamburg	Agency	Grey, Brussels
Creative Directors	Hermann Waterkamp	Creative Director	Philippe Thito
	Oliver Grandt	Copywriter	Sandrine Felot
Copywriter	Jan Wiendieck	Art Director	Emmanuel Colin
Art Director	Melanie Mertens	Client	Velux Blinds
Photographer	Heribert Schindler		
Client	Maglite		

146 **Homes, Furnishings & Appliances**

Agency	Forsman & Bodenfors, Gothenburg	Agency	Scholz & Friends, Berlin
Client	Ikea	Creative Directors	Jan Leube
			Matthias Spaetgens
		Copywriter	Edgar Linscheid
		Art Director	Marc Ebenwaldner
		Photographer	Ralph Baiker
		Graphic Artist	Anatolij Pickmann
		Client	Weru Windows

100% ORGANIC RAUN SOFA. ALMOST ORGANIC WOMAN.

raun

DON'T WORRY. RAUN SOFAS ARE AVAILABLE WITH FIVE-YEAR STAIN GUARANTEE.

raun

CUSTOMIZE YOUR RAUN SOFA.

raun

Agency	& Co., Copenhagen
Art Director	Jesper Schmidt
Photographer	Klavs Vedfeldt
Client	Raun Sofas

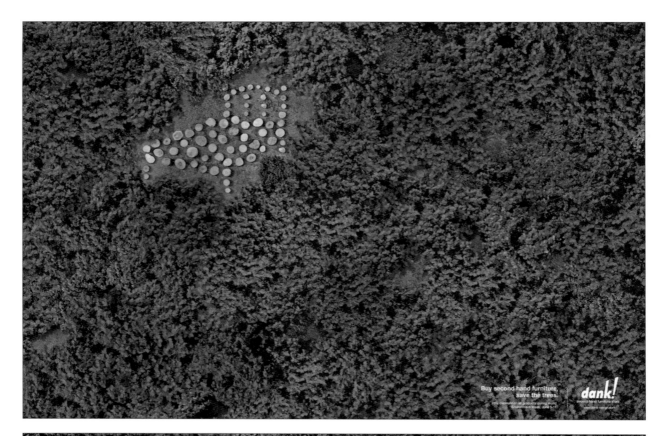

Homes, Furnishings & Appliances

Agency	DDB&Co., Istanbul
Creative Director	Karpat Polat
Copywriter	Volkan Karakasoglu
Art Director	Levent Yalgin
Client	Dank, Second-Hand Furniture

Agency	DDB Germany, Düsseldorf
Chief Creative Officer	Amir Kassaei
Executive CD	Eric Schoeffler
Copywriter	Dennis May
Art Directors	Kristine Holzhausen
	Tim Stübane
Photographer	Mikael Strinnhed
Client	Ikea

Agency	DDB Germany, Berlin
Chief Creative Officer	Amir Kassaei
Executive CDs	Stefan Schulte
	Bert Peulecke
Creative Directors	Tim Stübane
	Birgit van den Valentyn
Art Directors	René Gebhardt
	Björn Kernspeckt
Photographer	Mikael Strinnhed
Graphic Design	Peter Schönherr
Client	Ikea

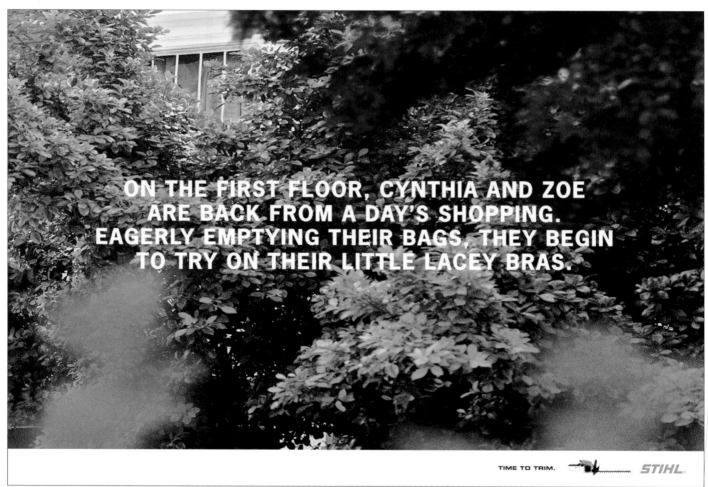

Agency	Publicis Conseil, Paris
Executive CD	Olivier Altmann
Creative Director	Hervé Plumet
Copywriter	Olivier Camensuli
Art Director	Frédéric Royer
Photographer	Hervé Plumet
Client	Stihl Trimmers

SAWING SEEMS HARDER WITHOUT A STIHL **STIHL®**

YEEEEHAA!! NEW VIKING RIDE-ON MOWERS. **VIKING**

Homes, Furnishings & Appliances **151**

Agency	Publicis Conseil, Paris	Agency	Publicis Conseil, Paris
Executive CD	Olivier Altmann	Executive CD	Olivier Altmann
Copywriter	Mathieu Degryse	Creative Director	Hervé Plumet
Art Director	Yves-Eric Deboey	Copywriter	Fabrice Dubois
Photographer	Marc Gouby	Art Director	Pascale Gayraud
Client	Stihl Chain-Saws	Client	Viking Mowers

ONE SECOND IS ENOUGH.

ONE SECOND IS ENOUGH.

ONE SECOND IS ENOUGH.

152 **Household Maintenance**

Agency	Serviceplan, Munich & Hamburg
Executive CD	Matthias Harbeck
Creative Director	Helmut Huber
Copywriter	Thorsten Voigt
Art Directors	Sandra Loibl
	Julia Pfund
Production	Wonderboys Film, Munich
Producers	Stefan Orb
	Alexandra Schulte
Client	UHU Super Glue,

These four very short commercials demonstrate the power of UHU glue. A collapsed building rights itself, a train un-plunges from a broken bridge, a car that has snapped in half glues itself back together and a disintegrating mummy is miraculously reassembled.. That's just how quick UHU is. One second is enough.

White wins.

Household Maintenance 153

Agency	Grey, Istanbul
Creative Directors	Tugbay Bilbay
	Engin Kafadar
Copywriter	Ergin Binyildiz
Art Directors	Dide Hersekli
	Gokce Sahbaz
Photographer	Lindsey Hopkinson
Illustrator	Taylor James
Client	Ace Bleach

Agency	Heimat, Berlin
Creative Directors	Guido Heffels
	Matthias Storat
Copywriters	Matthias Storath
	Susanne Düber
Art Directors	Kai Gerken
	Danny Baarz
Photographer	Markus Müller
Illustrator	Jennifer Schumacher
Client	Hornbach,
	Home Improvement Superstores

  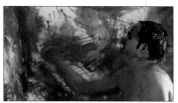 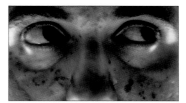

154 **Household Maintenance**

Agency	Heimat, Berlin
Creative Directors	Guido Heffels
	Matthias Storath
Copywriter	Susanne Düber
Art Directors	Kai Gerken
	Danny Baarz
Production	Trigger Happy, Berlin
Director	Ralf Schmerberg
Producers	Stephan Vens
	Nicolas Blankenhorn
	Kerstin Breuer
Client	Hornbach,
	"Imagination"

A man walks into an abandoned home. The place is a ruin, with insects crawling everywhere. But our undaunted hero mimes the actions he can imagine performing in the future. He climbs the stairs using a non-existent banister. He makes an invisible cup of tea. He acts out brushing his teeth and dancing – with an invisible woman – to the radio. Then he stretches out on the filthy floor, under imaginary covers. Hornbach home improvements: if you can imagine it, you can build it.

Agency	Heimat, Berlin
Creative Director	Guido Heffels
Copywriter	Matthias Storath
Art Director	Danny Baarz
Production	Stink, Berlin
Director	Robert Jitzmark
Producers	Jan Dressler
	Kerstin Breuer
Client	Hornbach,
	Home Improvement
	Superstores,
	"Painter"

Dressed only in his underwear, a man pours green paint over himself. He then indulges in a spot of "body painting", bouncing off the walls and putting hand prints everywhere, not to mention prints of (almost) every other part of himself. But when he strips away the protective paper that covers the top and bottom sections of the wall, we see that the resulting pattern is quite effective. Do the decorating any way you want – but get it done.

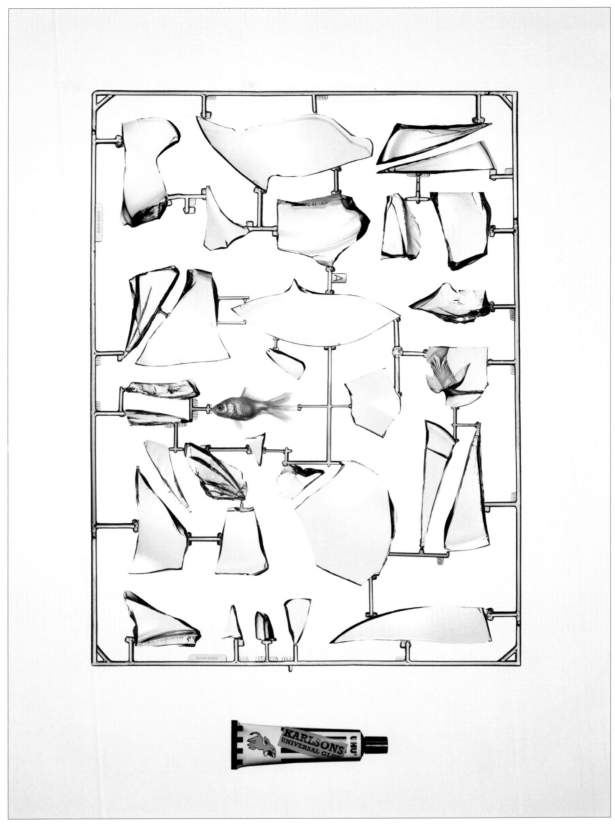

Agency	Storåkers McCann, Stockholm	Art Directors	Patrik Reuterskiöld
			Peter Eriksson
Copywriters	Brita Zackari		Mitte Blomkvist
	Christian Hening		Klaudia Carp
	Hanna Belander		Jonas Frank
	Mia Cederberg		Henric Almquist
	Björn Hjalmar		Ola Von Bahr
	Martin Johansen		Sofia Ekelund
		Photographer	Emil Larsson
		Final Art	Nico Paredes
		Client	Karlssons
			Universal Super Glue

Agency	Gitam BBDO, Tel-Aviv	Agency	DDB, Milan
Executive CD	Guy Bar	Creative Director	Vicky Gitto
Creative Director	Danny Yakobowitch	Copywriter	Sebastian Valenzuela
Copywriter	Matan Orian	Art Director	Hugo Gallardo
Art Director	Igal Ezra	Illustrator	Balalò
Client	Nikol Paper Towels	Client	Pattex Glue

Agency	Saatchi & Saatchi, London	Agency	FP7, Doha
Executive CDs	Paul Silburn	Creative Director	Fadi Yaish
	Kate Stanners	Copywriter	Kartik Aiyar
Creative Director	Howard Fretton	Art Directors	Fadi Yaish
Copywriters	Sarah Sturgess		Makarand Patil
	Lena Ohlsson	Photographer	Allen Dong
Art Directors	Lena Ohlsson	Client	Bayer
	Sarah Sturgess		Advanced Plant Food
Typographers	Scott Silvey		
	Roger Kennedy		
Client	Ariel		

158 **Household Maintenance**

Agency	Serviceplan, Munich & Hamburg
Creative Director	Ekki Frenkler
Art Directors	Pei-Jen Müller-Lierheim
	Miro Moric
Photographers	Felix Holzer
	Kevin Lee
	Antony Njuguna,
	Guido Alberto Rossi
Client	3M Scotch Magic Tape

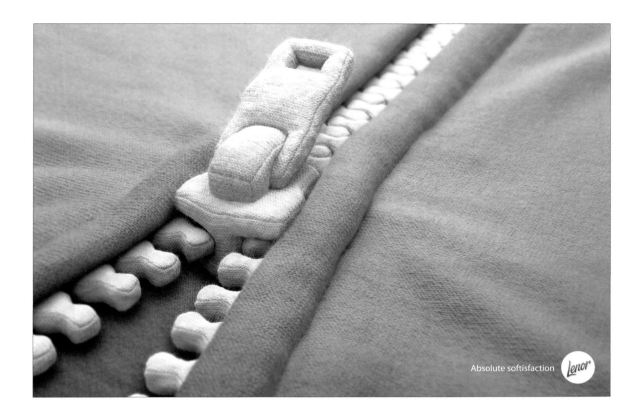

Absolute softisfaction *Lenor*

Agency	Grey, Moscow	Agency	Callegari Berville Grey, Paris
Creative Director	Oleg Lapshin		
Copywriter	Tatiana Yakusheva	Creative Director	Andrea Stillacci
Art Director	Oleg Panov	Copywriter	Luissandro Del Gobbo
Photographer	Igor Evstafiev	Art Director	Giovanni Settesoldi
Client	Lenor Fabric Softener	Photographer	Eugenio Recuenco
		Client	Saniterpen Pet Odor Remover

160   **Household Maintenance**

Agency	TBWA\Paris
Creative Director	Erik Vervroegen
Copywriter	Benoit Leroux
Art Directors	Philippe Taroux
	Benoit Leroux
Client	Mir Black

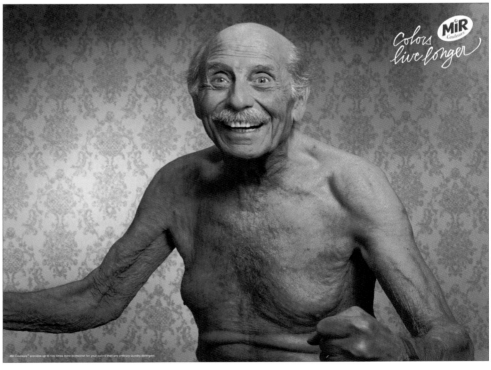

Agency	TBWA\Paris	Agency	TBWA\Paris
Creative Director	Erik Vervroegen	Creative Director	Erik Vervroegen
Copywriter	Pierre-Louis Messager	Copywriters	Thierry Buriez
Art Director	Ingrid Varetz		Alexandre Henry
Photographer	Vincent Fournier	Art Directors	Alexandre Henry
Client	Mir Wool		Thierry Buriez
		Photographer	Bruno Clément
		Client	Mir Couleurs

162   **Household Maintenance**

Agency	Jung von Matt, Stuttgart	**Agency**	DDB Germany, Düsseldorf
Creative Directors	Joachim Silber	**Chief Creative Officer**	Amir Kassaei
	Michael Ohanian	**Executive CD**	Eric Schoeffler
Copywriters	Lennart Frank	**Creative Directors**	Heiko Freyland
	Tassilo Gutscher		Alexander Reiss
Art Directors	Stefan Roesinger	**Art Directors**	Michael Kittel
	Dominic Stuebler		Simon Frembgen
Illustrator	Mark Khaisman	**Producers**	Michael Frixe
Client	Tesa Pack Ultra Strong	**Client**	Pattex Power Tape

Agency	Wächter & Wächter Bremen	Agency	Euro RSCG South Africa, Johannesburg	Vanish Stain Seeker finds stains faster than you can.
Creative Director	Andreas Rüthemann			
Copywriter	Veronika Weber	**Creative Director**	James Daniels	
Final Art	Litho Niemann + Steggemann	**Copywriter**	Laura May Vale	
Client	Pattex Adhesives	**Art Director**	Laura May Vale	
		Photographer	Clive Stewart	
		Client	Vanish	

PHILIPS
sense and simplicity

philips.com/ice

164 **Beauty Products & Services**

Agency	DDB London
Creative Director	Neil Dawson
Copywriters	Tim Charlesworth
	Neil Dawson
Art Director	Micheal Kaplan
Production	Sonny, London
Director	Fredrik Bond
Producers	Helen Kenny
	Richard Chambers
Client	Philips
	Satinelle Ice Epilator,
	"Karis"

We see a beautiful woman waking up in bed. Or is it a woman? A bass voice narrates: "My mom? Around the age of 7 she caught me wearing some of her clothes – and now she steals my make-up." We realise that Karis is a guy. Even so, he has no trouble blending in with pretty dancers and models. The most difficult part of being Karis? "All my hair." That's where the Philips Satinelle Ice Epilator comes in. It's gentle – and everyone knows men aren't great with pain.

47

Correct your age

OLAY

42

Correct your age

OLAY

33

Correct your age

OLAY

Agency	Saatchi & Saaatchi Russia, Moscow
Creative Director	Stuart Robinson
Copywriter	Alina Tskhovrebova
Art Directors	Julian Suetin
	Adrian Ely
Photographer	Tatyana Alekseeva
Designer	Lilia Absudova
Client	Olay Cream

Agency	JWT Russia, Moscow
Creative Director	Ivan Chimburov
Copywriter	Ivan Chimburov
Art Director	Ilya Bakerkin
Production	Dago, Moscow
Director	Alex Voitinsky
Producers	Olga Larionova
	Eugeny Romensky
	Maria Yakushina
Client	Rapira Razor Blades, "Scar"

A shaven-headed mercenary type tells us: "My face is my life." He takes us on a tour of his scars. "This is Angola, 1988…Mozambique, '91. It was hot and humid over there healing took long." His face is a veritable road map of wounds. "Nicaragua, '97… Afghanistan, a couple of years ago." An interviewer interrupts: "So why didn't you change your razor, man?" The mercenary glowers. Rapira: cut-free shaving.

Agency	Vega Olmos Ponce, Buenos Aires
Production	Gorgeous Enterprises, London
Director	Peter Thwaites
Producer	Flora Fernandez Marengo
Client	Impulse True Love, "Between a Rock and a Hard Place"

A car pulls up outside a house at the end of a first date. The girl suggestively removes her front door key from her handbag, giving us a glimpse of her Impulse spray. The guy walks around to open the door for her. Suddenly, they're in the middle of what looks like a police raid: cars, trucks, even a helicopter. In fact, the "cops" are trying to "save" him from a relationship. But even though he's kissing the bachelor life goodbye, the man succumbs to the inevitable. Impulse True Love: romance isn't dead.

Agency	WCRS, London
Production	Sonny, London
Director	Fredrik Bond
Producers	Ran Holst
	Lesley Williams
Client	Brylcreem, "Effortless"

Clever choreography and ingenious contraptions make a young man's morning routine stress-free. We follow him around his apartment as he spruces up his hair, catches a newspaper flung to him through the window, turns on the telly with an accurately kicked football, glides into a shirt that's waiting on a clothes line and arrives at the toaster just as it pops up. He finishes making his breakfast, slides into a chair and feeds his pet tortoise with similar ease. His life is effortless – just like great hair, with Brylcreem.

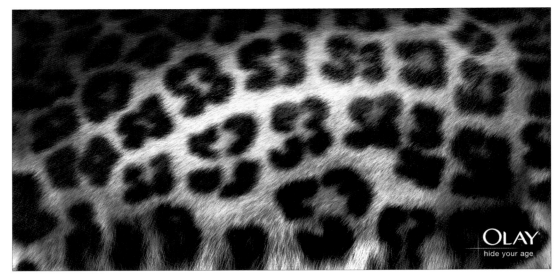

Beauty Products & Services   **167**

Agency	Saatchi & Saatchi, London
Executive CDs	Paul Silburn Kate Stanners
Creative Director	Daniel Malliard
Copywriter	Jonathan Benson
Art Director	Stanley Cheung
Typographer	Cris Jones
Client	Olay Cream

Beauty Products & Services

Agency	The Fan Club, Malmö	Agency	DDB Germany, Düsseldorf
Creative Directors	Ola Obrant Andreasson	Chief Creative Officer	Amir Kassaei
	Christian Barret	Executive CD	Eric Schoeffler
Copywriter	Ola Obrant Andreasson	Copywriter	Dennis May
Art Director	Christian Barret	Art Director	Kristine Holzhausen
Photographer	Thomas Persson	Illustrator	Maik Schrake
Client	Leep School of Hair	Client	Schwarzkopf Haircare

FOR STRONG HAIR
EXCLUSIVELY AVAILABLE AT THE EN VOGUE STORES IN ZURICH, SEEFELDSTRASSE 45, SCHIPFE 45, ZÄHRINGERPLATZ 11, LÖWENSTRASSE 12, TELEFON 01 211 66 66

Every face tells a story.

Edit yours.

Marks of time give your face character. But some fine lines are not so fine. With Restylane you can restore the volume of your skin and smooth away the appearance of lines and furrows. The procedure is safe and quick, with immediate benefits.
Restylane gives you flexibility and control over your looks, since it is long lasting, but not permanent. It does not affect facial expressions. Restylane is based on hyaluronic acid, a compound occurring naturally in our bodies.
Since the launch in 1996, more than 9 million treatments have been performed worldwide by authorised professionals. Restylane is the natural, easy way to look your best.

For more information and clinic locations: www.restylane.com/men   Restylane

Beauty Products & Services   **169**

Agency	Euro RSCG Group Switzerland, Zurich	**Agency**	King, Stockholm	When I thought my wife's private yoga instructor was gay...and prenuptial agreements weren't needed.
Executive CD	Frank Bodin	**Creative Director**	Frank Hollingworth	
Creative Director	Claude Catsky	**Copywriter**	Hedvig Hagwall Bruckner	When I thought late nights and weekends in the office would pay off.
Copywriter	Alexander Fuerer	**Art Director**	Alexander Elers	
Art Director	Charles Blunier	**Photographer**	Peter Gehrke	When I thought Anna was on the pill...When I thought twins were twicethe fun.
Photographer	Marco Grob	**Client**	Restylane	
Illustrator	Barney Rees			
Client	En Vouge			

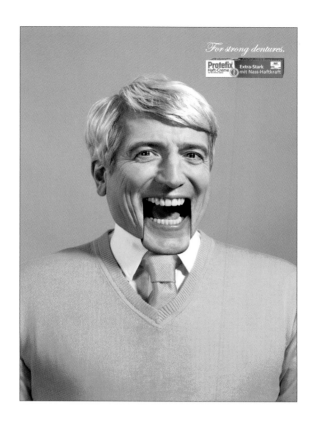

170 **Beauty Products & Services**

Agency	Scholz & Friends, Hamburg		Agency	Jung von Matt, Berlin
Creative Directors	Stefan Setzkorn		Creative Directors	Wolfgang Schneider
	Matthias Schmidt			Mathias Stiller
	Tobias Holland			Boris Schwiedrzik
Copywriter	Marc-Philipp Kittel			Christian Himmelspach
Art Directors	Pedro Sydow		Copywriter	Jens Daum
	Sven Janssen		Art Director	Fredrik Hofmann
Photographer	Rainer Elstermann		Client	Vichy Solar Protection
Client	Protefix Denture Adhesive			

Agency	DDB Germany, Berlin	Agency	BBDO Düsseldorf
Chief Creative Officer	Amir Kassaei	Creative Directors	Asi Shavit
Executive CDs	Bert Peulecke		Toygar Bazarkaya
	Stefan Schulte		Konstanze Bruhns
Creative Directors	Birgit van den Valentyn	Copywriter	Kai Hoffmann
	Tim Stübane	Art Director	Stephan Eichler
Copywriter	Jan Hendrick Ott	Photographer	Jochen Manz
Art Director	Gen Sadakane	Client	Diadermine
Photographer	David Cuenca		
Client	Schwarzkopf Got2be		

SHOULD'VE GONE TO SPECSAVERS

Specsavers

Opticians

Agency	Specsavers Creative, Guernsey	A rugged rural scene shot in black and white. A tough old shepherd controls his sheepdog with a series of whistles. Finally, thanks to the dog's energetic darting and sprinting, the sheep are safely in their pen. The shepherd shears them one by one. When he's done, the dog approaches him for a pat on the head. A second later, however, we see that the dog has been sheared too! The shepherd needs an optician. Should've gone to Specsavers.
Creative Director	Graham Daldry	
Copywriter	Graham Daldry	
Art Director	Steve Loftus	
Production	Gorgeous Enterprises, London	
Director	Chris Palmer	
Producers	Rupert Smythe Samantha Lock	
Client	Specsavers Opticians, "Collie Wobble"	

Toiletries & Health Care 173

Agencies	Saatchi & Saatchi Simko, Geneva
	Saatchi & Saatchi, Milan
Creative Directors	John Pallant
	Roger Kennedy
	Olivier Girard
	Jean-François Fournon
	Guido Cornara
	Agostino Toscana
Copywriter	Luca Lorenzini
Art Director	Luca Pannese
Photographer	Davide Bodini
Illustrator	Rob Perry
Client	Otrivin

Agency	Rocky Advertising, Helsinki	
Copywriter	Heikki Kärkkäinen	
Art Director	Aslak Bredenberg	
Production	Film Magica, Helsinki	
Director	Finn Andersson	
Producer	Tiina Butter	
Client	Aspirin Cardio, "Avoid Unnecessary Drama"	

We're at an auction, where a precious Ming vase is up for sale. The auctioneer names a starting price of € 500,000. The bids come in quickly: "€ 600,000 from the gentleman in the back row; € 700,000 on the phone; € 800,000 from the lady in the front." Soon it's up to one million. "Any other bids – no? One million for the first, second and third time – sold!" In an excited gesture, he shatters the vase with his gavel. Avoid unnecessary drama. Asprin Cardio can reduce the risk of a heart attack.

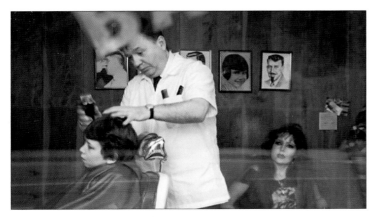

174   **Toiletries & Health Care**

Agency	Specsavers Creative, Guernsey	
Creative Director	Graham Daldry	
Copywriter	Simon Bougourd	
Art Director	Neil Brush	
Production	Rattling Stick, London	
Director	Danny Kleinman	
Producers	Johnnie Frankel	
	Sam Lock	
Client	Specsavers Opticians, "Eerie"	

A series of strange occurrences befall a small American town. A barber's clippers go dead in the middle of a haircut. A fountain dries up. A TV screen goes blank. Coffee stops boiling. A jukebox conks out. Traffic lights fail and telephone lines are dead. Is the town under attack? Cut to the solution: a myopic lumberjack who's blindly chopping down all the telegraph poles. Should've gone to Specsavers.

Agency	Leo Burnett, Milan	
Creative Directors	Sergio Rodriguez	
	Enrico Dorizza	
Art Director	Ermenegildo Rapetti	
Client	Clearblue	

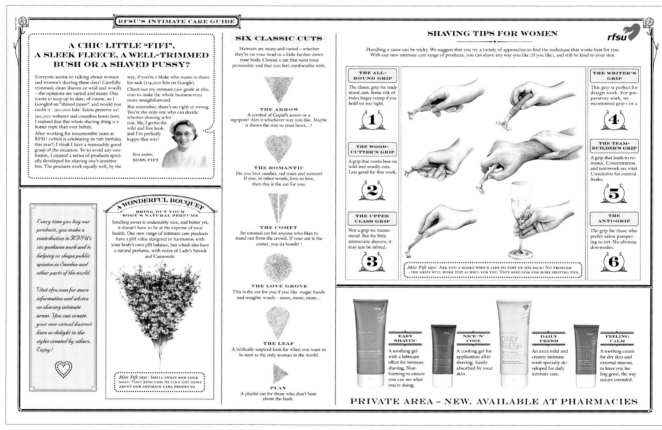

Agency	Euro RSCG, Madrid	Agency	Åkestam Holst, Stockholm
Creative Directors	German Silva	Copywriters	Hanna Björk
	Eva Conesa		Monica Born
	Felipe Crespo	Art Directors	Andreas Ullenius
Copywriter	Luis Munne		Paul Collins
Art Directors	Victor Martin	Illustrator	Torbjörn Krantz
	German Silva	Client	RFSU,
Client	Strepsils		The Swedish Association
			for Sexual Education

176 **Toiletries & Health Care**

Agency	Serviceplan, Munich & Hamburg		**Agency**	TBWA\Paris
Creative Director	Matthias Harbeck		**Creative Director**	Erik Vervroegen
Copywriter	Bernd Huesmann		**Copywriter**	Alban Gallé
Art Director	Christian Sommer		**Art Director**	Cyril Drouot
Illustrator	Jole Stamenkovic		**Photographer**	Dimitri Daniloff
Graphic Design	Ivo Hlavac		**Client**	Hansaplast Earplugs
Client	Apollo Optical Products			

Toiletries & Health Care   **177**

Agencies	Saatchi & Saatchi Simko, Geneva
	Saatchi & Saatchi, Milan & Frankfurt
Creative Directors	John Pallant
	Jean-François Fournon
	Guido Cornara
	Agostino Toscana
	Burkhart von Scheven
Copywriters	Giovanni Salvaggio
	Michael Muck
Art Directors	Williams Tattoli
	Petra Sievers
Photographer	John Parker
Client	Voltaren

Agency	BBDO Düsseldorf	Agency	Saatchi & Saatchi, Brussels
Creative Director	Toygar Bazarkaya	Creative Director	Jan Teulingkx
Art Director	Daniel Aykurt	Copywriters	Caroline D'Hont
Photographer	Ralf Gellert		Bouke Zoete
Client	Braun Nose Trimmer	Art Directors	Patrick Vermeylen
			Stijn Klaver
		Photographer	Tom Joye
		Client	Mebucaiine

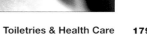

Agency	BBDO Düsseldorf		**Agency**	McCann Erickson, Madrid
Creative Directors	Marie-Theres Schwingeler		**Chief Creative Officer**	Leandro Raposo
	Toygar Bazarkaya		**Executive CD**	Luis Diez Muntane
	Ralf Zilligen		**Creative Directors**	Joaquin Barbero
Copywriter	Sonja Kleffner			Mario García Cadafalch
Art Director	Matias Mueller		**Copywriter**	Joaquin Barbero
Photographers	Mert Dueruemoglu		**Art Directors**	Mario García Cadafalch
	Markus Meuthen			Xavier Lorés
Illustrator	Peter Ruebenian		**Client**	Durex
Client	Aspirin Effect			

180 **Toiletries & Health Care**

Agency	BBDO Düsseldorf	Agency	KNSK Werbeagentur,
Creative Directors	David Lubars		Hamburg
	Toygar Bazarkaya	Creative Directors	Niels Holle
	Stefan Vonderstein		Tim Krink
Copywriters	Anno Thenenbach	Copywriter	Steffen Steffens
	Alexander Busch	Art Director	Thomas Thiele
Art Directors	Olaf Reys	Photographer	Christopher Koch
	Irina Schweigert	Client	Dolormin
	Joerg Tavidde		
	Lidia Pranjic		
Photographers	Frank Schemmann		
	Stefan Kranefeld		
Client	Gillette Fusion		

Agency	BBDO Düsseldorf
Creative Directors	Toygar Bazarkaya
	Stefan Vonderstein
Copywriter	Ingo Hoentschke
Art Directors	Ronald Liedmeier
	Olaf Reys
Photographer	Klaus Merz
Graphic Design	Lidia Pranjic
Client	Braun Series Shavers

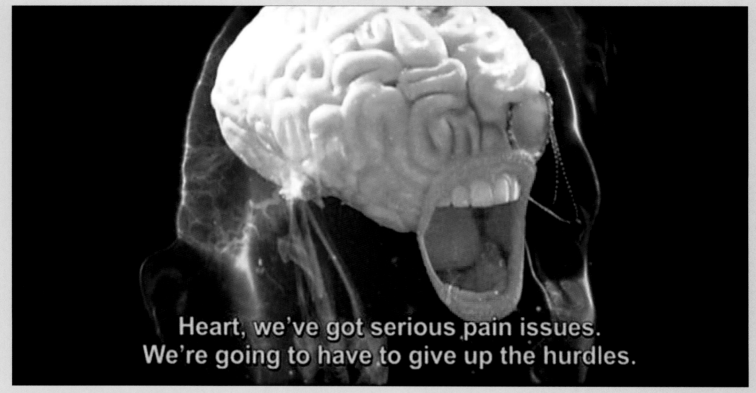

Heart, we've got serious pain issues.
We're going to have to give up the hurdles.

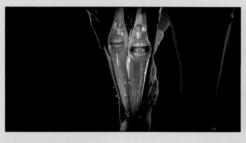

They're so perfect in their squareness and their...

The gun shot!

Legs, release!

Let the lactic acid flow, man!

We're the same age!

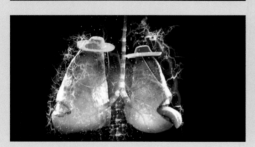

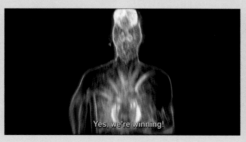
Yes, we're winning!

182   **Clothing & Fabrics**

Agency	Wieden+Kennedy, Amsterdam
Executive CDs	John Norman
	Jeff Kling
Creative Directors	Eric Quennoy
	Mark Bernath
Copywriter	Betsy Decker
Art Director	Anders Stake
Production	Paranoid, Los Angeles
Director	Luis Nieto
Producers	Anne Lifshitz
	Cat Reynolds
Client	Nike Women, "Sanders"

Here's what happens inside an athlete's body during a race. Her organs have developed cartoon-like characters, with the brain as a monocle-wearing dictator. We witness the dialogue between them as they persuade the reluctant legs to get pumping. "I should never have agreed to this," grumbles the heart. But it becomes enthusiastic when it realises that its owner is about to win. When the camera pans out, we see athlete Nicola Sanders. Get strong like Nicola, thanks to Nike Women.

▲ **Clothing & Fabrics** 183

Agency	Publicis Conseil, Paris
Executive CD	Olivier Altmann
Copywriter	Thierry Albert
Art Director	Damien Bellon
Photographer	David Harriman
Client	Wonderbra Nipples

Agency	Wieden+Kennedy
	Amsterdam
Executive CDs	John Norman
	Jeff Kling
Creative Directors	Eric Quennoy
	Mark Bernath
Copywriter	David Smith
Art Director	Sezay Altinok
Production	Rabbit @ Bonkers,
	New York
Directors	Brent Harris
Producers	Saskia Kok
	Gersom Middelink
	Erik-Jan Verheijen
	Elissa Singstock
Client	Nike, "Bad Listener"

"They told me that I'd never walk. That I'd never compete with other kids," says a voiceover, as the camera pans across a collection of trophies and medals. "They told me I'd never make the team…" We see prosthetic legs beside a swimming pool, the start of a rugby match and bikes on a motocross track. "And that a man with no legs can't run." The narrator is amputee athlete Oscar Pistorius, who is sprinting on his famous "blades". "Anything else you want to tell me?" That's Nike courage.

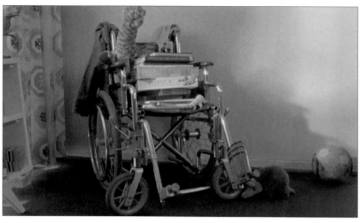

184 **Clothing & Fabrics**

Agency	BBH, London
Production	Sonny, London
Director	Jeff Labbe
Producers	Ran Holst
	David Karbassioun
Client	Levis 501s,
	"Secrets and Lies"

A girl and guy climb a stairwell on their way to the bedroom. "My name's not really Zane," the guy reveals, opening a button of his Levi's. "My name's not really Lucia," the girl retorts, doing the same. "I'm not in a band," says the guy, popping another button. "I don't really work for a label," the girl retorts. "I live in Detroit, not LA." "Well – I've never been to Manhattan." They're both down to one button now. The guy: "The truth is, I've been sleeping in my car." "That's all right – this isn't my apartment." Levi's – live unbuttoned.

Agency	1861 United, Milan
Creative Directors	Pino Rozzi
	Roberto Battaglia
Copywriter	Stefania Siani
Art Director	Federico Pepe
Production	H Films, Milan
Directors	Bill Barluet
	Tomaso Cariboni
Producer	Stella Orsini
Client	Freddy,
	"Olympics Beijing"

Italian sportswear brand Freddy's campaign uses mechanical contraptions to represent athletes' careers. Here, the machine represents different stages of a diver's life: the tube through which she is "born", the glass beakers containing tadpoles that stand for her "amphibious qualities", the bicycle tyre mimicking her aerial somersault, and the mirrors reflecting her face like the water she will enter. In another spot a runner's life is symbolized by a treadmill. These athletes have spent their whole lives getting to the Olympics.

It's the hat.

THE PRICE MAY GIVE YOUR HUSBAND A HEART ATTACK. BUT DON'T WORRY. IT ALSO COMES IN BLACK.

Agency	Serviceplan, Munich & Hamburg	Agency	JWT Dubai
Chief Creative Officer	Alexander Schill	Creative Director	Chafic Haddad
Creative Director	Axel Thomsen	Copywriters	Peter Moyse
Copywriter	Francisca Maass		Adrian An
Art Directors	Jonathan Schupp	Art Directors	Adrian An
	Imke Jurok		Peter Moyse
Illustrator	Jo van de Loo	Photographer	Tejal Patni
Client	Hut Weber	Illustrator	Adrian An
		Client	Nicola Finetti

Clothing & Fabrics

Agency	1861 United, Milan	Agency	Publicis Conseil, Paris
Executive CDs	Pino Rozzi	Executive CD	Olivier Altmann
	Roberto Battaglia	Copywriter	Olivier Camensuli
Copywriter	Luca Beato	Art Director	Frédéric Royer
Art Director	Micol Talso	Client	Wonderbra Swimwear
Photographer	Paolo Zambaldi		
Client	Darmon Milano		

Agency	Publicis, Frankfurt
Creative Directors	Nico Juenger
	Stefan Leick
Art Director	Hendrik Frey
Photographer	Johannes Krzeslack
Client	Wonderbra

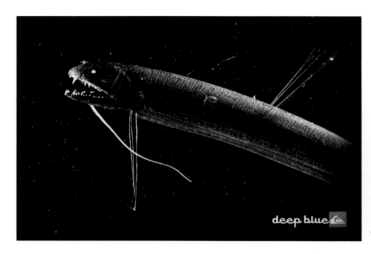

Clothing & Fabrics

Agency	Saatchi & Saatchi, Copenhagen
Creative Director	Simon Wooller
Copywriters	Rasmus Petersen
	Lasse Hinke
Art Directors	Rasmus Petersen
	Lasse Hinke
Graphic Design	Morten Meldgaard
Client	Quiksilver Deep Blue Jeans

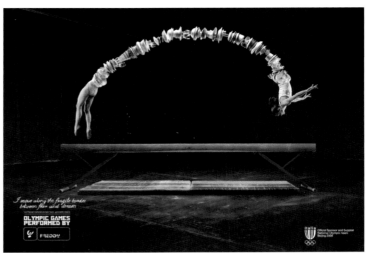

Agency	1861 United, Milan
Executive CDs	Pino Rozzi
	Roberto Battaglia
Creative Directors	Federico Pepe
	Stefania Siani
Copywriters	Stefania Siani
	Luca Beato
Art Directors	Federico Pepe
	Micol Talso
Photographer	Lorenzo Vetturi
Client	Freddy

Agency	1861 United, Milan
Creative Directors	Federico Ghiso
	Giorgio Cignoni
Copywriter	Federico Ghiso
Art Director	Giorgio Cignoni
Photographer	Riccardo Bagnoli
Client	Freddy

190   Clothing & Fabrics

Agency	Marcel, Paris
Creative Directors	Frédéric Témin
	Anne de Maupeou
Copywriters	Eric Jannon
	Dimitri Guerassimov
Art Directors	Nicolas Chauvin
	Romin Favre
Photographer	Laurie Bartley
Client	Diesel

WE ARE ANIMALS *Wrangler*®

Agency	& Co., Copenhagen	Agency	Fred & Farid, Paris
Creative Director	Thomas Hoffmann	Creative Directors	Fred & Farid
Art Directors	Thomas Hoffmann	Copywriters	Juliette Lavoix
	Martin Storgaard		Pauline de Montferrand
Photographer	Morten Laursen	Art Directors	Juliette Lavoix
Client	Ichi Jeans		Pauline de Montferrand
		Photographer	Ryan McGinley
		Client	Wrangler Jeans

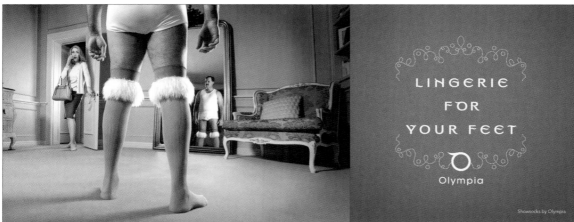

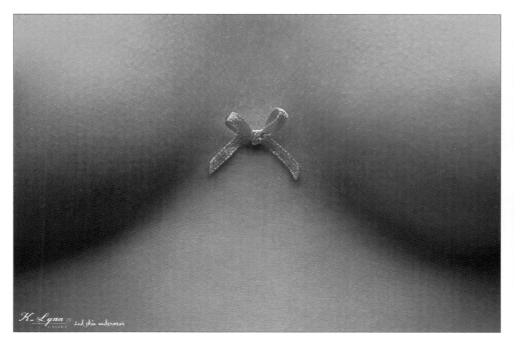

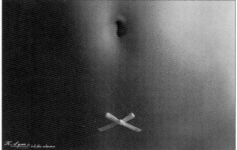

192   Clothing & Fabrics

Agency	Young & Rubicam, Paris	**Agency**	JWT, Dubai
Creative Directors	Les Six	**Creative Director**	Chafic Haddad
Copywriter	Jamie Standen	**Copywriters**	Rania Makarem
Art Director	Mark Forgan		Sally Tambourgi
Photographer	Ross Brown	**Art Directors**	Rania Makarem
Client	Olympia Socks		Sally Tambourgi
		Photographer	Tina Patni
		Client	K-Lynn, 2nd Skin Lingerie

Agency	Friendly Fire Communications, Vienna	Agency	KNSK Werbeagentur, Hamburg
Creative Directors	Thomas Schmid	Creative Directors	Niels Holle
	Norbert Horvath		Tim Krink
Copywriter	Thomas Schmid	Copywriter	Steffen Steffens
Art Director	Norbert Horvath	Art Director	Thomas Thiele
Photographer	Klemens Horvath	Client	Polarguard Outdoor Clothing
Graphic Design	Hannes Kosina		
	Manuel Godetz		
Client	Linda Zlok Fashions		

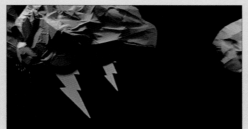

Footwear & Personal Accessories

Agency	Johannes Leonardo, New York	The film recounts how a young footballer's career went from glittering early success to an injury-plagued downfall as a result of ill-fitting sponsored boots. As a surreal dream sequence passes before our eyes, the player explains how the poorly fitting boots led to blisters, missed goals, injury and finally the end of his dream career. To escape the nightmare, he clutches onto the laces of a Nomis boot. Wearing the brand would have allowed him to avoid this disasterous chain reaction. Nomis boots – they're what your feet would choose.
Creative Directors	Leo Premutico Jan Jacobs	
Copywriter	Johannes Leonardo	
Art Director	Johannes Leonardo	
Production	Nexus Productions, London	
Director	Woof Wan-Bau	
Producers	Isobel Conroy Matthew Mattingly	
Client	Nomis Football Boots, "Damn Boots"	

STRADA
...like a little black dress.

Agency	New Moment New Ideas
	Company Y&R, Belgrade
Creative Director	Dragan Sakan
Copywriter	Slavisa Savic
Art Director	Slavisa Savic
Client	Strada Shoes

Agency   Jung von Matt,
         Hamburg
Creative Directors Dörte Spengler-Ahrens
         Jan Rexhausen
Copywriter   Henning Patzner
Production   Jo!Schmid
         Filmproduktion, Berlin
Director   Silvio Helbig
Producers   Jürgen Joppen
         Julia Cramer
Client   Runners Point,
         Asics Shoes, "Lion"

Two tribesmen walk through the African bush. "I'm no longer interested in Sandra Bullock," one of them reveals, as they amble past a giraffe. "Married women get sturdy legs." Then they stop dead, face to face with a lion. Gingerly, one of the men extracts his Asics running shoes from his bag and slips them onto his feet. "Do you think you're faster than a lion?" asks his friend. "No – but I'm faster than you!" Exit, pursued by the lion.

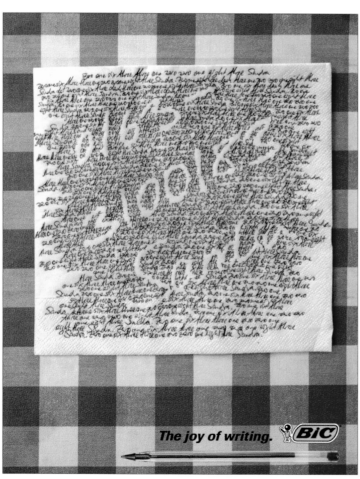

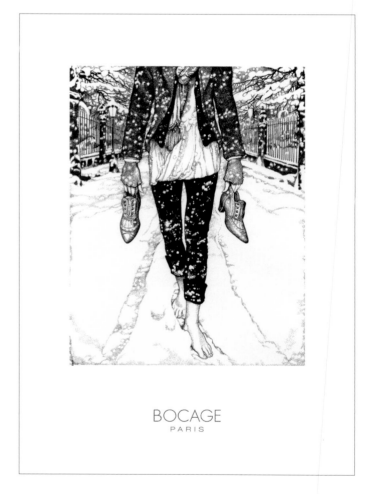

BOCAGE
PARIS

196   **Footwear & Personal Accessories**

Agency   Jung von Matt, Berlin
Creative Directors Wolfgang Schneider
         Mathias Stiller,
         Jan Harbeck
         David Mously
Copywriter   Nicolas Linde
Art Director   Duc Nguyen
Photographer Dan Zoubek
Illustrator   Oskar Strauss
Client   Bic Cristal

Agency   H, Paris
Creative Director Eric Galmard
Art Director   Philippe Rachel
Illustrator   Vania Zouravliov
Client   Bocage

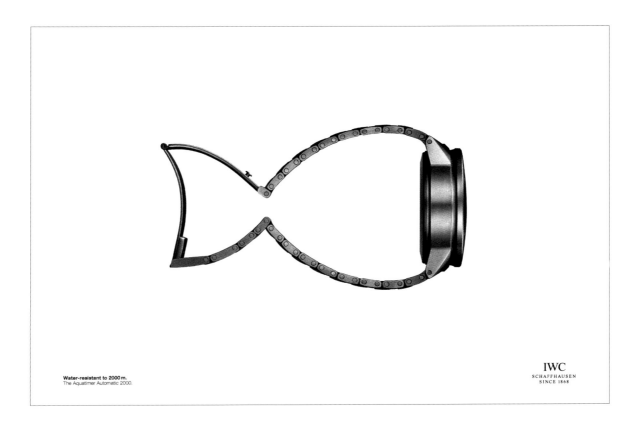

Water-resistant to 2000 m.
The Aquatimer Automatic 2000.

IWC
SCHAFFHAUSEN
SINCE 1868

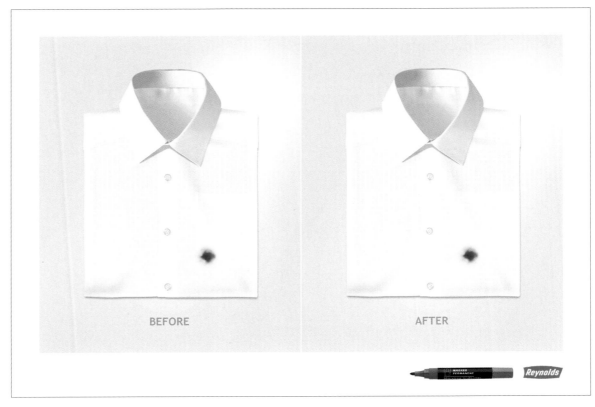

BEFORE

AFTER

Reynolds

Agency	Jung von Matt, Hamburg
Creative Directors	Dirk Haeusermann
	Wolf Heumann
Copywriter	Alexander Hansen
Art Director	Alexander Hansen
Photographer	Stephan Foersterling
Graphic Design	Lars Borker
Client	IWC Schaffhausen
	Aquatimer 2000

Agency	JWT Tunis
Creative Director	Georges Yammine
Copywriter	Georges Yammine
Art Director	Moez Tarifa
Client	Reynolds Permanent Marker

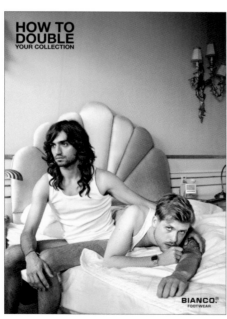

198 **Footwear & Personal Accessories**

Agency	& Co., Copenhagen
Creative Director	Thomas Hoffmann
Art Directors	Thomas Hoffmann
	Martin Storgaard
	Jesper Schmidt
Client	Bianco Footwear

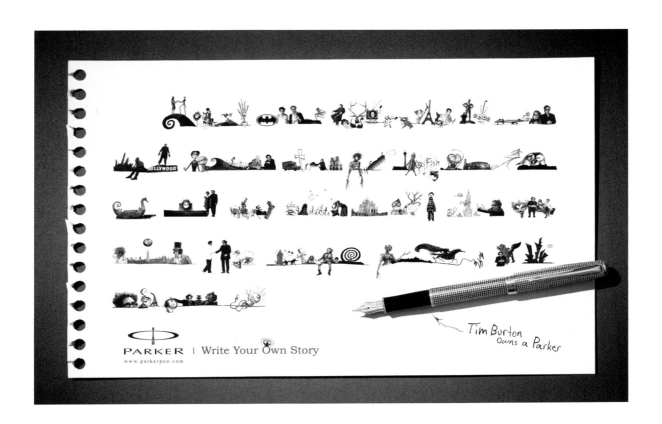

Agency	McCann Erickson, Paris	Agency	DDB Germany, Berlin
Creative Directors	Rémi Noël	Chief Creative Officer	Amir Kassaei
	Eric Holden	Executive CDs	Stefan Schulte
Copywriter	Sylvie Charhon		Bert Peulecke
Art Director	Gérald Schmite	Copywriters	Ricardo Wolff
Photographer	Jean-Noel Leblanc-Bontemps		Marian Goetz
Illustrator	Tim Burton	Art Directors	Gabriel Mattar
Client	Parker		Johannes Hicks
		Illustrator	Craig Zuckerman
		Client	Funk Sunglasses

200 **Automobiles**

Agency	DDB London	The VW Polo is so safe you can't help feeling confident. That idea is charmingly illustrated by this spot featuring a little dog with a split personality. Singing the Steve Winwood number "I'm A Man" at the top of his lungs while sitting next to his owner in her Polo, when he leaves the car he's reduced to a trembling, timorous little chap who can barely manage a whine. Back in the passenger seat, however, his pluck returns.
Creative Directors	Jeremy Craigen	
	Sam Oliver	
	Shishir Patel	
Copywriters & ADs	Dylan Harrison	
	Feargal Ballance	
Production	Independent, London	
Director	Noam Murro	
Producers	Richard Packer	
	Jay Veal	
	Lucy Westmore	
Client	Volkswagen Polo, "Dog"	

Agency	BBDO Düsseldorf
Creative Directors	Toygar Bazarkaya
	Ton Hollander
Copywriters	Markus Steinkemper
	Toni Selzer
Art Director	Sven Klasen
Client	Mercedes-Benz

Agency	Grabarz & Partner, Hamburg
Executive CD	Ralf Heuel
Creative Directors	Henning Patzner
	Christoph Stricker
Copywriter	Martin Grass
Art Directors	Djik Ouchiian
	Fabian Klingbeil
Production	Five Three Double Ninety Filmproductions, Hamburg
Director	Tibor Glage
Producers	Folko Hoheisel
	Patrick Cahill
Client	Volkswagen Touareg, "Garage"

A woman stands in a garage while a mechanic does something under her car. He's making grunting and straining noises. She looks worried: what on earth can he be doing under there? Even his boss shoots a concerned glance from the office. With a final violent wrench, the mechanic removes something stuck to the underside of the car. He stands up. And dumps a live octopus into the woman's arms. With a 580mm wading depth, the VW Touareg can go in deep – very deep.

202   Automobiles

Agency	DDB London
Creative Director	Jeremy Craigen
Copywriters	Graeme Hall
	Noah Regan
Art Directors	Graeme Hall
	Noah Regan
Production	Outsider, London
Director	Scott Lyon
Producers	Zeno Campbell-Salmon
	Richard Chambers
	Vicky Cullen
Client	Volkswagen Golf, "Enjoy the Everyday"

This remarkably edited spot shows how the VW Golf fits into your everyday life. We see a man leaving his house over and over again, in different outfits and seasons. The same process is repeated as he gets into his car, drives to work, leaves the office, goes on a somewhat tense road trip with his wife, gives a pal a lift and enjoys some well-earned leisure time. The dialogue and the sound of slamming doors form a beat that accompanies the rapid-fire images. VW: enjoy the everyday.

Agency	DDB España, Barcelona
Creative Director	José M. Roca de Viñals
Copywriter	Isahac Oliver
Art Director	Xavi Sitjar
Production	The Gang Films, Madrid
Director	Sebastian Grousset
Producers	Matt Grousset
	Raul Garcia
	Vicky Moñino
Client	Volkswagen Touran, "Magic"

A little boy tells his friends that his father has magic powers. His pals don't believe him – and nor do his teachers, who are not impressed by his fibs. "You'd like to carry on saying your father has magic powers in the principle's office, would you?" They march him off. From the window of the principle's office, we see his father arriving to sort the problem out. And sure enough, he parks his car without using his hands. The VW Touran comes with park assist – like magic, it parks itself.

Product recall.

Volkswagen Golf Type I, 1974 model

It has been shown that, due to vibration, the **closing mechanism of the glove compartment** can be subject to wear. In the long run, in some cases, this might result in a more difficult handling of this mechanism. Even though no complaints have been registered, Volkswagen is making Golf Type I owners aware of this, as a precaution.

As this is not in line with the high standards of quality that Volkswagen has for its products, owners of the above-mentioned model are requested to go to www.volkswagen.nl/recall before 12 January 2008. If necessary, Volkswagen will have the closing mechanism **replaced free of charge**. Volkswagen regrets any inconvenience caused. This is why Volkswagen offers dissatisfied customers **free servicing** for their car as compensation.

Volkswagen emphasizes that this only applies to the Volkswagen Golf Type I, 1974 model.

Once again, Volkswagen offers its apologies for any inconvenience caused.

Pon's Automobielhandel B.V. (Volkswagen importer)

The Tiguan. On request with rearview camera.

Das Auto.

Agency	DDB Amsterdam	**Agency**	Grabarz & Partner, Hamburg
Creative Directors	Joris Kuijpers	**Executive CD**	Ralf Heuel
	Dylan de Backer	**Creative Directors**	Ralf Nolting
Copywriter	Dylan de Backer		Patricia Pätzold
Art Director	Joris Kuijpers	**Copywriter**	Constantin Sossidi
Client	Volkswagen Golf	**Art Director**	Oliver Zboralski
		Photographer	Ernesto Martens
		Client	Volkswagen Tiguan

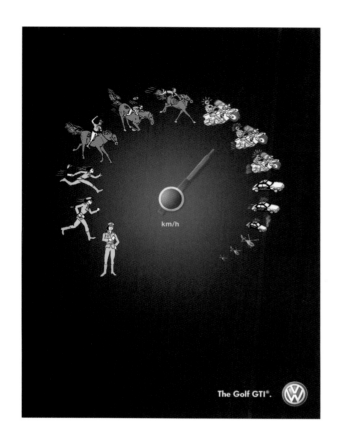

Agency	DDB Germany, Berlin	Agency	DDB Germany, Düsseldorf
Chief Creative Officer	Amir Kassaei	**Chief Creative Officer**	Amir Kassaei
Executive CD's	Stefan Schulte	**Creative Directors**	Heiko Freyland
	Bert Peulecke		Alexander Reiss
Copywriter	Birgit van den Valentyn	**Copywriters**	Jan Propach
Art Director	Tim Stübane		Shahir Sirry
Graphic Design	Jussi Jääskeläinen	**Art Directors**	Fabian Kirner
	Olivia Nowak		Michael Kittel
	Henri Paltemaa	**Photographer**	Michael Kittel
	Wulf Rechtacek	**Client**	Volkswagen Golf R32
Client	Volkswagen Golf GTI		

DSG 7 electronic gearbox. Shift fluently.

DSG 7 electronic gearbox. Shift fluently.

Das Auto.

Polo. Now with air conditioning as standard.

Das Auto.

Agency	DDB Brussels	**Agency**	Owens DDB, Dublin
Creative Director	Peter Aerts	**Creative Director**	Colin Murphy
Copywriter	Bart Van Goethem	**Copywriter**	Adrian Cosgrove
Art Director	Johan Van Oeckel	**Art Director**	Gordan Bent
Typographers	Isabelle De Vos	**Photographer**	Jo Sax
	Phil Bautzer	**Client**	Volkswagen Polo
Client	Volkswagen		

Automobiles

Agency	Grabarz & Partner, Hamburg
Executive CD	Ralf Heuel
Creative Directors	Henning Patzner
	Christoph Stricker
Copywriter	Constantin Sossidi
Art Director	Oliver Zboralski
Photographers	Yona Heckel
	Pim Vuik
Graphic Design	Eduardo Inderbitzin
Client	Volkswagen Touareg

An offroad car, not necessarily for offroad people.
The Cross Polo.

Makes dangers less dangerous.
The brake assist system. Now in the Passat.

Das Auto.

Automobiles **207**

Agency	DDB Germany, Berlin	Agency	Grabarz & Partner, Hamburg
Chief Creative Officer	Amir Kassaei	Creative Directors	Ralf Nolting
Executive CD's	Stefan Schulte		Patricia Pätzold
	Bert Peulecke		Ralf Heuel
Creative Director	Dennis May	Copywriter	Constantin Sossidi
Copywriters	Ricardo Wolff	Art Director	Oliver Zboralski
	Frederico Aramis	Illustrator	Sugar Power
Art Directors	Gabriel Mattar	Graphic Design	Julia Elles
	Izabella Cabral	Client	Volkswagen Passat
Photographer	Sven Schrader		
Client	Volkswagen Cross Polo		

Agency   Ogilvy, Cape Town
Creative Directors Gordon Ray
Art Director   Jamie Mietz
Production   Velocity Films,
                Cape Town
Film Director   Greg Gray
Producers   Helena Woodfine
                Emma Lundy
Client   Volkswagen GTI,
                "Dream"

Driving along a highway, a man is intrigued by the red lights and siren on a truck. Cut to a bedroom, where the same man is dreaming through the alarm. As his girlfriend gets ready, his dream is influenced by the noises she makes: a song on the radio is the same as the one in his car, her shower is rain on the windshield, the curtains being opened are the white light at the end of a tunnel. When she tries to jolt him awake, the car does stunts. Finally she jangles his car keys – and he wakes up.

208   **Automobiles**

Agency   Lowe, London
Creative Director Patrick McClelland
Copywriters   Simon Pearse
                Clive Pickering
Art Directors   Emmanuel St. M. Leux
                Andre Moreira
Production   Bakery Films,
                Hamburg
Director   Bruce St. Clair
Producers   Florian Sigl
                Dan Heighes
Client   Opel Meriva & Zafira,
                "Adjustable World"

On a bus, a pretty girl removes the entire aisle with one tug so she can sit next to a good-looking young guy. A man in swimming trunks transforms a car park into a pool by lifting some canvas. We see a whole bunch of people transforming the landscape to suit themselves: extending bus shelters, widening streets and making obstacles disappear. Welcome to a world that adjusts to your needs – at least, it does if you drive the flexible Opel Meriva or the new Zafira.

Agency   KNSK, Hamburg
Creative Director Claudia Bach
Copywriters   Lisa Port
                Fabian Tritsch
                Lennert Wendt
                Anna-Kristina Schroeder
                Nina Burmeister
Art Director   Michael Reissinger
Production   Deli Pictures, Hamburg
Director   Michael Reissinger
Producers   Sebastian Hellge
                Kerstin Arndt
Client   Chrysler Jeep

A song called Ten Little Vehicles accompanies a childlike animation of a line of cars. "Ten little vehicles were driving in a line: one engine broke, it had to stop, from then on there were nine." The song recounts how each of the cars comes to a sticky end: two of them lose control on a hillside, one skids on some ice, two more are hit by a truck in damp weather, three collide with trees. And the last little vehicle? With its safety features, the Jeep goes "on and on forever more".

		A scientist stands in an empty room making a cat's cradle with string. Then another scientist joins in. Pretty soon, the room is packed with boffins making ever more complex and extravagant constructions out of string supported by their fingers. Finally – almost inevitably – the camera pans back to show that they have sketched the shape of an entire Audi in a highly complex configuration of taut string. One tug, and it all unravels. Fortunately, the real Audi A4 is just as elegant – and built to last.
Agency	DDB España, Barcelona	
Creative Director	Alberto Astorga	
Copywriters	Alfredo Binefa	
	Carlos Lanzon	
Art Director	Jaume Badia	
Production	Agosto, Barcelona	
Director	Nacho Gayan	
Producers	Rafa Montilla	
	Toni Moreno	
	Vicky Moñino	
Client	Audi A4, "String"	

		In an office, a very annoying man creeps up behind people and taps them on the shoulder. They look around, but he slaps them from their blind side. He finds this hilarious. In one scene, he simply shoves an unsuspecting colleague to the floor. But the tables are turned when one particular colleague avoids the man's slaps effortlessly. The flailing hand flies over his head or to one side. The new Volvo is equipped with BLIS, the blind spot information system.
Agency	Gramm Werbeagentur, Düsseldorf	
Creative Directors	Uwe Köbbel	
	Norbert Streich	
Production	Laterna Magica, Düsseldorf	
Director	Kristian Gründling	
Producers	Michael Sieger	
	Norbert Streich	
Client	Volvo, "Slap"	

		In a Spanish bar, a dusky temptress is watching a good-looking guy making a selection on the jukebox. He sees that she's interested and decisively punches in the number of the tune he wants. He stands and waits for his cue. For a moment we expect him to grab her a hot flamenco clinch – but suddenly there's a pounding synthesiser and he begins dancing robotically like a member of Kraftwerk. Spanish and German is an odd combination. But the Seat is just that.
Agency	& Co., Copenhagen	
Art Director	Jesper Schmidt	
Production	Bacon, Copenhagen	
Director	Martin Werner	
Producer	Malene Dyhring	
Client	Seat, "Spanish and German"	

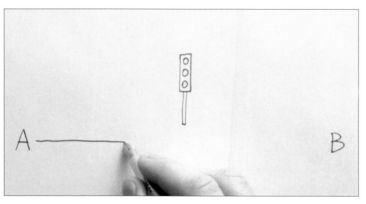

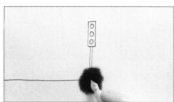

Agency   BBDO Düsseldorf
Creative Directors   Ton Hollander
                Sebastian Hardieck
                Ralf Zilligen
Copywriters   Markus Steinkemper
                Sebastian Steller
Art Director   Patrick Hahne
Production   Markenfilm, Hamburg
Directors   Ton Hollander
                Frank Sprung
Producers   Steffen Gentis
                Silke Rochow
                Nele Schilling
Client   Smart, "Pen"

A fountain pen draws a straight line across a page of white blotting paper, pausing below a drawing of some traffic lights. "Isn't it strange?" says the narrator. "You stop your car at a red light – and it still uses up fuel." Ink leaks out of the nib onto the white paper. Next we see a fresh sheet of blotting paper. "The new Smart Fortwo with start-stop generator has a slightly different approach," says the narrator. The pen stops at the traffic light. So does the flow of ink. "It turns off the engine while standing still. And back on as you proceed." Smart thinking.

This page is dedicated to all those who are looking for a space and can't see one. It is for everyone who has difficulty parking, for those who search and search and, finally, don't find a place. It is a tribute to those who drove round and round the block and in the end got fed up. It is also dedicated to those who, tired of driving, parked in a no parking spot for five minutes and when they came back, the car had gone. It's an homage of the "I want" (a parking space) and "never gets" (a parking space). It is dedicated to those optimists who decided to get up even earlier so that they could leave the car near work, and who didn't manage to get up earlier, let alone park. It is also for you, who are reading this, and can't find a gap. It's for all those who, after two hours driving round in circles in their car, have ever thought, in that little space, just between those two cars, you could fit a smart.

p. 23

Agency   Euro RSCG, Athens
Creative Directors   Manos Palavidis
                George Papoulias
Copywriter   Aspasia Amenta
Art Director   Matina Panagiari
Client   Smart

Agency   Contrapunto, Madrid
Creative Directors   Antonio Montero
                Carlos Jorge
                Félix del Valle
Copywriter   Félix del Valle
Art Director   Carlos Jorge
Client   Smart

Agency	BBDO Düsseldorf	Agency	Contrapunto, Madrid
Creative Directors	Toygar Bazarkaya	Creative Director	Antonio Montero
	Carsten Bolk	Copywriter	Pablo Castellano
	Ton Hollander	Art Director	Leandro Cacioli
	Ralf Zilligen	Producer	Javier Luján
Copywriters	Andreas Walter	Client	Smart
	Dennis Tjoeng		
Art Director	Jacques Pense		
Graphic Design	Lena Tuczek		
Client	Smart		

Agency	BETC Euro RSCG, Paris
Creative Director	Rémi Babinet
Copywriter	Jean-Christophe Royer
Art Director	Eric Astorgue
Client	Peugeot 407

Agency	BETC Euro RSCG, Paris
Creative Director	Rémi Babinet
Copywriter	Jean-Christophe Royer
Art Director	Eric Astorgue
Production	Les Télécréateurs, Paris
Director	Stylewar
Producers	Fabrice Brovelli Solène Frank
Client	Peugeot 407, "Postprod"

A car rolls along a country road to the sound of soaring opera music. Suddenly a voice says "Stop! What's that on the headlight?" Using a Photoshop-style tool, the post-production wizard zooms in on a fly and removes it. "I don't like the sky, can you change that?" says the director (or possibly the client). He then removes chewing gum stuck to the tyre, initials scratched onto the bark of a tree, and the actor's hairstyle. Even when the film rolls again, he starts fussing about the music. The Peugeot 407: made by perfectionists.

Agency	BETC Euro RSCG, Paris
Creative Director	Rémi Babinet
Copywriter	Jean-Christophe Royer
Art Director	Eric Astorgue
Production	Wanda, Paris
Director	Michael Downing
Producers	Fabrice Brovelli Solène Frank
Client	Peugeot 207, "Heartbeat"

We see a man driving his Peugeot 207 along a winding country road at night. The only sound is his heartbeat. The images are intercut with scenes of a beautiful woman taking a bath. The man's heartbeat quickens as he nears his destination, taking the curves rapidly. The woman dons a silky nightgown. By the time he arrives at her door, the man's heart is beating fast. But when he gets out of the car, it slows again. Clearly it wasn't the prospect of seeing the woman that was making his blood race.

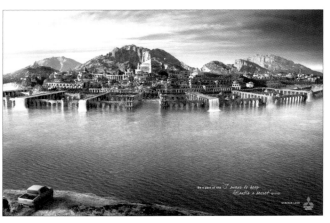

Automobiles 213

Agency   MSTF Partners, Lisbon
Creative Director Susana Sequeira
Copywriter   Rui Soares
Art Director   Aldenir Morais
Client   Mitsubishi Strakar L200

Automobiles

Agency	KNSK Werbeagentur, Hamburg
Creative Directors	Anke Winschewski
	Tim Krink
	Niels Holle
Copywriter	Kurt Müller-Fleischer
Art Director	Bill Yom
Client	Chrysler Jeep

Agency	KNSK Werbeagentur, Hamburg	Agency	Leagas Delaney Italia, Rome
Creative Directors	Anke WInschewski	Creative Directors	Stefano Campora
	Tim Krink		Stefano Rosselli
	Niels Holle	Copywriter	Valentina Maran
Copywriter	Kurt Müller-Fleischer	Art Director	Max Verrone
Art Directors	Bill Yom	Photographer	Fulvio Bonavia
	Wiebke Bethke	Client	Saab 9-3 TTiD
Client	Chrysler Jeep		

Agency	Jung von Matt, Hamburg		**Agency**	Rainey Kelly Campbell Roalfe/Y&R, London
Creative Directors	Jan Rexhausen			
	Dörte Spengler-Ahrens		**Creative Director**	Mark Roalfe
Copywriter	Sergio Penzo		**Copywriter**	Adrian Lim
Art Director	Hisham Kharma		**Art Director**	Steve Williams
Illustrators	Claudia Schildt, Fabian Zell		**Photographer**	Andy Green
Client	Mercedes-Benz G-Class		**Client**	Land Rover Defender

FEELS ITALIAN. WHEREVER YOU ARE.

LAMBORGHINI. BORN IN SANT'AGATA BOLOGNESE.

FEELS ITALIAN. WHEREVER YOU ARE.

LAMBORGHINI. BORN IN SANT'AGATA BOLOGNESE.

Deutsch Marque.

THE NEW C5. Unmistakeably German. (Made in France) ⋀ CITROËN

A touch of Klaus.

THE NEW C5. Unmistakeably German. (Made in France) ⋀ CITROËN

Très Bonn.

THE NEW C5. Unmistakeably German. (Made in France) ⋀ CITROËN

x

Agency	Philipp und Keuntje, Hamburg
Creative Directors	Diether Kerner
	Oliver Ramm
Copywriter	Daniel Hoffmann
Art Director	Sönke Schmidt
Photographer	Arthur Mebius
Client	Lamborghini

Agency	Euro RSCG, London
Creative Director	Mark Hunter
Copywriter	Justin Hooper
Art Director	Olly Caporn
Photographer	Kulbir Thandi
Graphic Design	Mark Osbourne
Client	Citroën C5

You'll be amazed at what we do

Automotive & Accessories

Agency	DDB London
Creative Directors	Sam Oliver
	Shishir Patel
Copywriter	Dave Henderson
Art Director	Richard Denney
Production	Rattling Stick,
	London
Director	Andy McLeod
Producers	Kirsty Dye
	Lucy Westmore
Client	Kwik-Fit, "Boy"

A Kwik-Fit mechanic is explaining the car repair firm's services to a woman. "We can offer you a combined MOT and service from just £99...." As the man talks, the woman's small boy repetitively bashes the water cooler with his toy. "...With a guarantee on parts and labour," finishes the mechanic. "That's great!" the woman exclaims. "What else can you do?" Turning to the annoying boy, the man flutters his fingers in the kid's face. Hypnotised, the boy instantly falls asleep. Kwik-Fit: you'd be surprised what they can do.

Navigation and entertainment in one.
The RNS 510 navigation system.

Navigation and entertainment in one.
The RNS 510 navigation system.

Navigation and entertainment in one.
The RNS 510 navigation system.

 Automotive & Accessories **219**

Agency	DDB Germany, Berlin
Chief Creative Officer	Amir Kassaei
Executive CD's	Stefan Schulte
	Bert Peulecke
Copywriters	Ricardo Wolff
	Philip Bolland
	Ludwig Berndl
Art Directors	Gabriel Mattar
	Kristoffer Heilemann
Photographer	Sven Schrader
Client	Volkswagen
	RNS 510 Navigation System

Agency | Jung von Matt, Berlin
Creative Directors | Wolfgang Schneider
 | Mathias Stiller
 | Jan Harbeck
 | David Mously
Copywriter | Christopher Ruckwied
Art Director | Marius Lohmann
Production | Radical Media, Berlin
Director | Sebastian Schipper
Producers | Kristin Hirt
 | Hermann Krug
DOP | Julian Hohndorf
Client | Mercedes-Benz,
 | "4Matics"

Four suited men stand in the road. Each of them poses a different part of the same question "What... is... the... benefit... of... a... superior... all-wheel... drive... system?" As they carry on with their explanation, we realise that the little quartet is perfectly in synch. "It reacts before you have to react." Immediately after one man says "Gesundheit", another one sneezes. "Each wheel knows what the other is doing," they explain, as they walk in perfectly coordinated movements. For safer driving in any weather conditions, try the 4Matics all-wheel drive system. From Mercedes, of course.

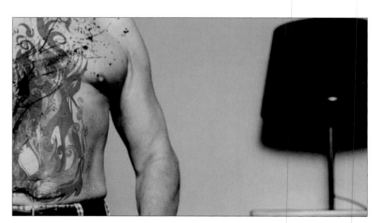

220   Automotive & Accessories

Agency | Saatchi & Saatchi, Paris
Creative Director | Christophe Coffre
Copywriter | Thimothée Gaube
Art Director | Julien Chesne
Production | Première Heure, Paris
Director | Bryan Little
Producers | Jérome Rucki
 | Antoine Grujard
Client | Total,"With You All the Way"

A car pulls up at a Total petrol station in an African city. An attendant fills up the car. But as the automobile leaves, the petrol station goes with it. We see the car and its accompanying petrol station taking a long journey through various African landscapes. Along the way, the duo pause to do good deeds, like pumping up a kid's football. Finally, when the car reaches its destination, the Total petrol station can stop looking after it. In real life, there's a Total petrol station at every stage of your trip. Total: with you all the way.

Agency | Young & Rubicam, Madrid
Creative Director | Nicolas Hollander
Production | Lee Films, Madrid
Director | Sega
Producers | Iván Fernandez Chapi
Client | Repsol, "Let's Invent the Future"

"We invented the wheel, we discovered fire, we reached the moon..." As the narrator describes the achievements of humankind, we see them replicated as tattoos. "We invented cars and motorcycles, zeros and ones, hugs and the alphabet...We invented the internet...We painted cathedrals, pyramids and aeroplanes....We invented rock, penicillin and telegrams." The list goes on. And yet, with all we've done, why can't we protect the thing that is most important to us? A palm opens to reveal...the planet earth. Repsol: let's invent the future.

Genuine Volkswagen Accessories®

The Transporter. Reliable partner of the police force.

Commercial
Vehicles

Agency	DDB, Milan	Agency	DDB, Brussels
Creative Directors	Vicky Gitto	Creative Director	Peter Aerts
Copywriter	Vicky Gitto	Copywriter	Tom Berth
Art Director	Massimo Valeri	Art Director	Geert De Rocker
Client	Volkswagen Accessories	Photographer	Gregor Collienne
		Client	Volkswagen Transporter

Agency	DDB, Brussels
Creative Director	Peter Aerts
Copywriter	Tom Berth
Art Director	Geert De Rocker
Photographer	Kris Van Beeck
Client	Volkswagen Transporter

Agency	DDB Germany, Berlin
Chief Creative Officer	Amir Kassaei
Executive CDs	Stefan Schulte
	Bert Peulecke
Copywriter	Birgit van den Valentyn
Art Director	Tim Stübane
Photographer	Matthias Koslik
Graphic Design	Jussi Jääskeläinen
	Olivia Nowak
Client	Volkswagen Recycling

Automotive & Accessories   **223**

Agency	DDB Germany, Düsseldorf
Chief Creative Officer	Amir Kassaei
Creative Directors	Heiko Freyland
	Alexander Reiss
Copywriter	Heiko Freyland
Art Director	Alexander Reiss
Client	Volkswagen Dynaudio

Of course it's a VW Van, ask your dad.

Frankly, what else could it possibly be? Sure, your little nephew sees two blue cats picking flowers on the sides but he's only six. Of course; your cousin Harriet sees a huge heart in the middle but remember the poor thing only reads silly romance novels and has lived alone 35 000 years. As for your cousin Oliver, he sees a horned mask--the type serial killers might wear. But your cousin Oliver is a pimply post-adolescent type whose main occupation is to watch horror movies when he's not feverishly paging through magazines he hides under his bed. So who's right? It's your dad, a man of experience who knows what he talks about, and to whom, by the way, you should listen more often.

The Van is 60.

It was already there when we lived naked in huts. In 1969.

In 1969, the Volkswagen Van was already 22 years old. And 1969, wotthat was a great year when you were that age. A great year to dream; lying in the grass watching the moon while Armstrong and Aldrin were hopping around on it. A great year to dance naked in the mud at Woodstock and put your clothes back on to walk the streets and protest the Vietnam war. A great year also to reread Kerouac who had just left the road for good, while listening to Abbey Road without knowing it would be the Beatles' last album. In France, it was a great year not to give a darn about newly-elected president Pompidou, or the very first flight of Concorde, because in 1969 in France, we knew before anyone it would be the erotic year. **The Van is 60.**

It's unusual to drive the vehicle you were conceived in.

Love was everywhere the year you were born. Love on sheepskins now moth-eaten. Love burned to ashes. Love in communes now long shut down. Love under trees that were cut down since. Love on beaches now washed away, in countries with new names. Love without even taking off their now outdated clothes. Love on music nobody remembers and following gurus now turned realtors. Come to think of it, apart from you and the Volkswagen Van, there isn't much left of those years. **The Van is 60.**

It has carried all the world's ideals. The door must not have been shut right.

Imagine all the people holding hands, the liberation of our comrades, sexual liberation, the end of capitalism, of profit, of oppression, the ongoing struggle, a free Vietnam, free love, the smell of incense burning, the smell of bras burning, the smell of goat cheese and patchouli, Cuba si, nuclear no thanks, nan trugarez, nein danke, gurus, chamans, chakras, little red books, the road to Katmandu, to Goa, the road again, Afghan jackets, Indian shirts, Swedish pretty hitchhikers, bell-bottoms, sheepskin vests... When you realize everything the VW Van has lost on the way, you wonder how its reputation has made it intact. **The Van is 60.**

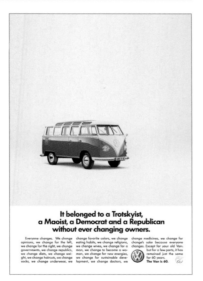

It belonged to a Trotskyist, a Maoist, a Democrat and a Republican without ever changing owners.

Everyone changes. We change opinions, we change for the left, we change for the right, we change governments, we change republics, we change diets, we change weight, we change haircuts, we change socks, we change underwear, we change favorite colors, we change eating habits, we change religions, we change wives, we change for a man, we change to become a woman, we change for new energies, we change for sustainable development, we change doctors, we change medicines, we change for change's sake because everyone changes. Except for your old Van: but for a few parts, it has remained just the same for 60 years. **The Van is 60.**

We know, it's a shock.

The Van is 60.

224 **Automotive & Accessories**

Agency	DDB, Paris
Creative Directors	Alexandre Hervé
	Sylvain Thirache
Copywriter	Patrice Dumas
Art Director	Aurélie Scalabre
Client	Volkswagen Van

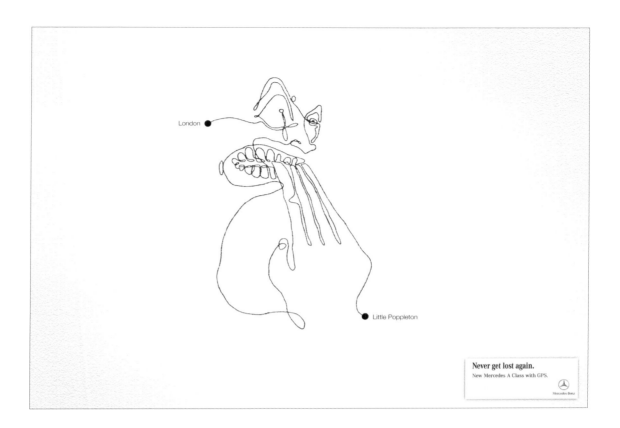

London

Little Poppleton

Never get lost again.
New Mercedes A Class with GPS.

Mercedes-Benz

THE NEW SPEED TRIPLE

TRIUMPH

GO YOUR OWN WAY

Agency	CLM BBDO, Paris	Agency	DraftFCB Deutschland, Hamburg
Creative Directors	Gilles Fichteberg		
	Jean-Francois Sacco	Creative Directors	Mario Anspach
Copywriter	Laurent Laporte		Nadja Hatzy
Art Director	Sophian Bouadjera	Copywriter	Glenn Erk
Illustrators	Yoanne Lemoine	Art Directors	Christiane Schmidt
	Sophian Bouadjera		Martin Krause
Client	Mercedes-Benz GPS	Client	Triumph Speed Triple

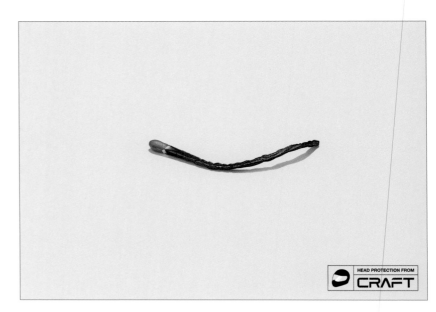

Automotive & Accessories

Agency	Euro RSCG Spain, Madrid
Creative Directors	German Silva
	Felipe Crespo
	Eva Conesa
Copywriter	Manolo Salgado
Art Director	Xavi Orquin
Client	Peugeot Spare Parts

Agency	DDB Germany,
	Düsseldorf
Chief Creative Officer	Amir Kassaei
Executive CD	Eric Schoeffler
Copywriter	Dennis May
Art Directors	Kristine Holzhausen
	Markus Rittenbruch
Photographer	Christian Stoll
Client	Craft Helmets

Agency	Serviceplan, Munich & Hamburg	Agency	TBWA\Istanbul
Executive CD	Matthias Harbeck	Creative Director	Ilkay Gurpinar
Copywriter	Oliver Palmer	Copywriter	Emre Kaplan
Art Directors	Therese Stüssel	Art Director	Gamze Ichedef
	Frank Weitzenbauer	Illustrator	Erol Gunes
Photographer	Felix Reidenbach	Client	Fiat Ducato
Client	BMW Motorcycle Sound Systems		

Agency	Leo Burnett, Cairo
Creative Director	Mohamed Hamdalla
Art Directors	Tameem Youness
	Mohamed Fouad
	Magd El Sherif
Production	The Producers, Cairo
Director	Mohamed Hamdalla
Producers	Hany Ossama
	Shereen Mostafa
Client	Melody Tunes Channel,
	"Madonna" &
	"Pussycat Dolls"

Normal Egyptian folk come on like pop stars in these two hilarious spots from Cairo. In the first execution, a group of middle-aged men (and one woman) are sitting around waiting for a bus. "Time-a goes by…so slowly," sings one of the men. The others join in, waving their arms in a bad re-enactment of Madonna's hit video. Clearly these guys are all addicted to the English-language videos on Melody Tunes channel.

In the second spot, a buxom young woman out on the town with her girlfriends sees a young couple having a quiet drink in the same bar. Taking a shine to the man, the maxi-sized chick sings "I know you like me…I know you do." Her friends join in as she jumps to her feet. "Don't you wish your girly-friend hot like me," she continues. Yes, she's been watching Pussycat Dolls on Melody Tunes. All English, all the time.

☑ Good job

☑ Funny (very)

☐ Charismatic

☑ Sensual

☑ A bit like De Niro

☑ Loves to party

The ideal man doesn't exist.

His magazine, maybe.

GQ
Gentlemen's magazine.

 Media   229

Agency	DDB, Paris
Creative Directors	Alexandre Hervé
	Sylvain Thirache
Copywriter	Fabien Teichner
Art Director	Faustin Claverie
Production	La Pac, Paris
Director	Minivegas
Producers	Sophie Mégrous
	Julie Mathiot
Client	Condé Nast,
	GQ Magazine,
	"The Ideal Man"

What is the ideal man like? Maybe like this guy, jogging down an open road. Subtitles suggest categories. Is the man "athletic"? That box is ticked. "Graceful?" The man begins to run elegantly: tick! Sexy? He's joined by hoards of admiring women. In fact, he acts out each category as it appears on the screen. He has a good job, he's funny, he's strong, he's charismatic, he's romantic, he's sensual, and he likes animals. He has a touch of De Niro. And by the way, he's a hard-partying rebel. Of course, the ideal man doesn't exist. His magazine, maybe: GQ.

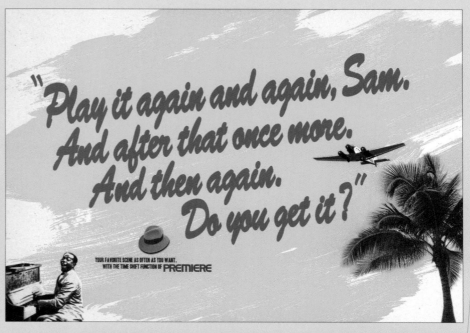

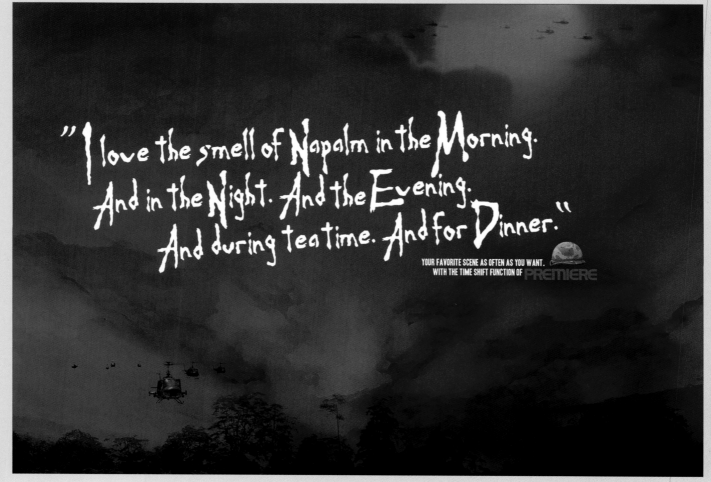

Agency	DDB Germany, Düsseldorf
Chief Creative Officer	Amir Kassaei
Executive CD	Eric Schoeffler
Copywriters	Dennis May
	Lena Reckeweg
Art Directors	Kristine Holzhausen
	Markus Rittenbruch
Photographer	Christian Stoll
Graphic Design	Marilyn Wolf
Client	Premiere TV

Agency	Selmore, Amsterdam
Creative Directors	Poppe van Pelt
	Diederick Hillenius
Copywriters	Poppe van Pelt
	Tomas Minken
Art Directors	Diederick Hillenius
	Albert Vegars
Production	Comrad, Amsterdam
Director	Willem Gerritsen
Producers	Jelani Isaacs
	Danielle van Berkel
Client	De Volkskrant,
	"Cucumbers"

A close-up of some appetising vegetables. But the narrator explains that much of our food today is genetically modified. Is that really good for us? What would we do if it became obvious that scientists were tampering with our food? We see what happens when question mark-shaped cucumbers are placed in a supermarket. Customers give the curvy 'cumbers a wide birth and pick the regular straight variety – also modified. De Volkskrant newspaper – because you need to know.

Need to know. de Volkskrant

beate-uhse
With child Lock

EXCLUSIVELY ON
PREMIERE

Media 231

Agency	TBWA\PHS, Helsinki
Creative Director	Tommy Makinen
Copywriters	Tommy Makinen
	Erkko Mannila
Art Directors	Mikko Torvinen
	Jouni Seppanen
Graphic Design	Aleksi Palomaki
Client	Sub Movie Channel

Agency	Kempertrautmann,
	Hamburg
Creative Directors	Jens Theil
	Gerrit Zinke
Copywriter	Michael Götz
Art Director	Florian Schimmer
Client	Premiere,
	Beate Uhse Erotic TV,
	"Parental Controls"

We see a blank page and a hand holding a pen. The hand begins to draw what at first looks like an erotic sketch. With a few deft additions it's quickly transformed into a harmless cartoon of a bird. Another blank page – and what's this? Is that somebody being…? Oh no, our mistake, in fact it's a horse. And surely that can't be an enormous…? No, of course not, it's a cartoon snowman. Beate Uhse erotic TV with child lock: you'll see it, but your children won't.

Agency	BETC Euro RSCG, Paris
Creative Director	Stéphane Xiberras
Copywriter	Nathalie Dupont
Art Director	Francis de Ligt
Production	Irène, Paris
Director	Xavier Gianolli
Producer	David Green
Client	Canal+, "Versailles"

We're at the palace of Versailles, where a marquis has an audience with Marie Antoinette. "So marquis," begins Marie, then interrupts herself with a strange puffing noise. "Did you meet...puff puff... this Princess d'Orleans?" He replies "Puff puff...yes your majesty." The dialogue continues like this. Even the revolutionary mob outside puffs en masse. Finally we cut to a present day jogger, who is relating the story to her fellow runner, complete with puffing. Canal+: films too good to keep to yourself.

232   Media

Agency	BETC Euro RSCG, Paris
Creative Director	Stéphane Xiberras
Copywriter	Arnaud Assouline
Art Director	Benjamin Le Breton
Production	Quad, Paris
Director	Reynald Gresset
Producer	Isabelle Menard
Client	Sci-Fi Channel, "Adopt Sci-Fi"

An alien child is abandoned on Earth when his spaceship leaves without him. He finds himself in a grim orphanage, where he's forced to suffer terrible food and the merciless teasing of the other kids. They lock him in the bathroom, beat him up and tell him in no uncertain terms: "Go home." At night he cries himself to sleep. At the end of the spot, he stands at a window watching a child leave with foster parents. Open your heart to science fiction: adopt sci-fi.

Agency	Rainey Kelly Campbell Roalfe/Y&R, London
Creative Director	Mark Roalfe
Copywriter	Paul Silburn
Production	Red Bee Media, London
Director	Vince Squibb
Producer	Sarah Caddy
Client	BBC iPlayer, "Penguins"

Former Monty Python Terry Jones narrates in this BBC "mockumentary" about the arctic. He introduces us to a colony of penguins with a special skill: they can fly. Sure enough, after a short, waddling run-up the penguins take majestically to the sky and migrate to the rainforests of South America. Missed something interesting on the BBC? Thanks to its new digital service, you needn't. Watch BBC shows from the past week, on your computer.

Agency	1861United, Milan
Creative Directors	Pino Rozzi
	Roberto Battaglia
Copywriter	Federico Ghiso
Art Director	Giorgio Cignoni
Production	Akita Film, Milan
Director	Guy Manwaring
	(Sonny, London)
Producers	Paolo Zaninello
	Carla Beltrami
Client	Sky Italy - Kids,
	"Teddy Bear"

A small boy wanders around town, putting up posters of his missing teddy bear. Everywhere he goes, we hear the little "tap tap" of his hammer as he nails up another picture of the bear. In sun and rain he continues his mission, practically wallpapering the town with posters. He carries on until sundown. The next day, he's at it again, nailing another poster to a tree. But then he hears another "tap tap", right behind him. He looks behind the tree and sees a teddy bear – putting up a poster of a small boy. TV drives the imagination.

Agency	Advico
	Young & Rubicam,
	Zurich
Creative Director	Christian Bobst
Copywriter	Martin Stulz
Art Director	Rob Hartmann
Production	Markenfilm, Zurich
Client	Sonntags Zeitung,
	"Bush"

A reporter asks George W. Bush: "Why did you really go to war?" Bush hesitates. Suddenly, his head peels away like a Russian doll, to reveal…Donald Rumsfeld. But Rumsfeld is also unable to answer, so he makes way for…Condoleeza Rice. She's equally lost for words, so Bush senior replaces her. He says: "We have before us…the opportunity to forge a new world order." The Matrioshka reassembles and we find W. again, looking relieved that dad was able to help out. Sonntags Zeitung gives you "the insight story".

Agency	Grey Beirut
Creative Director	Philippe Skaff
Copywriter	Philippe Skaff
Art Director	Ghassan Khairallah
Production	Spinifex, Sydney
Director	Kimble Rendal
Producers	Tracey Tailor
	Rania Khoury
Client	Al Arabiya,
	"Know More"

In a Middle Eastern restaurant, a man orders chicken. The narrator relates a chain of events: "For 60 million chicks, their diet of choice is soya, imported from Brazil on ships like this …" He goes on to explain how pollution from such ships causes ice caps to melt, flooding land and forcing people into refugee camps, where they are recruited by terrorist groups. The ensuing war stifles the global oil supply, meaning that ships can't put to sea, so chickens starve. "No chicken today," says the waiter. Al Arabiya news channel: know more.

234   **Media**

Agency	RBK, Stockholm
Creative Director	Fredrik Dahlberg
Copywriters	Ulf Rönnbäck af Luleå
Art Director	Johan Pihl
Photographer	Luka Mara
Illustrator	Lars Anéer
Client	Fokus

Agency	Marcel, Paris
Creative Directors	Frédéric Témin
	Anne de Maupeou
Copywriter	Eric Jannon
Art Directors	Dimitri Guerassimov
	Thomas Dimetto
Illustrators	Thomas Dimetto
	Dinny Nanja
	Wacyl Djender
Client	France 24

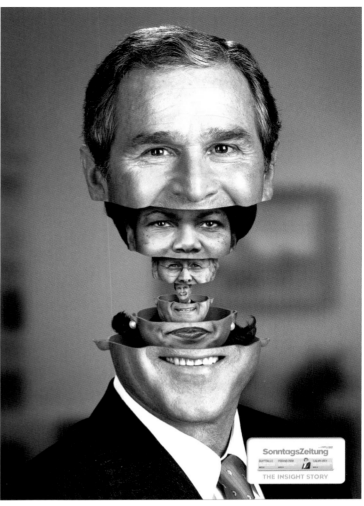

Agency	Advico Young & Rubicam, Zurich
Creative Directors	Philipp Skrabal
	Christian Bobst
Copywriter	Martin Stulz
Art Director	Rob Hartmann
Photographer	Scheffold Vizner
Client	Sonntags Zeitung

236 Media

Agency	BETC Euro RSCG, Paris
Creative Director	Stéphane Xiberras
Copywriter	Olivier Couradjut
Art Director	Rémy Tricot
Photographer	Cédric Delsaux
Client	13éme Rue (13th Street)

The seven deadly sins
Seven special programmes to lead you astray

13ème RUE
THE CRIME CHANNEL

Agency	BETC Euro RSCG, Paris
Creative Director	Stéphane Xiberras
Copywriter	Arnaud Assouline
Art Directors	Benjamin Le Breton
	Landry Stark
Illustrator	Landry Stark
Client	13éme Rue (13th Street)

After they died,
these guys have experienced worse than going to Hell.
They have turned into a *Junk de Luxe* t-shirt.

Blitzkrieg Bop (*The Ramones*) 2:10 © 1976

oui fm 102.3 - www.ouifm.fr - www.myspace.com/ouifm   © Ian Dickson/Redferns/musicpictures.com

It's high time you listened to a band
that is not compared to *The Clash*.

White Riot (*The Clash*) 2:08 © 1977

oui fm 102.3 - www.ouifm.fr - www.myspace.com/ouifm   © Virginia Turbett/Redferns/musicpictures.com

Erratum:
The *Christ* died at the age of 27 with a bullet in his head.

Smell Like Teen Spirit (*Nirvana*) 4:39 © 1991

oui fm 102.3 - www.ouifm.fr - www.myspace.com/ouifm   © Michel Linssen/Redferns/musicpictures.com

No young people,
this is not a picture
from *Dior Homme*'s latest fashion show.

The Modern World (*The Jam*) 2:30 © 1977

oui fm 102.3 - www.ouifm.fr - www.myspace.com/ouifm   © Ebet Roberts

Agency	Leg, Paris
Creative Director	Gabriel Gaultier
Copywriter	Gabriel Gaultier
Art Director	Stéphane Richard
Client	Oui FM

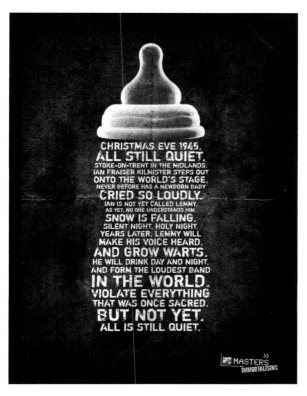

CHRISTMAS EVE 1945.
ALL STILL QUIET.
STOKE-ON-TRENT IN THE MIDLANDS.
IAN FRAISER KILMISTER STEPS OUT
ONTO THE WORLD'S STAGE.
NEVER BEFORE HAS A NEWBORN BABY
CRIED SO LOUDLY.
IAN IS NOT YET CALLED LEMMY,
AS YET, NO ONE UNDERSTANDS HIM.
SNOW IS FALLING.
SILENT NIGHT, HOLY NIGHT.
YEARS LATER, LEMMY WILL
MAKE HIS VOICE HEARD.
AND GROW WARTS.
HE WILL DRINK DAY AND NIGHT,
AND FORM THE LOUDEST BAND
IN THE WORLD.
VIOLATE EVERYTHING
THAT WAS ONCE SACRED.
BUT NOT YET.
ALL IS STILL QUIET.

Agency   BBDO Germany, Stuttgart
Creative Directors   Armin Jochum
                     Friedrich Tromm
Copywriters   Georg Baur
                     Torben Otten
Art Director   Sven Gareis
Illustrator   Sven Gareis
Client   MTV Masters

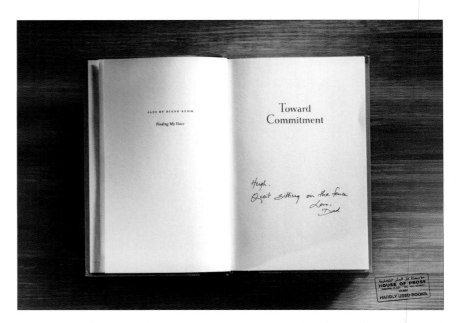

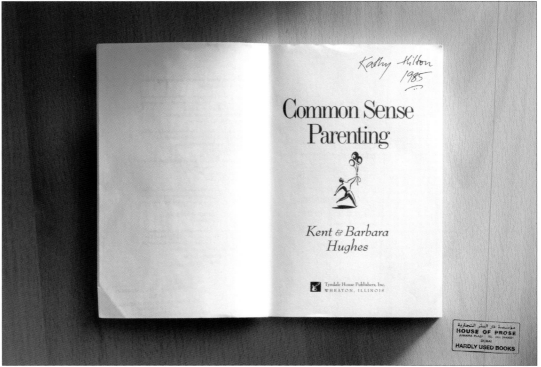

Media

Agency	Forsman & Bodenfors, Gothenburg	Agency	Brandcom Middle East, Dubai
Client	Göteborgs-Posten	Creative Director	Manoj Ammanath
		Copywriter	Manoj Ammanath
		Art Director	Sabina Mustafa
		Photographer	Sunil Raju
		Illustrator	Anil Palyekar
		Client	House of Prose

Agency   CLM BBDO, Paris
Creative Directors Gilles Fichteberg
                    Jean-Francois Sacco
Copywriter   Edouard Perarnaud
Art Director   Martin Darfeuille
Photographer   Jean-Yves Lemoigne
Client   Metro

Agency	Vitruvio Leo Burnett, Madrid
Executive CD	Rafa Antón
Creative Director	Javier Álvarez
Copywriter	Santiago Saiegh
Art Director	Julita Pequeño
Photographer	Raquel Quintana
Client	TCM

Agency	McCann Erickson Polska, Warsaw
Creative Directors	Iwona Kluszczynska
	Wojtek Dagiel
Copywriters	Iza Przepiorska-Kotlinska
	Lukasz Kotlinski
Art Directors	Lukasz Kotlinski
	Iza Przepiorska-Kotlinska
Photographer	Lukasz Murgrabia
Client	Jazz Radio

244 **Recreation & Leisure**

Agency	Publicis Yorum, Istanbul	The city of Istanbul literally becomes a jazz combo in this tuneful film. As the piano kicks in, a pedestrian crossing is trans-
Creative Director	Cevdet Kizilay	formed into a keyboard. Telegraph wires
Copywriter	Ebru Ataman Firat	are plucked, as if by an invisible hand, to
Art Director	Adnan Elmasoglu	provide the bass. Chimney pots are the
Production	PTT, Istanbul	valves of a trumpet and a spinning carousel
Director	Ozan Aciktan	is a cymbal. Abandoned oil drums are...
Producers	Tunay Vural	well, drums. The railings of a park become
	Asu Sipsak,	applauding audience members. The Akbank
	Arzu Koksal	Jazz Festival is bringing jazz to the heart of
	Banu Onuk	Istanbul.
Client	Akbank Jazz Festival, "Jazz of the City"	

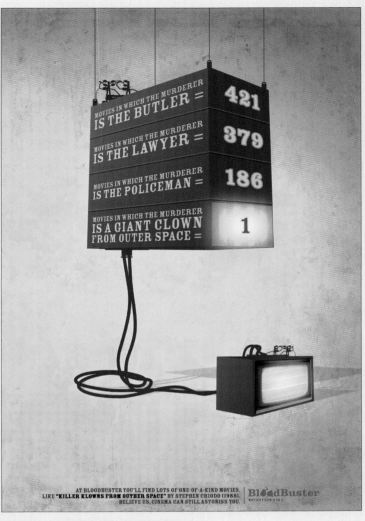

Agency	Leagas Delaney Italia, Rome
Creative Directors	Stefano Campora
	Stefano Rosselli
Copywriter	Stefano Campora
Art Director	Eustachio Ruggieri
Client	Bloodbuster

Agency	Try Advertising Agency, Oslo
Copywriter	Lars Joachim Grimstad
Art Director	Egil Pay
Production	Fantefilm, Oslo
Director	Mats Stenberg
Producers	Magne Lyngnern
	Eivind Moe
	Cecilie Thue
Client	Keno, "Bad Day, Good Day"

These two commercials are almost identical and were shown in the same commercial break. In the first, a man has a bad day. He drops his toast, which lands jam side down. The vending machine eats his coins. Work goes badly. He sits next to a smelly woman on the tram. His girlfriend slaps him. When buying his lottery ticket, he plays it safe. In the second version, however, the toast lands jam side up. The vending machine delivers two chocolate bars. He's a hero at work. The woman on the tram is a babe. And his girlfriend adores him. So he picks ten lottery numbers. He's feeling lucky.

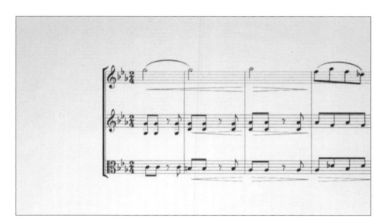 

Agency	Euro RSCG Group Switzerland, Zurich
Executive CD	Frank Bodin
Creative Director	Axel Eckstein
Copywriter	Nemanja Gajic
Art Director	Isabelle Buehler
Production	Virtual Republic, Düsseldorf
Director	Michael Klein
Producer	Gerhard Vetter
Client	Zurich Chamber Orchestra, "Roller Coaster"

This animated spot opens with a slow pan across a line of sheet music, backed by the appropriate classical piece (Ferdinand Ries's Symphony No. 2 in C minor, op. 80, from 1814). But as the music grows more dramatic, the lines of sheet music are transformed into a rollercoaster. The viewer is taken on an exhilarating ride as the coaster rises, falls, twists and plunges with the music, effectively mimicking the emotions that the piece provokes. This is what you can expect if you attend a performance of the Zurich Chamber Orchestra.

Agency	Vaculik Advertising, Bratislava
Creative Directors	Milan Hladky
	Dejan Galovic
Copywriter	Juraj Dvorecky
Art Director	Bohumil Dohnal
Production	Hitchhiker Films, Bratislava
Director	Roman Valent
Client	International Festival of Theatre Schools, "We Are Still Learning"

On a stage set, actors perform a Shakespearian scene. One of the actors draws his sword. His rival attempts to do the same, but his sword refuses to come out of its scabbard. When he pulls it free with a mighty wrench, he staggers back and accidentally severs the hand of a fellow cast member. The audience is sprayed with arterial blood. Everyone starts screaming. The director sighs and walks off. Welcome to the International Festival of Theatre Schools. The actors still have a lot to learn.

Agency	Try Advertising Agency, Oslo
Copywriter	Petter Bryde
Art Director	Thorbjørn Ruud
Production	Monster Commercials, Oslo
Director	Mathis Fürst
Producers	Sebastian Marcussen
	Eivind Moe
	Cecilie Thue
Client	Luck Lottery, "Been Around"

At a railway station, a man spots an old friend with a rucksack. He asks his pal where he's been. The friend replies with a rhyming song "I've been to…the United States, Mexico, Panama, Haiti, Jamaica, Peru, Republic Dominican, Cuba, Caribbean, Greenland, El Salvador too!" The man looks bemused, but his friend continues. "Puerto Rica, Colombia, Venezuela, Honduras, Guyana and still…Guatemala, Bolivia, then Argentina and Ecuador, Chile, Brazil!" The song seems to go on forever. Luck can take you a long way. Especially if you win the lottery.

Agency	Serviceplan, Munich & Hamburg
Chief CO	Alexander Schill
Executive CD	Matthias Harbeck
Copywriter	Oliver Palmer
Art Directors	Frank Weitzenbauer
	Therese Stüssel
Production	Cobblestone Filmproduktion, Hamburg
Director	Moritz Mohr
Producer	Bey-Bey Chen
Client	Boris Becker & Co., "High Precision Rackets"

A tennis coach is shouting at his student as he serves ball after ball at her. "Faster… Go!" The balls zip back over his head. "Too high! You make me sick!" She fires back another speeding ball, which like the others sticks into the wire mesh fence behind the coach. He yells: "Move your fucking legs! You're wasting my time!" The girl returns one final serve and strides off the court. The camera pans back. Behind the coach, we see that the balls stuck into the mesh spell out the words: "Fuck you!" Precision tennis rackets, from Boris Becker & Co.

Agency	Upset, Athens
Creative Director	Nikos Vavakis
Copywriter	Manos Moschonas
Art Director	Eleni Tempelou
Production	Le Spot, Athens
Director	Harry Patramanis
Producers	Eleni Asvesta
	Vicky Kanelaki
	Evelyn Nanou
Client	OPAP, "Mixed Up"

A football match is in progress. The commentator breathlessly details each pass. Suddenly, one of the players snatches up the ball and begins dribbling it like a basketball. After dodging two players he throws the ball to a teammate – who hits it with a tennis racket. Meanwhile, a motocross bike has roared onto the pitch to intercept the ball and send it, with a flick of the tyre, towards a pyramid of acrobats. The man on top does a back flip and sends the ball into the goal. With OPAP, you can bet on anything. More sport – more fun.

Agency	TBWA\PHS, Helsinki
Creative Director	Erkko Mannila
Copywriters	Erkko Mannila
	Tommy Makinen
Art Director	Mikko Torvinen
Production	B-Rappu, Helsinki
Director	Petri Kotwica
Producers	Yrjo Nieminen
	Olli Korpiala
Client	Lotto,
	"Hiding Millionaires"

A man is reluctant to leave his own home. He checks the coast is clear before stepping out to pick up his mail. He looks upset when a neighbour appears. "Going on holiday?" the neighbour inquires, spotting a brochure. "No…no holidays here." The man scurries back into his home. His wife accuses him of not being able to keep his mouth shut. "Now the news spreads, Michael!" On the other side of the street, the neighbour is equally paranoid. He tells his wife "They know it, Rachel, they know it!" The lotto is creating more millionaires than ever.

THE LAST WEEK WITH ANDY WARHOL

Other Voices, Other Rooms
9 February – 4 May 2008

MODERNA MUSEET

Agency	Publicis QMP, Dublin
Creative Directors	Carol Lambert
	Ger Roe
Copywriter	Darragh Carey
Art Director	Ciaran McCarthy
Production	Speers Films, Dublin
Director	Richard Chaney
Producers	Jonny Speers
	Rachel Murray
Client	TG4,
	"The More You Watch, the More You See"

A small Irish language broadcaster wanted to say a lot with one commercial. So the agency shot a pub scene unlike any other. The more viewers watched the commercial, the more strange things they noticed. A spy handing over a file, a woman in handcuffs, beer drinking aliens – even a life-sized marionette. And who are those two people in wartime army uniforms? Through a doorway, a violent argument is taking place. No doubt other things remain to be spotted. There's much more to TG4 than you might expect. The more you watch, the more you see.

Agency	Storåkers McCann, Stockholm
Copywriter	Hanna Belander
Art Director	Jonas Frank
Client	Moderna Museum

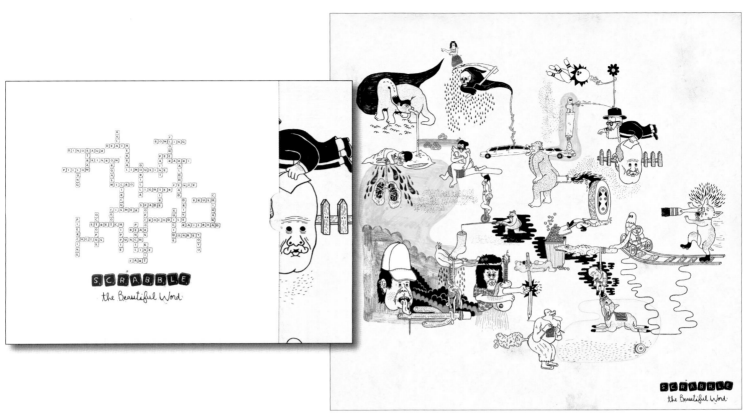

Agency	Ogilvy & Mather, Paris	The words used in different games
Creative Director	Chris Garbutt	of Scrabble were shown on the front
Copywriters	Arnaud Vanhelle	of envelopes that were inserted into
	Benjamin Bregeault	magazines. Posters inside the envelopes
	Mihnea Gheorghiu	unfolded to visualise the various words
Art Directors	Antoaneta Metchanova	used in each game.
	Alex Daff	
	Najin Ha	
Illustrators	Am I Collective	
	David Ho	
	Ekta	
Client	Scrabble	

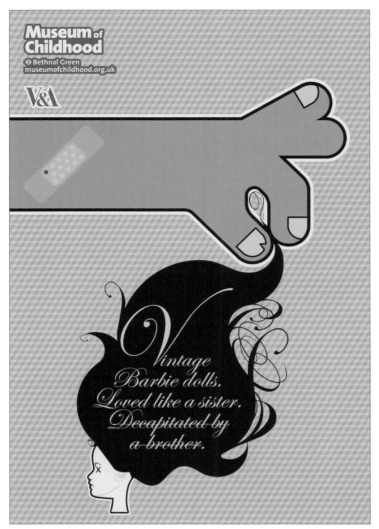

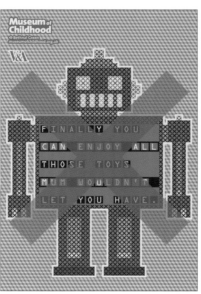

Agency	Abbott Mead Vickers BBDO, London
Creative Director	Paul Brazier
Copywriter	Mike Nicholson
Art Director	Paul Pateman
Illustrator	Paul Pateman
Client	Museum of Childhood

The **INSTANT CRITIC** Collection

Your boss, your aunty, the vice-president of Paraguay. Whoever it may be, you're coming to Tate Britain with someone you want to impress. This Collection is designed to turn your visit into a glittering walk-through advertisement for your intelligence. First, a heads-up: don't say 'next to,' say 'juxtaposed with,' don't say 'lots of,' say 'multitude' and whatever you do, don't say 'nice,' say 'visionary.' After memorising these, lead your companion to the lesser known works as true genius always goes against the grain. On your way, nod at our attendants like you know them (they'll play along) and stop at Paul Nash's *Kinetic Feature*. Examine it so closely your nose hairs threaten to brush the canvas and then study it from so far away it becomes a blur. Move on, with hands clasped behind your back, to *Harvest Home* by John Linnell. Stand before it and say something like, 'It really displays his admiration for Turner, even if the technique and style are quite different.' Then read the painting's label and look unsurprised when it says exactly the same thing. Now glide off to the still-lifes (the pictures of stuff on a table). These are perfect for referring to later in dinner party conversation when you can compare the dining table in front of you with say, the table in Edward Collier's *Still Life with a Volume of Wither's Emblemes*. Saunter on in meditative silence. When you spot Reynolds's *Lady Bampfylde* approach it as though being pulled in by some sort of tractor beam. Praise the remarkable artistry but also the model. Say, 'To remain so poised when Reynolds's pet macaw was running amok in the studio shows incredible self-discipline.' As the laughter subsides and before any tricky questions (you'll need to come to one of our specialist talks to handle those) suggest closing the tour with a trip to the café. They have a multitude of sandwiches juxtaposed with cakes and the scones are really visionary.

Create your own Collection
BP British Art Displays 1500 – 2008

Supported by BP

Admission Free ⊖ Pimlico
www.tate.org.uk ⬤ Millbank Pier

BRITAIN
TATE

The **I WANT TO BE SWEPT OFF MY FEET** Collection

Hey you. What say you and me leave this hurly-burly world and go on a little adventure around Tate Britain? I'll be by your side the whole way, guiding you firmly yet tenderly through a Collection that will lead us to realms of wonder and joy. Let's begin with JMW Turner's sublime *Sunrise, with a Boat between Headlands* where a brand new day dawns. Did you get a tingle too? Here, I want to show you something else – it's *Youth on the Prow, and Pleasure at the Helm* by William Etty where sensual nudes on a boat snatch at bubbles of pleasure. Enjoy that moment of wild abandon, whilst carefully ignoring those killjoy clouds on the horizon. Now imagine you and I are high above them. Spread out your arms. Take my hand and let's fly from the ocean to the rolling countryside of John Linnell's *Contemplation*. Look, can you see? We're not the only ones to be swept up in its bucolic beauty. The little shepherd is looking up from his book awe-struck by the scenery in which he will forever remain. This is how I felt when I first caught sight of you. Your to-die-for nose and dazzling smile beckon me like James Ward's *Gordale Scar* with its imposing rock and troubled skies. Its dangerous allure is almost impossible to resist. I feel like Richard Smith's *Vista*. Yes, it may be a picture of a humble cigarette packet but its hypnotic pattern makes me dizzy and light on my feet. Oh, there's a bench nearby. Shall we? Do you need a foot massage? You've got a beautiful little toe. But I've confessed too much. Good-bye, my sweet. Everything must come to an end, but our memories needn't. Let's treat ourselves to a little postcard from the bookshop. A small trinket of an afternoon, in another place. Remember me, my love.

Create your own Collection
BP British Art Displays 1500 – 2008

Supported by BP

Admission Free ⊖ Pimlico
www.tate.org.uk ⬤ Millbank Pier

BRITAIN
TATE

Agency	Fallon London	**Agency**	Jung von Matt, Stockholm	The Royal Swedish Opera's new version of the biblical story Samson & Delilah takes place in Israel; from 1948 to the present day. The agency went to the Gaza Strip to spray-paint stencils on abandoned buildings. The Gaza graphics were photographed and these images were used as press ads.
Executive CD	Richard Flintham			
Creative Director	Juan Cabral	**Copywriter**	Magnus Andersson	
Copywriters	Selena Mckenzie	**Art Directors**	Max Larsson von Reybekiel	
	Toby Moore		Jacob von Corswant	
Art Directors	Selena Mckenzie	**Client**	The Royal Swedish Opera,	
	Toby Moore		Samson & Delilah	
Typographer	Hugh Tarpy			
Client	Tate Britain			

Agency	SCP, Gothenburg
Creative Director	Tommy Östberg
Copywriter	Neil Clark
Art Director	Tommy Östberg
Client	Gothenburg Symphony Orchestra

Go wherever the music takes you - just sit tight.

Agency	Ogilvy & Mather, Copenhagen		**Agency**	Ogilvy, Frankfurt
Art Directors	Thomas Boldsen		**Creative Director**	Stephan Junghanns
	Claus Collstrup		**Copywriter**	Peter Strauss
Production	A-Film, Tallinn		**Art Director**	Ralf Richter
Client	Scrabble		**Photographer**	Michael Schnabel
			Typographer	Annika Goepfrich
			Client	Mattel Hot Wheels

Recreation & Leisure

Agency	Bates Pangulf, Dubai
Creative Directors	Prasanna Hegde
	Richard Nugent
Copywriter	Prasanna Hegde
Art Directors	Richard Nugent
	Rajaram Ojha
Client	Al Ain Desert Wildlife Park

Agency	Young & Rubicam, Prague
Creative Director	Daniel Ruzicka
Copywriter	Don
Art Director	Don
Photographer	Jaime Mandelbaum
Client	Museum of Communism

Agency	Cheil Communications, Schwalbach im Taunus
Creative Director	Patrick Thiede
Copywriter	Berend Enslin-Lohmann
Art Director	Jennifer Graf
Photographer	Tim Thiel
Client	Bad Soden Riding School

Industrial & Agricultural Products

Agency	The Jupiter Drawing Room, Cape Town
Executive CD	Graham Warsop
Creative Director	Tom Cullinan
Copywriter	Peter-John Eales
Art Directors	Julie Thorogood
	Justin Joshua
Production	Velocity Films, Cape Town
Director	Keith Rose
Producers	Karen Kloppers
	Hazel Neuhaus
Client	Sasol, "Questions"

A marionette explores an imaginary museum. "It's not answers that change the world, but questions," says the narrator, as we follow the puppet on her tour. "What if that crazy guy never said, 'But can't we do better than a horse and cart?' Or if no-one ever asked, 'Why can't we harness energy?'" What if Shakespeare, Socrates and Darwin had not been curious? "Einstein said that we were only ever one step away from the next big question. So let's start with a little one: what if?" Energy and chemical firm Sasol is reaching new frontiers.

Advanced Industrial Freezer Systems **HEINEN** FREEZING Hf

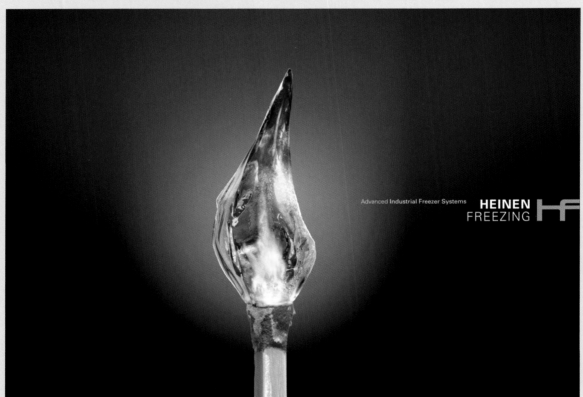

Advanced Industrial Freezer Systems **HEINEN** FREEZING Hf

 Industrial & Agricultural Products 257

Agency	Wächter & Wächter, Bremen
Creative Director	Andreas Rüthemann
Copywriter	Jan Portius
Final Art	Litho Niemann + Steggemann
Client	Heinen Freezing Systems

Great wash!
Water purification systems by
SIEMENS

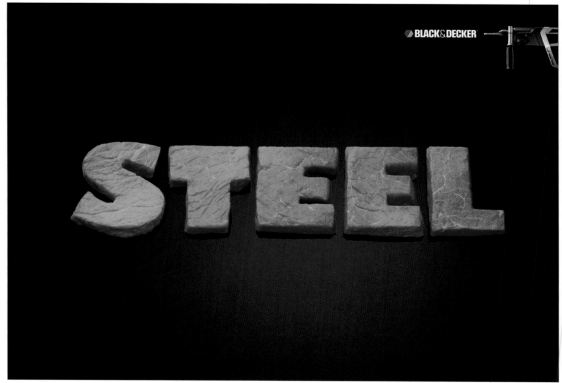

258 **Industrial & Agricultural Products**

Agency	Publicis EAD, Sofia	**Agency**	Serviceplan, Munich & Hamburg
Client	Siemens	**Executive CD**	Matthias Harbeck
	Water Purifying Systems	**Copywriter**	Oliver Palmer
		Art Directors	Frank Weitzenbauer
			Therese Stuessel
		Photographer	Jan Steinhilber
		Client	Black & Decker Hammerdrill

Agency	Publicis, Helsinki	Agency	D'Adda, Lorenzini, Vigorelli, BBDO, Milan
Creative Director	Anthony Wolch		
Copywriter	Tomi Winberg	Creative Director	Gianpietro Vigorelli
Art Director	Sami Anttila	Copywriter	Alessandro Fruscella
Photographer	Thomas Herbrich	Art Director	Letizia Ziaco
Client	SRV Construction	Client	Cattlemaster 4

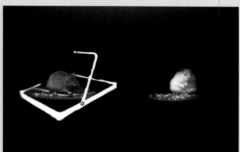

Professional Equipment & Services

Agency	JWT Russia, Moscow
Creative Director	Ivan Chimburov
Copywriter	Ivan Chimburov
Art Director	Ilya Bakerkin
Production	Park Production
	Trehmer Studio,
	Moscow
Director	Dmitry Venikov
Producers	Alex Farber
	Maria Yakushina
DOP	Michail Gershfeld
Client	Salvador-D,
	"Mice vs Hamsters"

"This is a mouse," says the narrator, as a spotlight falls on the small creature. "And this is a hamster," he adds, as a very similar creature is illuminated. "But while mice are hunted and killed, hamsters are loved and cared about." Lines draw on the screen depict a trap over the mouse – but a cosy cage over the hamster. "You know why? Because hamsters have better PR." The spot is for the Salvador-D public relations agency, naturally.

We're looking for engineers who like to solve difficult problems. Call us on this number now:

$x = 24$, $y = 30$

Phone $= 044.(y^2 - x).(y^2 - 10^2) \times 10.$

Professional Equipment & Services **261**

Agency	Ruf Lanz Werbeagentur, Zurich
Creative Directors	Markus Ruf
	Danielle Lanz
Copywriter	Thomas Schoeb
Art Director	Marcel Schlaefle
Client	McKinsey & Company

262　**Professional Equipment & Services**

Agency	Scholz & Friends, Berlin
Creative Directors	Matthias Spaetgens
	Oliver Handlos
Copywriter	Daniel Boedeker
Art Director	David Fischer
Production	Entspanntfilm, Berlin
Producers	Nic Niemann
	Anke Landmark
Client	Jobsintown.de,
	"Screensaver"

A bright light circulates on the screen, reminiscent of a fairly primitive screen saver. Suddenly there is a clattering noise. A light comes on and we see a bare room in what looks like a warehouse. A young man curses and extricates himself from the metal shelving unit he's just bumped into. Resigned, he picks up a fishing rod with a torch tied to the end of it. He begins waving it around. When he switches off the light, the "screen saver" is back in action. Life's too short for the wrong job. Find a new one on the Jobsintown website.

Agency	Scholz & Friends, Berlin
Creative Directors	Matthias Spaetgens
	Oliver Handlos
Copywriters	Daniel Boedeker
	Axel Tischer
Art Directors	David Fischer
	Tabea Rauscher
Photographer	Hans Starck
Graphic Design	Ferdinand Ulrich
	Julia Hauch
Client	Jobsintown.de

You don't have to eat British food
to learn proper English

CAMBRIDGE CENTAR
NOW IN BANJA LUKA

Agency	TBWA\Vienna
Creative Directors	Bernhard Grafl
	Gerda Reichl-Schebesta
Copywriter	Tanja Trombitas
Art Director	Maik Wollrab
Photographer	Robert Staudinger
Illustrator	Peter Jani
Client	CPT Couvert

Agency	New Moment New Ideas
	Company Y&R, Belgrade
Creative Directors	Dragan Sakan
	Svetlana Copic
Copywriter	Svetlana Copic
Art Director	Ivana Veljkovic
Client	Cambridge Center

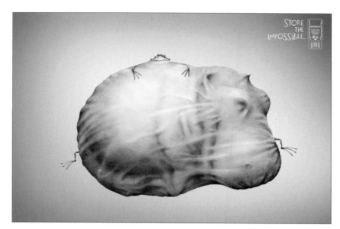

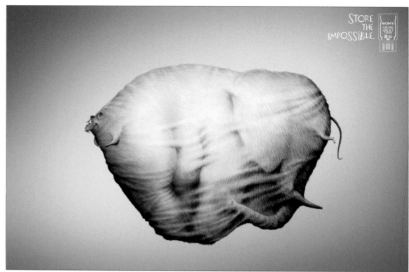

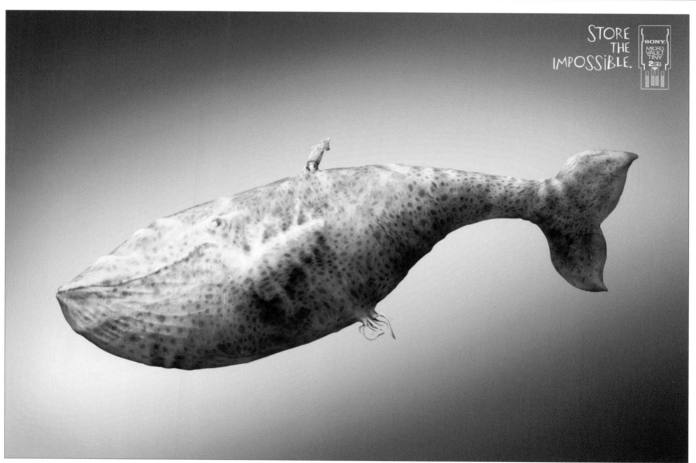

Professional Equipment & Services

Agency	Fortune Promoseven, Dubai
Creative Director	Marc Lineveldt
Copywriters	Ali Ali
	George Azmy
Art Directors	Ali Ali
	George Azmy
Photographer	Furia
Client	Sony Microvault 2GB

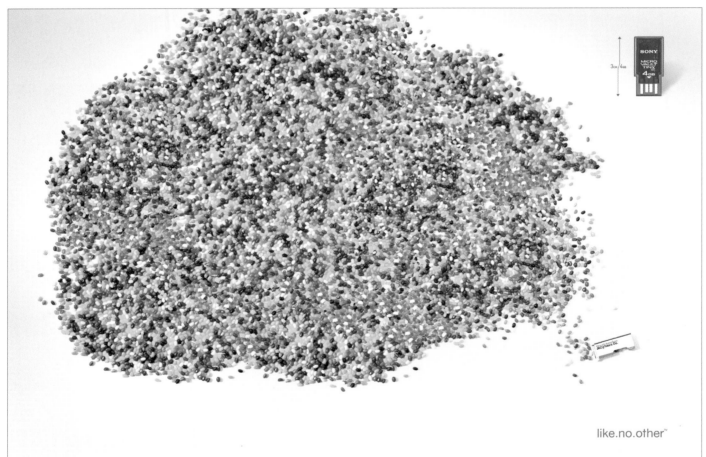

Agency	Fortune Promoseven, Dubai
Creative Director	Marc Lineveldt
Copywriter	Vincent Fichard
Art Director	Matthew Jones
Photographer	Adam Browninghill
Client	Sony Microvault 4GB

We let Josephine
write this ad instead
of Steve.

Should the fee be
20% lower then?

Women generally have 20% lower salary than men.
How come? Have an opinion at manpower.se

Manpower

Professional Equipment & Services

Agency	Grey Stockholm	**Agency**	Publicis, Helsinki
Copywriters	Josephine Adner	**Creative Director**	Anthony Wolch
	Steve Söderlund	**Copywriter**	Tomi Winberg
Art Director	Lars Hörnström	**Art Director**	Sami Anttila
Client	Manpower	**Photographer**	Koen Demuynck
		Client	Tieturi Business Courses

The fastest way from Beijing **DHL** EXPRESS

Just look at what a campaign on Radio Contact can do. **CONTACT** feel good

Agency	Ogilvy, Amsterdam
Creative Director	Carl Le Blond
Copywriter	Edsard Schutte
Art Director	Jan-Willem Smits
Photographer	Arno Bosma
Client	DHL

Agency	Leo Burnett, Brussels
Creative Directors	Jean-Paul Lefebvre
	Michel De Lauw
Copywriter	Jean-Paul Lefebvre
Art Director	Arnold Hovart
Graphic Design	Benoît Germeau
Client	Radio Contact

Professional Equipment & Services

Agency	Kolle Rebbe Werbeagentur, Hamburg
Creative Directors	Ulrich Zuenkeler Ingo Müller
Copywriters	Thomas Rendel Sascha Petersen
Art Director	Benjamin Allwardt
Client	Inlingua

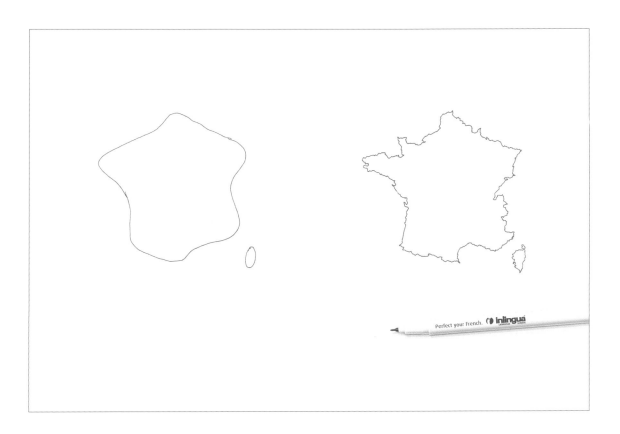

Agency	Kolle Rebbe Werbeagentur, Hamburg	Agency	DDB Germany, Düsseldorf
Creative Directors	Ulrich Zuenkeler	Chief Creative Officer	Amir Kassaei
	Stefan Wübbe	Executive CD	Eric Schoeffler
	Rolf Leger	Creative Directors	Heiko Freyland
Copywriter	Florian Ludwig		Alexander Reiss
Art Director	Florian Schmucker	Copywriter	Shahir Sirry
Client	Inlingua	Illustrator	Maren Esdar
		Client	Berlitz

HERE YOU ARE. Another day at the office. Time to go home. Remember how proud you were when you landed that great job at that famous agency. And now? Well, your work's o.k., your colleagues are pretty nice and the office parties get pleasantly out of hands at times. Of course you're keeping your eyes open (for job opportunities and to see if that tram is coming already). You're still very ambitious. You want something else. You're looking for new energy, in yourself and in an agency. That's great, especially if you're an Account Manager with FMCG-experience, a strategist or a DTP-artist. Because that's what we're looking for. So get your Blackberry or iPhone and mail us at werken@eurorscg.nl to make an appointment. Don't wait any longer! You might miss the tram.

Professional Equipment & Services

Agency	Euro RSCG, Amsterdam	This one-off recruitment ad was posted in a tram shelter used by the employees of four large Amsterdam agencies for their daily commutes.
Creative Directors	Laurens Boschman	
	Joost van Praag Sigaar	
Copywriter	Joost van Praag Sigaar	
Art Director	Laurens Boschman	
Client	Euro RSCG	

Agency	TBWA\PHS, Helsinki
Copywriters	Eka Ruola
	Erkko Mannila
Art Director	Minna Lavola
Photographer	Jere Hietala
Illustrator	Olli Repo
Typographer	Margit Mardisalu
Client	CFP & Shots,
	Young Director Award

Professional Equipment & Services **271**

Agency	Abbott Mead Vickers BBDO, London	Agency	Fortune Promoseven, Dubai
Creative Director	Paul Brazier	Creative Directors	Marc Lineveldt
Copywriter	Diane Leaver		Ali Ali
Art Director	Simon Rice	Copywriters	Ali Ali
Client	Royal Mail		Marc Lineveldt
		Art Director	Ali Ali
		Photographer	Jaime Mandelbaum
		Client	Fortune Promoseven

272 **Professional Equipment & Services**

Agency	MSTF Partners, Lisbon
Creative Directors	Susana Sequeira
	Lourenço Thomaz
Copywriter	Susna Sequeira
Art Director	Lourenço Thomaz
Client	Corbis

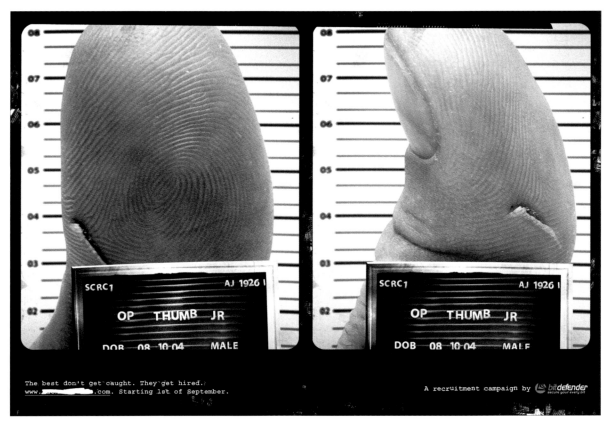

The best don't get caught. They get hired.
www._____.com. Starting 1st of September.

A recruitment campaign by bitdefender

Professional Equipment & Services 273

Agency   Publicis Romania,
               Bucharest
Creative Director Razvan Capanescu
Copywriter   Cezar Panait
Art Director   Dragos Ometita
Client   Bitdefender

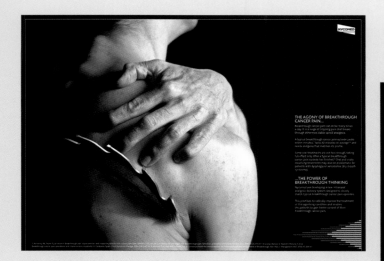

THE AGONY OF BREAKTHROUGH CANCER PAIN...

Breakthrough cancer pain can strike many times a day. It is a surge of crippling pain that breaks through otherwise stable opioid analgesia.

A typical breakthrough cancer pain episode peaks within minutes,[1] lasts 30 minutes on average[2,3] and needs analgesia that matches its profile.

Some oral treatments are not fast enough, taking full effect only after a typical breakthrough cancer pain episode has finished.[4] Oral and orally dissolving treatments may also be problematic for patients with dysphagia or xerostomia (dry mouth syndrome).

...THE POWER OF BREAKTHROUGH THINKING

Nycomed are developing a new intranasal analgesic delivery system designed to closely match typical breakthrough cancer pain episodes.

This promises to radically improve the treatment of this agonising condition and enables the patients to gain better control of their breakthrough cancer pain.

1. Portenoy RK, Payne D, Jacobsen P. Breakthrough pain: characteristics and impact in patients with cancer pain. Pain. 1999;81(1-2):129-34. 2. Portenoy RK and Hagen NA. Breakthrough pain: definition, prevalence and characteristics. Pain. 1990;41(3):273-81. 3. Gomez-Batiste X, Madrid F, Moreno F, et al. Breakthrough cancer pain: prevalence and characteristics in patients in Catalonia, Spain. J Pain Symptom Manage. 2002;24(1):45-52. 4. Bennett D, Burton AW, Fishman S et al. Consensus Panel Recommendations for the Assessment and Management of Breakthrough Pain. Part 2: Management. P&T 2005;30:354-61.

274   Prescription Products

Agency	Sentrix Global Health Communication, Milan
Creative Directors	Clayton Love
	Silvana Vescovi
Copywriter	Clayton Love
Art Directors	Silvana Vescovi
	Marco Adelfio
	Nathalie Garcia
Client	Nycomed

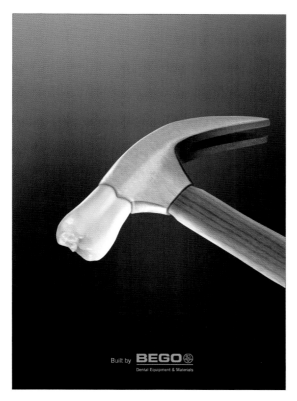

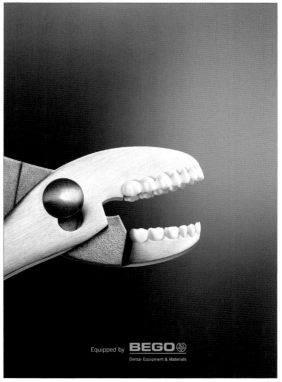

Built by **BEGO** 🔾
Dental Equipment & Materials

Equipped by **BEGO** 🔾
Dental Equipment & Materials

TAKING PPIs OR ANTACIDS WITH CERTAIN PIs COULD CAUSE A SERIOUS CUT IN POWER

TELZIR®
fosamprenavir calcium
700 mg TABLETS

POTENCY YOU CAN RELY ON IN HIV

Agency	Wächter & Wächter, Bremen		**Agency**	Junction 11, London
Creative Director	Andreas Rüthemann		**Creative Directors**	Richard Rayment
Copywriters	Christine Elfers			John Timney
	Jan Portius		**Copywriter**	Richard Rayment
Client	Bego		**Art Director**	John Timney
	Dental Equipment & Materials		**Client**	Telzir

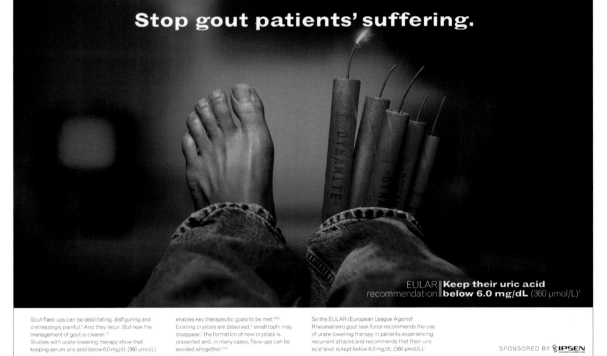

Agency	Publicis, Amsterdam	Agencies	Junction 11, London
Creative Directors	Marcel Hartog		GSW Worldwide, Columbus
	Jeroen van Zwam	Creative Directors	Randall Montgomery
Copywriter	Arnout Robbe		Dave Bowers
Art Director	Fred Rosenkamp		John Timney
Photographer	Dennis Beerling		Richard Rayment
Client	Publicis Healthcare	Copywriters	Richard Rayment
			Randall Montgomery
		Art Directors	John Timney
			Andy Spitzer
			Dennis Leahy
		Photographer	Dennis Manarchy
		Client	Ipsen

Agency	Paling Walters, London
Creative Director	Adrian Parr
Copywriter	Carmel Thompson
Art Director	Adrian Parr
Photographer	Andy Mac
Client	Xenical

Agency	Jung von Matt, Hamburg	The two-dimensional Ikea catalogue was transformed into a three-dimensional in-stallation by creating a real-life replica of the living room depicted on its cover. The "cover" stage set went on a tour of German shopping malls, where visitors could have their picture taken on the set. A few days later, participants in the photo shoot could go to Ikea and pick up a catalogue featuring themselves as the cover models!
Creative Directors	Arno Lindemann	
	Bernhard Lukas	
	Tom Hauser	
	Soeren Porst	
Copywriters	Caroline Ellert	
	Tom Hauser	
Art Director	Joanna Swistowski	
Graphic Design	Julia Stoffer	
	Julia Jakobi	
	Matthias Grundner	
Client	Ikea	

Agency	Ogilvy, Frankfurt
Creative Directors	Simon Oppmann
	Peter Roemmelt
Copywriter	Peter Roemmelt
Art Director	Simon Oppmann
Client	German Foundation
	for Monument
	Protection

Germany's historical monuments must be saved from disrepair. The German Foundation for Monument Protection urgently needs donations. So it put to work those who were most likely to suffer from underfunding: sculptures from historic buildings. Replica sculptures were placed in subway stations and pedestrian underpasses, "begging" for help. The German Foundation for Monument Protection registered a 40% increase in donations.

Agency	Goss, Gothenburg
Copywriters	Elisabeth Berlander
	Micke Schultz
	Ulrika Good
Art Directors	Gunnar Skarland
	Mattias Frendberg
	Mimmi Andersson
	Jan Eneroth
	Albin Larsson
Client	Gothenburg
	Homeless Aid

To draw attention to the homeless in Gothenburg at Christmas time, letters addressed to "Lasse Persson, a doorway/tunnel/stairwell, Hisingen" were sent out. The name of the supposed "sender" was written on the back. The Swedish post office couldn't find Lasse because he had no home, so the mail went back to the "sender" with a post office stamp saying "Not known at this address". Of course, the "sender" was the intended recipient all along. A Christmas card and donation form inside the envelope explained everything.

Agency	OgilvyOne Worldwide, Frankfurt
Creative Director	Michael Koch
Copywriter	Markus Toepper
Art Director	Thomas Knopf
Client	Evangelical Church

Five thousand families belonging to Frankfurt's Protestant community have children under the age of 12 who have not been baptised. The church wanted to get young and adult family members alike to think about baptism in a way that made them curious. The church sent out a letter made from special paper. As soon as the paper was submerged in water, the message appeared. The act of baptism and the "change" caused by water thus become tangible for parents and children alike.

Agency	BBDO Düsseldorf
Creative Directors	Toygar Bazarkaya
	Sebastian Hardieck
	Ton Hollander
	Ralf Zilligen
Copywriter	Elias Kouloures
Art Director	Vera Schuchardt
Client	Smart

These "smart glasses" gave recipients an idea of how it felt to drive the new Smart Fortwo, without having to go all the way to a dealer. Enjoy the perfect test drive in your own living room!

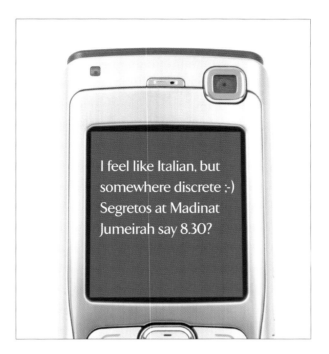

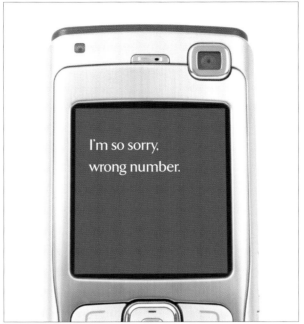

Agency	Face To Face, Dubai	Segreto ("secret") is a discrete Italian restaurant. Recipients received what appeared to be a text sent by an individual requesting they meet "somewhere discrete tonight at 8.30". The author of the text suggested a specific restaurant "Segretos, the Italian at the Madinat Jumeirah". A second text was sent 10 minutes later apologizing for sending the text to a wrong number. A high proportion of recipients replied. Some even called the number, where a recording explained that this message was in fact part of a marketing campaign for the restaurant.	
Creative Directors	Ralph Roden Mike Sands		
Copywriter	Ralph Roden		
Art Director	Mike Sands		
Client	Segreto Italian Restaurant		

Agency	JWT, Dubai	These "Guard Dog Sounds" CDs were sent to high net worth individuals to encourage them to take out home insurance. The CDs featured the barks of various ferocious dogs; Rottweilers, Pit-Bulls, Great Danes etc. An audio message on the CD made its purpose clear; if you don't have your home insured, play this to keep burglars away.	
Creative Directors	Chafic Haddad Rani El Khatib		
Copywriter	Ranadip De		
Art Director	Firas Medrows		
Client	AIG Home Insurance		

Agency	TBWA\Germany, Berlin	Everybody hates chain mails. They are time-consuming and fill your inbox with junk. In the context of its brand campaign "In an Absolut World" – which depicts a world as perfect as its vodka – Absolut wanted to humorously comment on this problem. The mail reads: "If you forward this message to 10 of your friends great misfortune will overtake you. If you delete it immediately you will gain love, money and infinite wisdom."
Creative Directors	Stefan Schmidt Dirk Henkelmann Philip Borchardt	
Copywriters	Frederick Kober Djamila Rabenstein	
Art Directors	Djamila Rabenstein Frederick Kober	
Graphic Design	Erik Scholz	
Client	Absolut Vodka	

Agency	JWT, Dubai	Women who experience domestic abuse in the UAE are hesitant to speak out. City of Hope is the only organisation of its kind in Dubai that cares for them. It wanted the agency to tackle this issue in a sensitive yet effective manner and encourage women to speak up. The agency distributed a different kind of beauty kit to women shopping in malls. It offered make-up solutions "if hit with a remote control", "dragged across a room" or "smacked in the eye".
Creative Director	Chafic Haddad	
Copywriters	DV Hari Krishna Doug Mackay Rami Abu Ghazeleh	
Art Directors	Kedar Damle Arnoldfelix Fabella Tarek Samaan	
Client	City of Hope Women's Shelter	

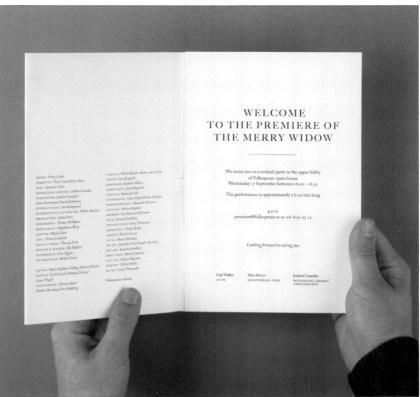

Agency	Lowe Brindfors, Stockholm
Creative Director	Håkan Engler
Copywriter	Martin Ericson
Art Directors	Kalle dos Santos
	Petter Lublin
Client	Folkoperan

To promote a new version of "The Merry Widow" to opinion leaders and potential sponsors, the Folkoperan embarked on a major campaign. The operetta is about Hanna, who becomes a rich (and merry) widow when her elderly husband dies. In print ads, her feelings were symbolised by the image of a wreath with the text "At last!". The invitation to the premiere was in the form of an invitation to a funeral. When the card was opened, the recipient was treated to the tune of "Celebration" by Kool and the Gang.

Agency	DraftFCB Kobza, Vienna
Creative Directors	Patrik Partl
	Andreas Gesierich
Copywriters	Patrik Partl
	Florian Schwab
Art Directors	Andreas Gesierich
	Daniel Senitschnig
Client	Dr. Alfred Kriesler
	Divorce Lawyer

This divorce lawyer caused havoc by slipping pictures of pretty half-naked women into envelopes of family snaps that had been returned by the developing studio. On the back of the picture, a note bearing the lawyer's logo reassured: "This picture was attached by us. Should you ever receive a similar one, contact..." followed by the lawyer's address and phone number.

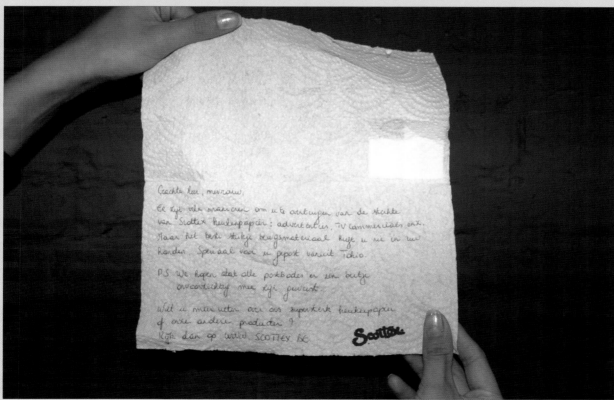

Business to Business Direct

Agency	Duval Guillaume, Antwerp	To demonstrate the strength of Scottex kitchen towels to its target market of
Creative Directors	Geoffrey Hantson Dirk Domen	Belgian restaurateurs, the agency sent out a mailing made of the product itself. Some of
Copywriters	Carsten Van Berkel Stefan Leendertse	the Scottex envelopes travelled thousands of miles to reach their recipients: as far away
Art Directors	Stefan Leendertse Carsten Van Berkel	as New York, Tokyo or Ushuaia, the world's most southern city. And 98% arrived at their
Client	Scottex	destinations in a perfect state.

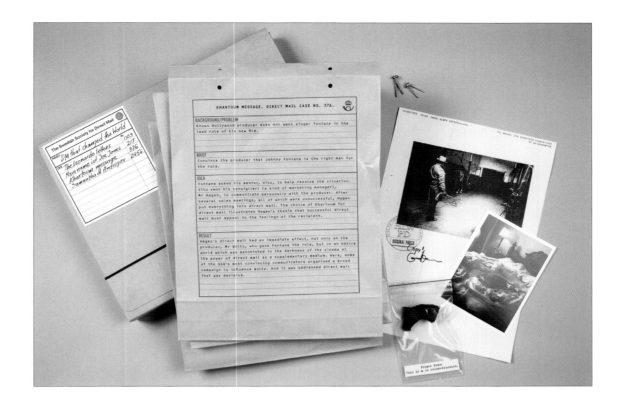

Agency	Åkestam Holst, Stockholm	
Copywriter	Mark Ardelius	
Art Director	Andreas Ullenius	
Project Leader	Peter Bergendahl	
Production	Katarina Johansson	
Graphic Design	Torbjörn Krantz	
Client	Posten	

Posten, the Swedish Post Office, wanted to get marketing directors in Sweden to consider direct marketing. To make the point it searched for examples of direct communication that changed history. It treated the examples as if they had been collected and archived for hundreds of years. It also created "The Swedish Society for Direct Mail" as a source of DM know-how, led by three executives. This unit sent targets "original" files from its archive, together with a letter inviting the receiver to book a meeting by phone.

Agency	ANR BBDO Sweden, Gothenburg & Stockholm
Creative Director	Håkan Larsson
Copywriter	Håkan Larsson
Art Directors	Rosita Johnson
	Jonas Sjövall
Client	Västra Vetinary Clinic

To mark its launch, Västra Veterinary Clinic managed to capture the individual scent of each of its five vets in aerosol cans. Since the centre specialises in dogs, they thought it might be a good way of putting the olfactory sensitive animals at ease, even before they visited the new practice for the first time. The aerosol cans – which were decorated with pictures of the vets – were then sent out to 100 kennels with a note explaining the areas each vet specialised in. As a result referrals to the new service were 450% more than anticipated.

wonderbra

Walker Werbeagentur
Pius Walker
Blaufahnenstrasse 14
8001 Zurich
Switzerland

International pitch of 22 May 2008

Dear Mr Walker,

It is with regret that we have to inform you that you have won the pitch for the
WONDERBRA budget. This applies not only to the national but also to the international
launch campaign in 34 countries.

We also wish to inform you that we will be entrusting you with all international
below-the-line measures in addition to the international image campaign.

We hope that you appreciate our position.

Best regards,

Harris S. Thornton
CMO & Member of the Board

A lack of staff can spoil even
the best news. You'll find
reinforcements quickly on
www.freelancerportal.ch

FREELANCER
PORTAL.CH

Wonderbra. Hanesbrand Inc., 4505 Metropolitan East blvd., Montreal / Quebec. Canada

Krieg, Schlupp, Bürge /
Springer & Jacoby Werbeagentur AG
Daniel Krieg, Uwe Schlupp
Seestrasse 367
CH-8038 Zurich

In the matter of: Our competition

Dear Mr Krieg,
Dear Mr Schlupp,

We regret to inform you that you have won the competition for the "Diesel Jeans"
budget for 43 national markets around the world.

Nonetheless, we would like to wish you all the best for the future and thank you
for your efforts.

Best regards,

Franco Ballotta
Director of International Brand Management

A lack of staff can spoil even
the best news. You'll find
reinforcements quickly on
www.freelancerportal.ch

FREELANCER
PORTAL.CH

Diesel S.p.A.
Via dell'Industria, 7 | 36060 Molvena (VI) | Italy | Phone +39.0424.457766 | Fax +39.0424.458866

---

286   **Business to Business Direct**

Agency	DDB Amsterdam	
Creative Directors	Sanne Braam	
	Sikko Gerkema	
Copywriter	Ruben Sonneveld	
Art Directors	Robert van der Lans	
	Niels de Wit	
Client	Swift Mega Couriers	

Swift sent its own personnel manager a registered envelope using competing courier companies (TNT, UPS, DHL). In this way, the competing couriers took the envelope right to the personnel manager's desk. He then immediately offered the couriers a job by taking an application form out of the same just-delivered envelope. The courier had unwittingly just delivered his own job application form.

Agency	Ruf Lanz
	Werbeagentur,
	Zurich
Creative Directors	Markus Ruf
	Danielle Lanz
Copywriter	Thomas Schoeb
Art Director	Grit Wolany
Client	Freelancerportal.ch

Freelancerportal.ch is a site where freelancers in the Swiss advertising industry can offer their services to agencies in the event of staff shortages. Personal letters from some of the world's most attractive clients were sent to the CEOs of top Swiss agencies. The letters announced that the agencies had won huge, dream budgets – but in a strangely regretful tone. The reason was provided by an attached message: "A lack of staff can spoil even the best news. You'll find reinforcements quickly on freelancerportal.ch."

Hi, this is Andreas Ullenius.
I want to be your friend.

I have visited 215 cities in
33 different countries, but my
travel-IQ is below average.

Nemo saltat sobrius, nisi forte insanit.

Hi, this is Calle Lewenhaupt.
I want to be your friend.

My social status is Groupie
and I'm throwing a sheep at you.

Hi, this is Göran Åkestam.
I want to be your friend.
I've tagged myself in 6
pictures. If I were a
stripper my name would
be "Big Bad Baldwin".

Hi, this is Jesper Holst.
I've added you as a friend.
My two nicknames are
"Das grose Lederwurst" and
"Papa Peach".
Check out my private holiday pictures!

Agency	Åkestam Holst, Stockholm	The Swedish Post Office wanted to communicate the power of direct mail to its target group in the Swedish ad industry, while at the same time inviting them to their yearly DM award ceremony. As Facebook had become trendy, it was the perfect vehicle. "Friend" requests of the type familiar to Facebook users were sent as physical mail-outs. This clearly showed that direct mail was more personal than the web.
Copywriter	Monica Born	
Art Directors	Andreas Ullenius Jesper Holst	
Producer	Marie Höglin	
Graphic Design	Torbjörn Krantz	
Client	Posten	

Agencies	Amp Communications, London	The Telegraph has more upmarket readers with high disposable income than any other paper in the UK. And as they are less likely to be affected by the credit crunch, there's no better place for businesses to advertise. The agency targeted media planners with creative that literally stood out, in the form of dolls representing its customers. As media planners effectively "buy" audiences, they appreciated the irony of seeing consumers as commodity goods.
	Adam & Eve, London	
Creative Directors	Simon Haslehurst	
	Ben Priest	
Copywriter	Kristian Wheater	
Art Director	Simon Haslehurst	
Client	The Daily Telegraph	

Agency	BBDO Düsseldorf	To recruit literature graduates as junior copywriters BBDO created the "world's first napkin book" that students could pick up in their campus cafeterias. The napkin book celebrated love of the written word and explained how one can make copywriting their chosen profession.
Creative Directors	Toygar Bazarkaya	
	Sebastian Hardieck	
	Ralf Zilligen	
Copywriters	Helmut Bienfuss	
	Douglas Tracy	
	Yvette Bradley	
Art Directors	Lidia Pranjic	
	Caroline Kunsemueller	
Photographer	Jost Hiller	
Illustrator	Lidia Pranjic	
Client	BBDO	

SUDDENLY, THERE'S MORE ROOM ON THE ROAD.

WITH THE COMPACT NEW FIAT FIORINO THERE'S EASIER PARKING, BETTER ACCESS AND MORE MANOEUVRABILITY.

THE BEST GET WHERE OTHERS CAN'T.

Working in town might offer you big business opportunities, but it can also put you in a tight spot. Narrow streets, small spaces and tricky corners are all problems you face daily. But with the arrival of the new Fiorino everything just became a lot easier – not to mention wider, bigger and faster.

Being only 3.86m long and 1.7m wide, there aren't many places the Fiorino can't get to. (And with a turning circle of 9.95m, it can also back out again.) But just because the Fiorino is compact on the outside doesn't mean it's small inside. With a roof height of 1.72m and up to 2.8m³ of load space it makes light work of even the bulkiest objects.

Loading and unloading should prove no trouble too, thanks to the wide opening rear doors and optional sliding side access panels. A loading floor height of just 53cm and regular shape also helps.

But while getting things in and out of the Fiorino won't be a problem for you, undesirables don't have it so easy. Thatcham, the leading independent research centre for vehicle security, has awarded the Fiorino four stars for break-in resistance and five stars from being stolen altogether.

And they are not the only ones to be impressed with the Fiorino. Van Fleet World has just announced it 'Best New Van' in their 2008 honours.

SCARED, MISTER LAUPERT?

Just wait for the SHOCKING SHORTS AWARD.

You're invited. Please confirm on www.shockingshorts.de/VIP

Agency	Leo Burnett, London
Executive CD	Jon Burley
Creative Director	Garry Munns
Copywriter	Paul Faulds
Art Directors	Chris Rambridge
	Martin Lawson
Producer	Jo Alexander
Client	Fiat Fiorino

Fiat Professional launched the new compact Fiorino van in May 2008. The task was to inform businesses of its compact size, create standout against competitors and to generate sales. Creative was developed using the proposition "roads feel wider". The piece emulated an official letter advising of road widening in the area of the recipient's business.

Agency	Jung von Matt, Berlin
Creative Directors	Mathias Stiller
	Wolfgang Schneider
	Florian Kitzing
	Michael Haeussler
	Lennart Witting
Copywriter	David Missing
Art Director	Viktor Wahl
Producer	Nadja Catana
Client	13th Street

Every year, the TV station 13th Street presents the Shocking Shorts Awards: the short film festival for mystery and horror. In order to attract talented young directors, 21 very personal invitations were sent out. Each of the invitees received an unmarked letter in their mailbox. The only content a DVD labelled: "Play me". On the DVD, the recipients saw their own homes, filmed secretly, for minutes. In some cases they even saw themselves, walking past the window, coming home or going out. The clip ended with a personal invitation to attend the awards.

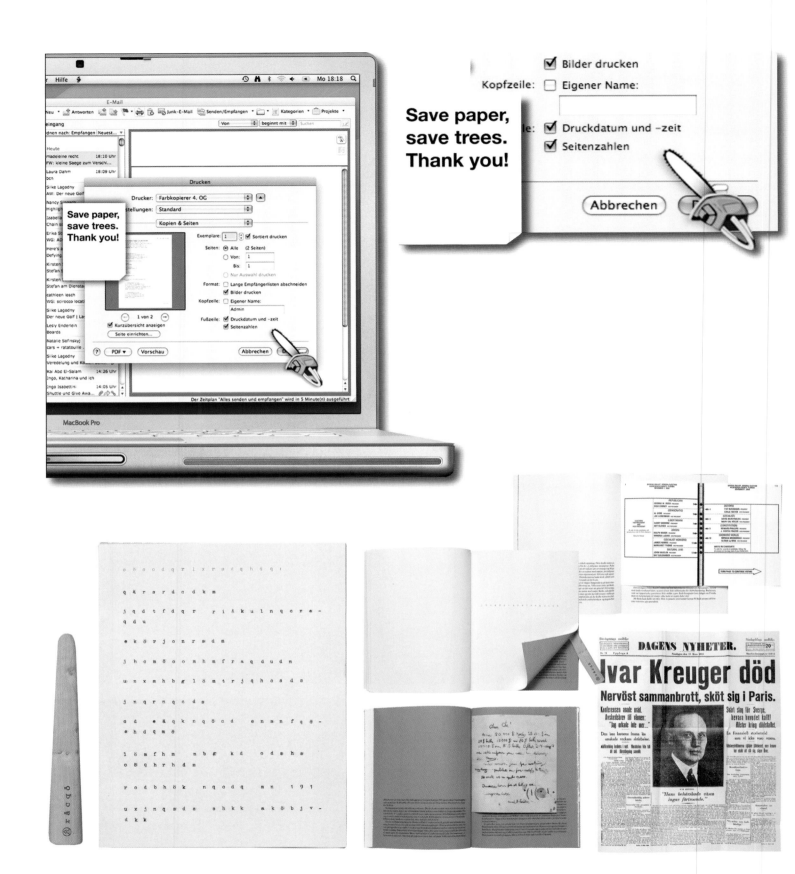

Agency	DDB Germany, Berlin
Chief Creative Officer	Amir Kassaei
Executive CDs	Bert Peulecke
	Stefan Schulte
Creative Director	Thomas Bober
Copywriters	Axel Tischer
	Nina Faulhaber
Art Directors	Eva Bajer
	Johannes Hicks
	Philip Simon
Graphic Design	Andreas Barhainski
Client	DDB Worldwide

Printing out e-mails is a waste of paper. An application was installed on the agency's computers. It turned the mouse arrow into a buzz saw icon accompanied by the appropriate sound every time the user pressed the print button. At the same time a small description field popped up with the message: "Save paper, save trees. Please do not print out this e-mail." Users who went ahead heard the sound of creaking timber and a falling tree. But when users pressed "cancel" the saw stopped buzzing and birds began to sing.

Agency	Garbergs Reklambyrå, Stockholm
Copywriter	Rebecka Osvald
Art Director	Karin Ahlgren
Graphic Design	Beatrice Stanzska
Client	Södra Cell Paper Pulp

Paper pulp producer Södra's long-term marketing strategy has been to develop products that reflect the power of paper. Here it reproduced ten of the world's most mysterious documents and bound them in a mysterious book - everything from lost photographs to the Lindbergh kidnapping letter. So the book itself would be a paper mystery it was sent anonymously, encrypted and with uncut pages. The accompanying paperknife with the Södra logo provided a solution to the code.

Dear Mr. De Meuter,
if you need extreme precision,
just give us a call.

Kind regards,
the Komatsu team.

KOMATSU®
+32 (0)2 255 25 28

Agency	AdmCom, Bologna
Creative Director	Maurizio Cinti
Copywriters	Massimiliano Pancaldi
	Silva Fedrigo
Art Director	Manuel Dall'Olio
Illustrator	Manuel Dall'Olio
Client	AdmCom

The "Year of Creativity Box" was a self-promotional tool created by the agency to encourage people to reinvent themselves every day. It contained 366 illustrated business cards showing 366 imaginative professions, all of them featuring the name of the recipient.

Agency	Duval Guillaume,
	Antwerp
Creative Directors	Geoffrey Hantson
	Dirk Domen
Copywriter	Kristof Snels
Art Director	Sebastien De Valck
Client	Komatsu

To demonstrate the precision of Komatsu's construction machinery a personalised letter was placed in the mailboxes of Belgium's five biggest construction companies. It invited the recipient to watch an on-line movie that showed the actual letter being placed in their – clearly recognisable – mail boxes by a large Komatsu machine and concluding with the message, "If you need extreme precision, just give us a call".

Come on TV and advertise the item you are selling on eBay.

I'm selling this table football that was used in the last World Cup

I'm selling this guitar previously owned by Charlelie Couture (*french rock star*).

Bids start at 1 euro.

I am selling this car. Fancy a ride ?

Let's go, hyper speed !

You are eBay.

292   **Media Innovation (Traditional Media)**

Agency	BETC Euro RSCG, Paris
Creative Director	Stéphane Xiberras
Copywriter	Olivier Apers
Art Director	Hugues Pinguet
Production	Cosa, Paris
Director	Denis Thybaud
Producers	David Green Fabrice Brovelli
Client	eBay

For eBay France's first TV campaign, the agency created a strategy that captured the new brand signature: "You are eBay." Its intent was to put faces to the usually anonymous users of the auction site and to promote its diversity and richness. It held its own ad auction and gave ten real eBay users the opportunity to star in their own TV commercials for the items they wanted to sell on the site. The resulting ads were then broadcast instead of more conventional advertising spots.

Agency	DDB Amsterdam
Creative Director	Martin Cornelissen
Copywriters	Dieuwer Bulthuis
	Maarten van Kempen
Art Directors	Marco Sluijter
	Daniel Ashkol
Photographer	Ernst Yperlaan
Client	Centraal Beheer Insurance

Agency	Leo Burnett,
	Frankfurt
Executive CD	Andreas Pauli
Associate Exec. CD	Kerrin Nausch
Creative Directors	Ulf Henniger von Wallersbrunn
	Andreas Stalder
Copywriter	Andreas Stalder
Art Director	Ulf Henniger von Wallersbrunn
Client	Fiat 500

The goal was to demonstrate that the Fiat 500 isn't an object but a character full of life. Passers-by could text a message to this interactive billboard at the famous Check-Point Charlie in Berlin. Seconds later, their message appeared on the poster. Users of Fiat's website could also send messages and see them appearing "live" via a feed on the site. Instead of John F. Kennedy's famous phrase "Ich bin ein Berliner" (I'm a Berliner), the slogan on the poster said "Ich bin ein Turiner."

Agency	Leo Burnett, Frankfurt	Tide is a detergent that provides long-lasting whiteness. To reinforce the positioning of Tide as a detergent you can trust, clothes were printed on a billboard using a special "self-cleaning" material. While the billboards became more and more blackened with traffic fumes, the printed parts stayed clean and white.
Regional CD	Don Bowen	
Executive CD	Andreas Pauli	
Associate Exec. CD	Kerrin Nausch	
Creative Directors	Andreas Stalder Ulf Henniger von Wallersbrunn	
Copywriter	Volker Mueller	
Art Director	Daniela Ewald	
Photographer	Ramona Heinze	
Client	Tide	

Agency	Leo Burnett, Frankfurt	In order to communicate the whiteness of Tide in a unique way, city light posters were turned into Tide boards. Attached to the boards passers-by found a pen with which they could express themselves on the white surface. By pushing down the bar with the Tide logo, the boards became bright white again.
Executive CD	Andreas Pauli	
Associate Exec. CD	Kerrin Nausch	
Creative Director	Peter Buck	
Copywriter	Collja Lorig	
Art Director	Collja Lorig	
Production	Thorsten Zeh	
Client	Tide	

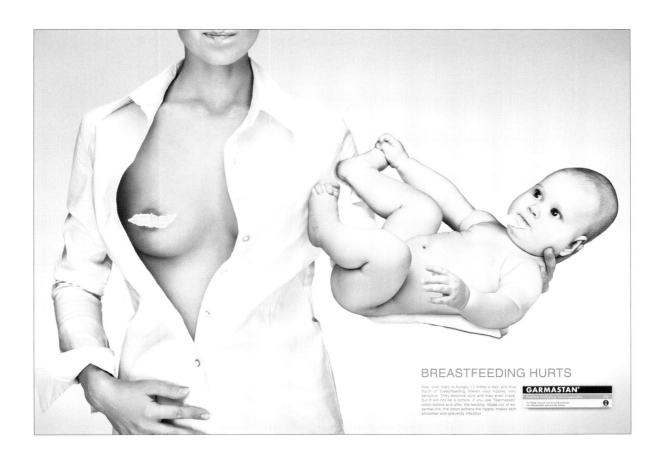

BREASTFEEDING HURTS

See, your baby is hungry 12 times a day, and that much of breastfeeding makes your nipples very sensitive. They become sore and may even crack. But it will not be a torture, if you use "Garmastan" lotion before and after the feeding. Made out of essential oils, the lotion softens the nipple, makes skin smoother and prevents infection.

GARMASTAN®

Agency	Milk Agency, Vilnius
Creative Director	Rimantas Stanevičius
Copywriters	Rimantas Stanevičius
	Rokas Tarabilda
Art Directors	Asta Budukevičiūtė
	Marius Kneipferavičius
Photographer	Tomas Kauneckas
Client	Garmastan

Garmastan is medicinal lotion used to soften nipples, preventing bleeding and infection during breast-feeding. This print campaign ran in maternity magazines. The double-page spread portrays a breast-feeding woman and her baby. The two pages are glued together. Once you tear them apart, the baby's mouth tears from the nipple, thus demonstrating how painful breast-feeding can be – unless you use Garmastan.

Agency	Leo Burnett, Beirut
Creative Directors	Bechara Mouzannar
	Celine Khoury
Art Directors	Areej Mahmoud
	Caroline Farra
	Yasmina Baz
Production	Pikasso
Client	Koleston Naturals

This billboard is positioned on a promenade. It has an unspoiled view of the sea and skyline behind it. Women often go there for their daily jog and stay at the cafés opposite to watch the sunset. The woman's hair is cut out of the billboard to capture the variations of Koleston Naturals colours through the different phases of the day and night.

296 **Media Innovation (Traditional Media)**

Agency	DDB Stockholm	Swedes drink more coffee, per capita, than any other country in the world except Finland. They depend on the drink to stay alert and concentrate on their daily tasks. This poster site was transformed into a giant puzzle that enabled passers-by to 'sort out their heads' and check that their caffeine levels were sufficient for the challenges of the day.
Creative Director	Andreas Dahlqvist	
Copywriter	Martin Lundgren	
Art Directors	Simon Higby	
	Viktor Arve	
	Ted Harry Mellström	
Photographer	Alexander Pihl	
Graphic Design	Daniel Lars Friberg	
Client	McDonald's Coffee	

Agency	DDB Stockholm	Eurosize posters were turned into huge serviette dispenses with giant napkins to promote McDonald's largest hamburger ever, the Big 'n' Juicy.
Creative Director	Andreas Dahlqvist	
Copywriter	Martin Lundgren	
Art Directors	Simon Higby	
	Ted Harry Mellström	
Photographer	Alexander Pihl	
Graphic Design	Patrik Oscarsson	
Production	Lagerholm & Co.	
Client	McDonald's	

SP

Doelstelling: Aandacht genereren voor een menselijke thuiszorg
Media: Televisie en internet.
Opdrachtgever: SP
Bureau: Thonik
Strategie: Thonik en SP
Realisatie: Thonik en Hazazah
Regie: Krijn van Noordwijk
Foto: Krijn van Noordwijk
Verantwoordelijk bij klant: Agnes Kant en Hans van Heijningen
Verhaal: De huidige regering neemt steeds meer maatregelen, waardoor de kwaliteit van de thuiszorg volgens de SP achteruit gaat. In deze nieuwe campagne doet een vrouw van 88 op indringende wijze verhaal van haar situatie en stelt zij een daad door zich voor heel Nederland uit te kleden, als symbool voor de uitgeklede thuiszorg.

DDB

Doelstelling: Maak duidelijk dat DDB op zoek is naar een ervaren media strategy director.
Medium: Tv
Bureau: DDB
Creatie: Niels de Wit, Jakko Achterberg, Niels Westra
RTV: Sophie van Pelt, Nikaj Gouwerok
Design: Daniël Samama
Account: Paul Blok
Verhaal: DDB komt weer met een traditionele tv-commercial omdat ze nog op zoek zijn naar een ervaren media strategy director de zodat onze klanten kan adviseren over wat er allemaal nog meer mogelijk is op mediagebied.

Usual Suspects

Doelstelling: Ontwikkel voor de Usual Suspects een nieuwe huisstijl + communicatiestijl die past bij de nieuwe positionering
Medium: Huisstijl
Opdrachtgever: Usual Suspects
Bureau: The Stone Twins
Fotografie: Krijn van Noordwijk
Verantwoordelijk bij klant: René van Dijk
Verhaal: Het ontwerp roept met een flinke knipoog de sfeer op van de criminele onderwereld. Het logo, waarin de bureaunaam verborgen zit in een serie setters en initialen, maakt toespelingen op vermomming en bedrog. Het typografische patroon dat zo ontstaat, leent zich perfect voor gebruik op zelfklevende tape. Voor de huisstijlelementen en het campagnemateriaal benaderden The Stone Twins fotograaf Krijn van Noordwijk om een serie portretten te maken waarop de medewerkers vastgebonden en gekneveld zijn.

ADFORMATIE 6, 7 FEBRUARI 2008

Sky Radio

Doelstelling: Communiceren dat Sky Radio 101 FM het station is in de Valentijnsperiode
Media: Tv, radio, internet, print, outdoor
Opdrachtgever: Sky Radio 101 FM
Verantwoordelijk bij de klant: Bart van Hal, Dennis Kuyer
Creatie: Yvo van Koppenhagen, Dennis Kuyer
Regie: Yvo van Koppenhagen
Productiemaatschappij: Creamm
Productie: Patrick Bakker, Marianne Dubois, Sandra Smit den Hollander
Muziek: James Blunt (Warner Music)
Verhaal: In het kader van komende Valentijnsdag roept de Britse wereldster James Blunt de kijkers op de luisteren naar Sky Radio 101 FM. De stage in Wolverhampton, voorafgaand aan zijn optreden in de concert, waar hij dat met een overnachting, een diner voor twee en kaarten voor zijn concert in Parijs kan winnen.

Forbo

Doelstelling: Forbo Flooring positioneren als een hoogwaardige werkgever met een inspirerend arbeidsklimaat.
Medium: Print
Opdrachtgever: Forbo Flooring
Bureau: Bridgevest
Strategie: Edzko Smid
Creatie: Gilli Atmodimedjo, Edwin Regterschot, Edzko Smid
Beeldbewerking: Hunk
Account: Edwin Regterschot
Verantwoordelijk bij klant: Lex Vogel

RTL4

Doelstelling: Nieuwe huisstijl RTL4
Medium: Tv
Opdrachtgever: RTL4
Bureau: Afdeling creatie RTL Nederland
Verhaal: RTL4 heeft een komende nieuwe station idents. Na de profilering met de RTL4-gezichten is nu gekozen voor grafische rustmomenten tussen de reclameblokken en programma's waarbij de 4 altijd centraal staat. Binnen de nieuwe huisstijl van de zender kunnen idents gelinkt worden aan programma's (bijvoorbeeld 'Goische Vrouwen', 'TV Makelaar' en 'RTL Nieuws') en thema's (film, wonen, koken of datum- of eventgerelateerde thema's). Het eerste datumgerelateerde thema dat de zender benadrukt is Valentijnsdag op donderdag 14 februari.

Nieuwe campagnes naar susanne@adformatie.nl. Zie www.adformatie.nl.

ADFORMATIE 6, 7 FEBRUARI 2008

Agency	DDB Amsterdam	DDB was looking for a new media strategy director. But instead of disappearing amongst all the other job advertisements in the local advertising trade press, the agency used the press in a totally different way. It developed a simple TV commercial and showed it once on a local station, it then submitted the spot to the new campaigns section of Adformatie where it reached the target audience in a more cost-effective and original way.
Creative Directors	Sanne Braam	
	Sikko Gerkema	
Copywriter	Niels Westra	
Art Directors	Jakko Achterberg	
	Niels de Wit	
Client	DDB Amsterdam	

Agency	Kempertrautmann, Hamburg	Recycling saves the forest.
Creative Directors	Jens Theil	
	Gerrit Zinke	
Copywriter	Michael Götz	
Art Director	Florian Schimmer	
Client	Robin Wood	

Media Innovation (Traditional Media)

Agency	Jung von Matt, Hamburg
Creative Directors	Jan Rexhausen Dörte Spengler-Ahrens
Copywriter	Sergio Penzo
Art Director	Hisham Kharma
Illustrators	Claudia Schildt Fabian Zell
Producer	Philipp Wenhold
Client	Mercedes-Benz G-Class

Agency	Cayenne, Vienna
Creative Director	Felicitas Prokopetz
Art Director	Sandra Lehninger
Client	Catholic Church

The brief was to promote the Catholic Church among a young audience while benefiting from high media attention during the Pope's visit to Austria. The unusual combination of the church and the latest communication tools achieved buzz within the target group. Users simply sent an SMS to the number on the ads and then received the Papal blessing on their cell phones. Additional services, such as "The thoughts of the day" or relevant ringtones (e.g. the famous church bell of the dome of St. Stephan's in Vienna) could also be ordered. The headline says: "This service is a blessing".

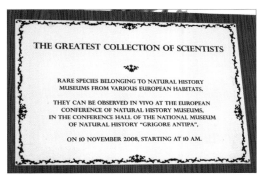

THE GREATEST COLLECTION OF SCIENTISTS

RARE SPECIES BELONGING TO NATURAL HISTORY
MUSEUMS FROM VARIOUS EUROPEAN HABITATS.

THEY CAN BE OBSERVED IN VIVO AT THE EUROPEAN
CONFERENCE OF NATURAL HISTORY MUSEUMS,
IN THE CONFERENCE HALL OF THE NATIONAL MUSEUM
OF NATURAL HISTORY "GRIGORE ANTIPA",

ON 10 NOVEMBER 2008, STARTING AT 10 AM.

Agency	Shalmor Avnon Amichay\	Agency	Leo Burnett & Target,
	Y&R Interactive		Bucharest
	Tel Aviv	Creative Director	Mihai Iliescu
Creative Directors	Gideon Amichay	Copywriter	Stefan Munteanu
	Tzur Golan	Art Director	Liviu Toader
	Yariv Twig	Photographer	Lucian Simion
Copywriters	Eyal Padan	Producer	Catalin Zota
	Geva Kochva	Client	Grigore Antipa,
Art Directors	Shirley Bahar		Romanian Natural
	Eyal Padan		History Museum
Client	Yellow Pages,		
	"Chiropractors"		

Bow ties replace butterflies to announce the "greatest collection of scientist's" that are scheduled to speak at the Natural History Museum's 100th anniversary conference.

Media Innovation (Alternative Media)

Agency	Mortierbrigade, Brussels	Every 15 seconds a child dies due to a lack of drinkable water. The annual charity event Music for Life raises money to help solve this global problem. To promote it, a small boy interrupted Flanders' best-watched TV station "één" several times over three days. Live and in prime time, he dashed onto the set, drank the host's glass of water and ran off. The story took on a life of its own online and in the press. When the agency had the attention of the audience, the campaign was officially unveiled.
Creative Directors	Joost Berends Philippe DeCeuster Jens Mortier	
Copywriters & ADs	Dieter Vanhoof Tim Driesen Joeri Van den Broeck	
Production	Caviar, Brussels	
Producer	Patricia Van de Kerckhove	
Client	Studio Brussel, Music for Life	

Agency	DDB Germany, Berlin	To promote the new Ikea catalogue, the agency used a Vienna railway station. The box-shaped windows of the façade were converted into a giant rack filled with new Ikea products. The installation covered 480 square meters in total.	
Chief Creative Officer	Amir Kassaei		
Executive CDs	Stephen Kimpel		
	Patrick Baschinski		
Creative Directors	Birgit van den Valentyn		
	Tim Stübane		
Copywriter	Anke Röll		
Art Director	Wulf Rechtacek		
Graphic Design	Peter Schönherr		
Client	Ikea		

Agency	Ogilvy, Frankfurt	To promote Ikea storage solutions, the agency decorated balconies on the front of a whole apartment block in one of the busiest streets in Frankfurt with giant-size mock-ups of Ikea drawers and cardboard boxes. This gained maximum attention and linked the products to where they belong: small flats and apartments. The three-dimensional installation had an extreme "stopping power" among passers-by.	
Creative Directors	Lars Huvart		
	Thomas Hofbeck		
Copywriter	Lars Huvart		
Art Director	Kerstin Eberbach		
Graphic Design	Kerstin Eberbach		
Production	Fabian Schrader		
Client	Ikea		

Life's too short
for the wrong job.

jobsintown.de

Media Innovation (Alternative Media)

Agency	Scholz & Friends, Berlin
Creative Directors	Matthias Spaetgens
	Oliver Handlos
Copywriters	Daniel Boedeker
	Axel Tischer
Art Directors	David Fischer
	Tabea Rauscher
Photographer	Hans Starck
Producer	Soeren Gessat
Graphic Design	Ferdinand Ulrich
	Julia Hauch
Client	Jobsintown.de

Agency	Euro RSCG Group Switzerland, Zurich
Executive CD	Frank Bodin
Creative Director	Axel Eckstein
Copywriter	Alexander Fuerer
Art Director	Isabelle Buehler
Client	Riposa Mattresses

This poster responds to the body like a mattress from Riposa. Inspired by a well-known game, it was a life-size construction whose 2000 aluminium rods could transform any body into an instant sculpture. Accompanied by a promotional team, the interactive poster was taken on a tour through Swiss cities. At trade fairs, in shopping centres and in train stations, it always aroused the interest of visitors and the press and served as an ideal icebreaker for sales discussions.

Agency	Serviceplan, Munich & Hamburg
Creative Director	Karsten Gessulat
Copywriter	Susanna Schreibauer
Art Director	Holger Breit
Graphic Design	Julia Bücheler
Client	Catholic Church

By covering this pool with a sheet of Plexiglas, the impression is created that users can walk on water. It's a playful way of promoting the church.

Agency	Leo Burnett, Frankfurt
Executive CD	Andreas Pauli
Associate Exec. CD	Kerrin Nausch
Creative Directors	Ulf Henniger von Wallersbrunn Andreas Stalder
Copywriter	Volker Mueller
Art Director	Daniela Ewald
Photographer	Ramona Heinze
Client	Fiat Ducato

The Fiat Ducato is a lightweight truck with the lowest loading height in its class. To communicate this, the rear of the Ducato appeared as a frame around the entry of a retail trolley shelter. Each time a customer removed or returned a trolley, they experienced easy loading. The USP was written as a headline on the ground. Brochures were offered inside the trolley shelter.

Agency	Leo Burnett, London	To launch an anti drink-driving campaign, a convicted driver was positioned under a giant pint glass, evoking the way he had been 'trapped' by the seemingly innocuous decision to have a pint. When the media showed up he explained how his life had been ruined: he lost his license, his job, his girlfriend, his car and a significant amount of money.
Executive CD	Jon Burley	
Creative Directors	Tony Malcolm	
	Guy Moore	
Copywriters	Bertie Scrase	
	Philip Deacon	
Art Directors	Bertie Scrase	
	Philip Deacon	
Production	Lime	
Producer	James Barnes	
Client	UK Department for Transport - Anti Drink-Drive	

Agency	JWT London	To publicise HSBC as the official banking partner of Wimbledon, this installation focused on the thing that makes the tennis tournament unique: grass. Because grass is light sensitive, by projecting a negative image onto a patch as it grows (in a dark room), it is possible to reproduce photographs. From a distance they look like photos, yet up close they're revealed to be perfectly ordinary grass. The people chosen for the portraits were those who contribute to the tournament on a local level: for instance head grounds man Eddie Seaward takes care of the grass!
Global CD	Axel Chaldecott	
Executive CD	Russell Ramsey	
Copywriters	Laurence Quinn	
	Phillip Meyler	
	Darren Keff	
Art Directors	Mark Norcutt	
	Phillip Meyler	
	Darren Keff	
Producers	Heather Ackroyd	
	Dan Harvey	
Client	HSBC, Wimbledon Sponsorship	

NEVER FEEL A BUMP AGAIN,
WITH VOLVO'S OPTIONAL
ACTIVE FOUR-C SUSPENSION.

Agency	Saatchi & Saatchi, London
Creative Directors	Paul Silburn
	Kate Stanners
Copywriter	Jonathan Benson
Art Director	Stanley Cheung
Production	MPH, London
Directors	Rupert Bryan
	Toby Clifton
Producer	Toby Clifton
Client	Carlsberg Lager

This live event at a soccer match reflects Carlsberg's positioning as "Probably the best lager in the world". As the crowd waits expectantly for the match to kick off there is an announcement over the public address system. At first, the message starts fairly typically. However, as it continues, the announcer goes on to describe the perfect wife of a football fan. He finishes with: "This announcement was brought to you by Carlsberg. Carlsberg don't do wives but if they did, they'd probably be the best wives in the world."

Agency	Ogilvy, Dubai
Creative Director	Till Hohmann
Copywriter	Sascha Kuntze
Art Director	James Purdie
Producer	Sukesh Babu
Client	Volvo

In the UAE the roads are cluttered with speed bumps and drivers need good suspension. The agency produced very special speed bumps for the entrance to dealership parking lots. They looked like the real thing, but in fact they were made of a soft sponge material. People slowed down expecting a bounce. But they felt nothing. A sign explained: "Never feel a bump again, with Volvo's Active Four-C suspension."

Media Innovation (Alternative Media)

Agency	Leo Burnett, Frankfurt	Landmines still claim thousands of innocent victims each year, among them many children. A special table football game was placed next to the Unicef booth at a Frankfurt exhibition. But as soon as people started to play, they realised that something was wrong: most of the players were missing one leg, some even two.
Creative Directors	Andreas Heinzel Peter Steger, Andreas Pauli Kerrin Nausch	
Copywriter	Florian Kroeber	
Art Director	Claudia Boeckler	
Photographer	Tobias Nientiedt	
Client	Unicef	

Agency	Interone Worldwide, Munich	You can only fully appreciate the driving thrills offered by a Mini Clubman if you experience them firsthand. But you don't necessarily need to get behind the wheel. The first ever "gesture controlled" test drive in German cinemas saw to that. After a brief explanation, the cinema audience was in the driving seat. Optical sensors ensured that their movements to left and right were translated into the movements of the Mini on screen. It made for a memorable driving experience.
Creative Directors	Silke Gottschalck Michael Ploj	
Copywriter	Uwe Grossecossmann	
Art Director	Michael Ploj	
Photographer	Manuel Casuela	
Graphic Design	Stefan Schulz Christoph Siebelt	
Programming	Patrick Decaix Wolfgang Mueller	
Client	Mini Clubman	

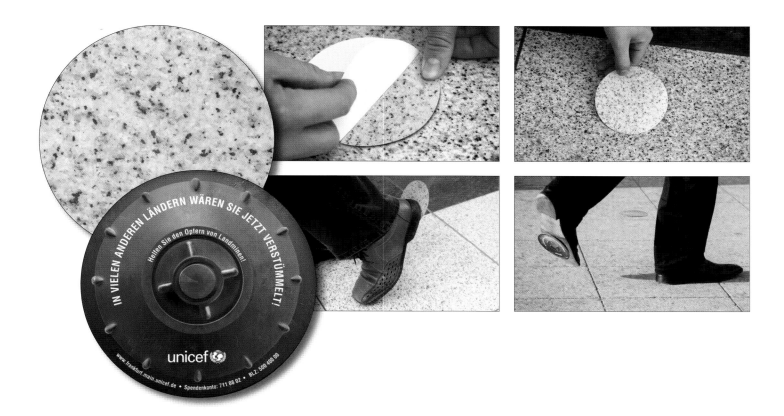

Agency	Leo Burnett, Frankfurt	In many countries, landmines are still an insidious danger to civilians. Unicef placed "invisible" adhesive landmine stickers on the floor. People who walked over them got the stickers stuck to their feet. While removing the stickers, they discovered a picture of a landmine on the underside with the message: "In many countries you would now be maimed."	Agency	Abbott Mead Vickers BBDO, London	Counselling service The Samaritans can be seen as a last resort: a number to call when you're desperate and contemplating suicide. The Samaritans want people to phone before things get that bad. To illustrate that point it hired a stuntman to play the part of a man who posts billboards for a living. He clung to the poster site as his ladder, brush and bucket lay on the pavement below. People rushed to help but the man politely told them he was fine. When the public stepped back they could read the poster and its message.
Creative Directors	Andreas Heinzel Peter Steger Andreas Pauli Kerrin Nausch		**Executive CD**	Mark Fairbanks	
			Creative Director	Paul Brazier	
			Art Director	Andy Sewell	
			Copywriter	Andy McAnnaney	
Copywriter	Florian Kroeber		**Production**	Rogue, London	
Art Director	Claudia Boeckler		**Director**	Daniel Wolfe	
Client	Unicef		**Producers**	Adam Saward Yvonne Chalkley Adam Walker	
			Client	Samaritans	

Media Innovation (Alternative Media)

Agency	Euro RSCG Group Switzerland, Zurich	If global warming continues at the same rate, most glaciers will be nothing more than heaps of rubble by the year 2080. On August 18, 2007 hundreds of men and women posed naked on Switzerland's Aletsch Glacier to foster awareness of the need to protect the climate. With this living sculpture, US installation artist Spencer Tunick and the agency created a symbolic link between the fragility of the receding glacier and that of human beings.
Executive CD	Frank Bodin	
Creative Directors	Juerg Aemmer Claude Catsky	
Art Director	Charles Blunier	
Client	Greenpeace Switzerland	

Agency	Philipp und Keuntje, Hamburg	To demonstrate that you can take sharper photos with the Leica D-Lux 3, the agency showed what ill-defined objects look like. To do this, it placed objects made of thousands of pixels in everyday surroundings. For example, a life-sized yet pixelated dog was tied up outside a Meister Camera shop. A poster next to it said: "See it in more detail with the Leica D-Lux 3."
Creative Directors	Diether Kerner Oliver Ramm	
Copywriter	Daniel Hoffmann	
Art Director	Sönke Schmidt	
Producer	Jörg Nagel	
Client	Meister Camera, Leica D-Lux 3	

Agency	Scholz & Friends, Berlin
Creative Directors	Oliver Handlos
	Matthias Spaetgens
Art Directors	Jens-Petter Waerness
	Erik Dagnell
Photographer	Torsten Roman
Producer	Soeren Gessat
Graphic Design	Annika Stierl
Client	Ravensburger Puzzles

Agency	gkk DialogGroup, Frankfurt
Creative Directors	Roman Kretzer
	Jan Steffen Nussbaum
Copywriter	Stefan Magin
Art Directors	Joerg Wiedemann
	Julia Lottmann
Producer	Arnulf Reichert
Client	Sabina Stobrawe, Divorce Lawyer

Jingle Bells (Trojan Girls) - Th...
Trojan Men

USC's **The Trojan** Men sing their version of ...
Bells at their holiday concert. UCLA
SUCKS...holiday christmas jingle bells acapp...
acapella cappella capela USC **trojan girls**

Tags: holiday christmas jingle bells acap...
acapella cappella capela USC trojan g...
men

Time: **01:20**

THE TROJAN GIRL

Now that's what I call a movie with a messag...
hot sexy lips blonde **girl** surprise extreme fu...
amazing viral impressive amnesty preview p...
erotic

Tags: red hot sexy lips blonde **girl** s...
extreme funny amazing viral impressiv...
amnesty preview picture erotic

Time: **00:49**

Show more videos recently added: Today | This week

California **Girls** - The Trojan Men ★★★★★
USC's **The Trojan** Men sing California **Girls** at the

Agency	DDB Germany, Berlin	
Chief Creative Officer	Amir Kassaei	
Executive CDs	Bert Peulecke	
	Stefan Schulte	
Copywriters	Nina Faulhaber	
	Marian Götz	
	Kai Abd El-Salam	
Art Directors	Lisa Berger	
	Johannes Hicks	
	Marc Isken	
Client	Volkswagen, Bologna Motor Show	

Volkswagen wanted to attract visitors to its stand at the Bologna Motor Show. It took advantage of Bologna's typical architecture by placing imitations of a Volkswagen's front and back wheel in archways to create the silhouette of a New Beetle.

Agency	Saatchi & Saatchi, Frankfurt
Chief Creative Officer	Burkhart von Scheven
Creative Directors	Anne Petri
	Mathias Henkel
Copywriter	Mathias Henkel
Art Director	Anna-Marina Pirsch
Production	Kamerad Film, Düsseldorf
Director	Sven Stausberg
Producers	Michael M. Maschke
	Julia Kallmeyer
Client	Amnesty International

Amnesty International placed a video on YouTube that worked in the same way as the Trojan horse. The film shows a spokesperson from Amnesty who explains the organisation's mission and asks viewers for support. Half way through, for a brief moment he holds up a poster showing the sensual lips of a blonde beauty. This is exactly the point from which YouTube's server automatically picks the image that will appear as the preview picture on the site menu. Guaranteed higher viewing figures for the Amnesty pitch.

Agency	TBWA\Germany, Berlin
Creative Directors	Stefan Schmidt
	Markus Ewertz
Copywriter	Markus Ewertz
Art Directors	Erik Gonan
	Hendrik Schweder
Production	Move it Media
Producers	Viola Thies
	Thomas Adam,
Client	Adidas Football

To emphasise the link between its client Adidas and the Euro 2008 soccer tournament, TBWA installed a colossal "huddle" in Zurich's main railway station. This 14-tonne homage to "the beautiful game" and its top players was ten times larger than the wax figures on display at Madame Tussaud's in London, Hollywood or Berlin, but every bit as detailed.

Agency	TBWA\Germany, Berlin
Creative Director	Stefan Schmidt
Copywriter	Emiliano Trierveiler
Art Director	Marco Bezerra
Photographers	Johann Sebastian Hänel
	Ragnar Schmuck
Production	Limes, Berlin
Producers	Gunnar Heinze
	Karolin Klevenhagen
Client	Adidas Football

TBWA created another channel that embodied the idea that "Impossible is nothing" for Adidas. The agency took Vienna's foremost landmark and converted it into an ambassador for the brand. It installed a 60-meter tall version of top goalkeeper Petr Cech, with eight spinning arms, on the Prater ferris wheel. An unbeatable goalkeeper you could take a ride with, the installation generated massive press coverage.

Media Innovation (Alternative Media)

Agency	Contrapunto, Madrid
Creative Directors	Antonio Montero
	Jaime Chávarri
	Iván de Dios
Copywriters	Guillermo Santaisabel
	Jaime Chávarri
Art Director	Clara Hernández
Photographer	Alvaro Guzmán
Client	WWF/Adena

Inserts announcing "The End" appeared in the middle of books in libraries and Madrid bookstores. The message was that "the end" could come sooner than we'd like for all of us, if we don't do something about climate change.

Agency	Grabarz & Partner,
	Hamburg
Creative Director	Ralf Heuel
Copywriter	Paul von Mühlendahl
Art Director	Fedja Kehl
Producer	Patrick Cahill
Client	Stern.de

The goal was to establish the Stern website as the fastest source of news in Germany. In a stunt staged in a cinema, a pregnant woman complained loudly of contractions before the main feature and hurried out with her husband. While the audience was still discussing this event, a cinema ad showed a screenshot of the Stern.de website. It was a photo of the woman and her husband in the foyer of the cinema with newly born twins in their arms, under the headline: "Twins born at a cinema in Hamburg." News has never been this fast: Stern.de

AirPort: On	AirPort: On	AirPort: On
Turn AirPort Off	Turn AirPort Off	Turn AirPort Off
No network selected	No network selected	✓ BuyaLargeLatteGetBrownieForFree
Feel Like Flying	**BuyAnotherCupYouCheapskate**	flying_high
flying_high	Feel Like Flying	GONET
GONET	GONET	kirsten de Lange
HaveYouTriedTheCarrotCake?	kirsten de Lange	linksys_OW_44630
kirsten de Lange	linksys_OW_44630	Marinke2
Laar	Marinke2	UPC26389
linksys_OW_44630	UPC26389	UPC87698
		Y2719PO

AirPort: On	AirPort: On	AirPort: On
Turn AirPort Off	Turn AirPort Off	Turn AirPort Off
No network selected	No network selected	Feel Like Flying
flying_high	**BuyCoffeeForCuteGirlOverThere?**	GONET
GONET	Feel Like Flying	Laar
Laar	GONET	Marinke2
linksys_OW_44630	kirsten de Lange	✓ **Mmm...YummyMuffinOnly2Euro**
Marinke2	linksys_OW_44630	SX551DA11D2
SX551DA11D2	Marinke2	UPC26389
TodaysSpecialEspresso1,60Euro	UPC87698	UPC87698
UPC26389	Y2719PO	Y2719PO

Media Innovation (Alternative Media) 313

Agency	BBDO, Düsseldorf
Creative Directors	Ton Hollander
	Toygar Bazarkaya
	Ralf Zilligen
Art Directors	Thomas Schmiegel
	Ariane Foerschler
Client	Smart

To show that a Smart "fits everywhere", this execution suggests that the car is parked between the pages of Deutsch magazine.

Agency	They, Amsterdam
Client	CoffeeCompany

As part of its bid to attract students, CoffeeCompany arranged free Wi-Fi access in its cafés. The only problem was that when students came in they didn't order anything and just used the Internet. To remedy this the Wi-Fi network was given names like "Order Another Coffee Already" or "Yummy Muffin Only 2 Euros", so that these suggestions appeared on laptop users' Wi-Fi menus when they wanted to go online. When confused customers asked the barista for the name of the café's Wi-Fi network, they were often told: "Buy Large Latte, Get Brownie For Free."

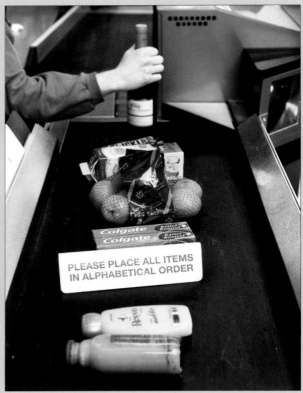

PLEASE PLACE ALL ITEMS
IN ALPHABETICAL ORDER

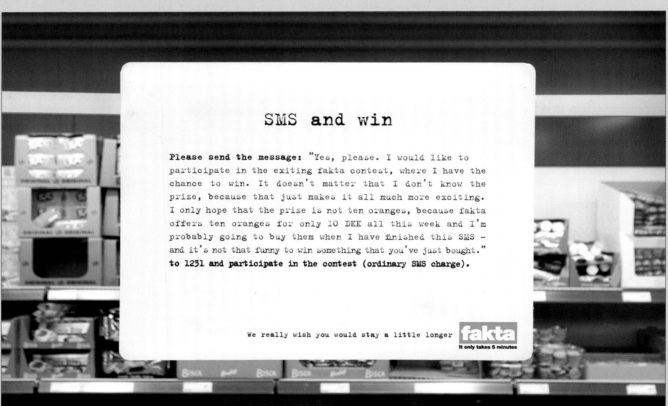

SMS and win

Please send the message: "Yes, please. I would like to
participate in the exiting fakta contest, where I have the
chance to win. It doesn't matter that I don't know the
prize, because that just makes it all much more exciting.
I only hope that the prize is not ten oranges, because fakta
offers ten oranges for only 10 DKK all this week and I'm
probably going to buy them when I have finished this SMS –
and it's not that funny to win something that you've just bought."
to 1231 and participate in the contest (ordinary SMS charge).

We really wish you would stay a little longer **fakta**
It only takes 5 minutes

314 **Promotions & Incentives**

Agency	Uncle Grey, Aarhus
Creative Director	Per Pedersen
Copywriter	Michael Paterson
Art Directors	Jesper Hansen
	Rasmus Gottliebsen
Client	Fakta

Although shopping at Fakta only takes
five minutes, the supermarket would really
like customers to stay a little longer. So it
installed a whole range of devices to delay
them, including price tags in the form
of puzzles, store announcements that
resembled riddles, and a sign at the till
saying: "Please put all items in alphabetical order."

Agency	Uncle Grey, Aarhus	Shortly after the starting pistol went off to launch Europe's largest running race for women only, a man in an Axe T-shirt jumped over the fence several meters ahead of the competitors. He sprayed himself with Axe deodorant and set off, the crowd of women not far behind. From the point of view of the spectators lining the route, here was one man – wearing an Axe T-shirt – being chased by approximately 6.000 women.	
Creative Director	Per Pedersen		
Copywriters	Michael Paterson		
	Ida Kinch		
Art Directors	Jesper Hansen		
	Rasmus Gottliebsen		
Client	Axe		

Agency	Uncle Grey, Aarhus	Hitchhikers waiting by roadsides held cards suggesting that they only wanted to be given lifts in Peugeot cars.
Creative Director	Per Pedersen	
Copywriter	Michael Paterson	
Art Director	Jesper Hansen	
Client	Peugeot	

Agency	Åkestam Holst, Stockholm	The core values of the Norrlands Guld brand are male bonding and friendship. In order to reach a slightly younger target group and give them something to talk about, the brand teamed up with jeans designer Örjan Andersson (of successful label Cheap Monday) to create Norrlands Guld Jeans. The jeans were branded from buttons to labels – and they even had beer openers sewn into them. Priced at the equivalent of €120 and sold in jeans stores all over Sweden, they sold out quickly and generated buzz on blogs and in the mainstream media.
Copywriter	Göran Åkestam	
Art Director	Fredrik Josefsson	
Producer	Helena Holmberg	
Project Leader	Stefan Öström	
Client	Norrlands Guld	

Agency	Åkestam Holst, Stockholm	Is it possible to hatch an egg in a down jacket? This was the challenge set by Swedish outdoor equipment retailer Playground, which wanted to promote the warmth and comfort of its down jackets. A human "hen" kept a fertilised egg wrapped in a sports bra in the lining of his coat and settled into a tent outside the store to brood. The media closely monitored the situation. And, sure enough, a healthy baby chick was born. Sales of down jackets soared – and the chicken population of Sweden spiked.
Copywriter	Hanna Björk	
Art Directors	Johan Baettig	
	Lars Holthe	
Photographer	Carl-Johan Paulin	
Project Leader	Jerker Winther	
Producer	Lotta Linde	
Client	Playground	

Agency	Serviceplan, Munich & Hamburg Plan.Net, Hamburg
Chief CO	Alexander Schill
Creative Directors	Axel Thomsen Maik Kaehler Christoph Nann Friedrich von Zitzewitz Daniel Koennecke
Copywriters	Marietta Mandt-Merck Frances Rohde
Art Director	Till Diestel
Client	Serviceplan

Say hello to Shen International Advertising: a Chinese advertising agency that takes well-known ad campaigns and adapts them for its own clients. Examples of pirated ads were shown on its homepage and on YouTube. The agency also announced a tool called the "AdConfigurator", which allows users to remix thousands of different ads. There was even a video presentation by agency CEO Shen Ken-Yi. All this generated lots of buzz. But finally it became clear that it was all a hoax perpetrated by Serviceplan. "Only new ideas are good ideas."

Agency	Lowe Brindfors, Stockholm
Creative Directors	Håkan Engler Tove Langseth
Copywriter	Ulrika Eriksson
Art Directors	Kalle dos Santos Petter Lublin
Photographer	Anton Ahlenius
Production	MorganKane, Stockholm
Producer	Sofia Bellini
Client	Folkoperan

Zarah is a new opera about Zarah Leander, a Swedish actress who became the greatest star of the Third Reich. That stardom made her highly controversial in Sweden. The debate rages to this day: was she a careerist or a Nazi? The campaign featured posters of Zarah with a Hitler moustache, as if in protest. Some days before the premiere, an event took place at a cinema in Stockholm. On the screen a German bomber dropped propaganda leaflets. And at the same time real flyers for the opera showered the audience.

Promotions & Incentives

Agency	TBWA\Germany, Berlin	
Creative Directors	Stefan Schmidt	
	Markus Ewertz	
Copywriter	Markus Ewertz	
Art Director	Hendrik Schweder	
Production	Magictouch	
Graphic Design	Harald Renkel	
	Gussi Kim	
Project Manager	Tanja Kurr	
Client	Adidas Football	

Even though the German national soccer team was narrowly beaten in the final of the Euro 2008 tournament, the public stood behind them. In recognition of this support, the players wanted to say "thank you" in front of the Brandenburg Gate in Berlin. In order to welcome the team home and allow the public to express its gratitude, Adidas and its agency TBWA created and installed 26 enormous postcards addressed to the German team, which thousands of fans could sign.

Agency	Ogilvy Kosovo, Pristina
Creative Directors	Fisnik Ismaili
	Jeton Morina
Copywriter	Fisnik Ismaili
Art Director	Jeton Morina
Producers	Jehona Serhati
	Yll Vuçitërna
	Bes Bujupi,
	Artan Zeneli
	Valon Xhaferi
Client	Kosovo Government

Only ten days before Kosovo officially declared its independence, the Kosovar government briefed Ogilvy to prepare an event. The agency responded with the giant sculpture NEWBORN. Three meters high, 24 meters long, 1 meter thick and weighing 9 tonnes, this English word was chosen to globally spread the message of a new country being born. But it was also a tool that enabled people to express their emotions via black permanent markers, which the agency provided. On 17 Feb 2008 over 150,000 people wrote on the sculpture, starting with the President.

The
BABY
NAMES
Collection

Tate Britain displays British art

Tate Britain
Millbank
London SW1P 4RG

You've examined the closing credits of your DVD collection, thumbed through countless baby name books and that precious little wide-eyed lump staring up at you is still without a name. Don't worry, your dilemma may be as easily solved by following this Collection.

Chances are you're over-thinking it. Keeping things simple is often the way to go. For instance, walk around our gallery and you'll come across 17 overachieving artists named John. Not to mention some splendid Marys. Then again, you may prefer something more exotic. Consider the name of the artist who painted *Covent Garden Market*. His name was Balthazar Nebot.

Or perhaps *Oriana*, a young woman immortalized by Frederick Sandys.

If you're still a bit stuck, try making a choice based on matching your newborn's personality with that of a work of art. For instance, an attention-seeking child could be named after *Marcus Gheeraerts II's Thomas Lee*, the only portrait in the whole gallery without trousers.

Perhaps your child is the more thoughtful type. In which case, think about naming it after the bookish *Sir Brooke Boothby* by Joseph Wright of Derby.

If strangers stop to admire your little one, you probably have a genuinely adorable baby. In which case you may like to choose a name of someone who is also adorable, like Dante Gabriel Rossetti's *Proserpine* or Thomas Gainsborough's *Giovanna Baccelli*.

If after all this, you still can't decide, have your little bundle select a name itself. Simply carry them aloft through the gallery and they'll eventually giggle at a piece of art. And in so doing, give themselves a name. That way, if they choose something like Daniel Mytens the Elder's *James Hamilton, Earl of Arran, Later 3rd Marquis and 1st Duke of Hamilton* they'll have no one to blame but themselves.

Whatever you do, don't beat yourself up about it, we have 975 works that are untitled so we've got much the same problem.

BP British Art Displays 1500 - 2008
Supported by BP

BRITAIN
TATE

The
BABY
NAMES
Collection

		When Leo Burnett launched the new Fiat 500 in London, it made sure everyone could see the little vehicle. The Fiat was placed inside one of the pods of the revolving London Eye. The Fiat 500: an everyday masterpiece.
Agency	Fallon London	
Executive CD	Richard Flintham	
Creative Director	Juan Cabral	
Copywriters	Toby Moore	
	Selena Mckenzie	
Art Directors	Toby Moore	
	Selena Mckenzie	
Typographer	Hugh Tarpy	
Client	Tate Britain	

Agency	Leo Burnett, London
Executive CD	Jon Burley
Creative Director	Garry Munns
Copywriters	Paul Faulds
	Kevin Travis
Art Directors	Chris Rambridge
	Ian Mitchell
Client	Fiat 500

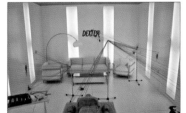

320   **Promotions & Incentives**

Agency	DDB Germany, Berlin
Chief Creative Officer	Amir Kassaei
Executive CDs	Bert Peulecke Stefan Schulte
Copywriters	Birgit van den Valentyn
Art Director	Tim Stübane
Graphic Design	Jussi Jääskeläinen
Client	Volkswagen Recycling

People in Germany are used to Volkswagen vehicles. But nobody has ever seen a washing machine driving through traffic. The stunt expressed the idea that 95% of all scrapped Volkswagens can be recycled.

Agency	Bungalow25, Madrid
Creative Director	Pablo Pérez-Solero
Copywriter	Pablo Pérez-Solero
Art Director	Julio Gálvez
Client	Fox Television

In order to promote the Fox television channel in Spain, the agency took over a large house in Madrid. It worked with set designers to recreate the settings of popular series (from Lost and House to Desperate Housewives and Dexter) and planned a complete agenda of themed activities over two weeks, including some celebrity visits. In this way, journalists, bloggers and the public could get closer to their favourite shows.

Agency	Spillmann/Felser/ Leo Burnett, Zurich
Creative Director	Martin Spillmann
Copywriter	Peter Brönnimann
Art Director	Tabea Guhl
Photographer	Serge Hoeltschi
Producer	Sebahat Derdiyok
Client	Migros Mode

Migros Mode decided to have its underwear line modelled by ordinary single people rather than by professional models. The singles were featured in TV ads, posters, print and on the internet, with the possibility of contacting them via a website. This platform also tracked which of the singles was still available and which of them had found romance thanks to the operation.

Agency	Saatchi & Saatchi, Copenhagen
Creative Director	Simon Wooller
Copywriters	Cliff Kagawa Holm
	Silas Jansson
Art Directors	Cliff Kagawa Holm
	Silas Jansson
Production	Sisomo, Copenhagen
Producer	Anna-Marie Elkjaer
Client	Danish Parkinson's Disease Association

To educate people about Parkinson's Disease, a non-traditional "ambush" event was created in an apartment that had been advertised for sale. With 70,000 white plastic balls and numerous specially adapted utilities in place, the tour gave unsuspecting visitors a hands-on experience of what it means to suffer from Parkinson's disease. The world looks different when you suffer from Parkinson's.

(SFX: Keys)

Man (shouting): "Hello, I'm home."

Woman (angry:) "Get in here! I found a text message on your cell phone."

Man (getting nervous): "What?"

Woman (reading loud): "The night with you was incredible?"

Man (getting scared): "Erm, now … now, let me explain. Please, please put that down."

Off (advertises): "Cup: 2.99."

(SFX: cup crashing)

Man (scared): "Are you out of your mind? You almost hit my head!"

Off (in a sales-like manner): "Plate: 3.99."

(SFX: plate crashing)

Off (advertises): "Plate: 3.99."

(SFX: plate crashing)

Woman (angry): "Who is it? Do I know her?"

Man (scared): "Please just put down the …"

Off (in a sales-like manner): "Vase: 29.99."

(SFX: vase crashing)

Woman (very angry): "Who is it?"

Man (whispering): "Monica."

(Silence)

Woman (going berserk): "My sister? Ahhhh!"

Off (in a sales-like manner, fast): "Shelf: 59.99. Set of 18 glasses: 8.99. Serving tray: 14.95. Set of 60 dishes: 97.90."

(SFX: Pottery and furniture crashing)

Woman (furious): "Come here!"

Man (whining): "Aaahhh."

Off (in a sales-like manner): "Nose: not available."

Off: "Find lots of affordable stuff. Now at IKEA."

Woman (drunk): "Helloooo."

(Man sighs)

Woman (drunk): "You're still up."

Man (worried and angry): "Of course I'm still up. Where have you been? It's one o'clock in the morning."

Woman (drunk): "I was out with the girls."

Man (annoyed): "Are you drunk? Come here."

Woman (giggles): "No. I have to use the bathroom first."

Off (in a sales-like manner): "Shower curtain: 3.99."

(SFX: shower curtain tearing)

Woman (drunk): "Wow, everything is spinning."

Off (in a sales-like manner): "Towel rail: 12.99."

(SFX: towel rail crashing)

(Woman giggles)

Off (in a sales-like manner): "Tooth brush holder: 3.99."

(SFX: tooth brush holder crashing)

Woman (drunk): "Oh, oh."

Off (in a sales-like manner): "Toilet seat: 14.95."

(SFX: toilet seat crashing)

Woman (drunk): "I got to hold on to something."

Off (in a sales-like manner): "Bathroom cabinet: 74.99."

(SFX: Bathroom cabinet crashing)

Man (shouting): "Janet, come to bed!"

Woman (drunk): "Coming. Oh, god. I feel I'm going to … going to be sick."

Man (screaming): "Ah, no, no, no!"

Off (in a sales-like manner): "Bed linen set: 19.95."

Off: "Find lots of affordable stuff. Now at IKEA."

Agency	DDB Germany, Berlin
Chief Creative Officer	Amir Kassaei
Executive CDs	Bert Peulecke
	Stefan Schulte
Copywriters	Marian Götz
	Ingo Isabettini
	David Oswald
	Kai Abd El-Salam
Production	Studio Funk, Berlin
Producers	Jens Mecking
	Hendrik Raufmann
Client	Ikea, "Text Message" & "Late"

(SFX: Synthesiser music)

ANN: "Jim Morrison died in 1971 at the age of 27 in Paris.

27-year-old Janis Joplin died due to a drug overdose in California.

In 1994 Kurt Cobain committed suicide. He was 27 years old.

One year after Woodstock, Jimi Hendrix died age 27 in London.

In 1969, Brian Jones drowned in a swimming pool. He was 27 years old.

Pete Doherty is 27."

SFX: Concert atmosphere

MVO: "Hurry up!"

ANN: "Pre-order tickets for his upcoming tour. At ticket.com"

This ad consists of an adult reading from a script and being copied by a child.

MVO: "If you don't wear your seat belt…"

CVO: "If you don't wear your seat belt…"

MVO: "If you use your mobile phone whilst crossing the road…"

CVO: "If you use your mobile phone whilst crossing the road…"

MVO: "If you cross the road where you can't see the traffic coming…"

CVO: "If you cross the road where you can't see the traffic coming…"

MVO: "If you disobey traffic signs when cycling…"

CVO: "If you disobey traffic signs when cycling…"

MVO: "Your kids will copy you."

CVO: "Your kids will copy you."

MVO: "Be aware of your actions on the road. THINK!"

MVO: "THINK!"

CVO: "THINK!"

Agency	.start, Munich
Creative Directors	Marco Mehrwald
	Thomas Pakull
Copywriter	Bernd Nagernauft
Production	Studio Funk, Hamburg
Client	München Ticket, "27"

Agency	Leo Burnett, London
Executive CD	Jon Burley
Creative Directors	Tony Malcolm
	Guy Moore
Copywriters	Daniel Fisher
	Richard Brim
Producer	Adam Furman
Client	UK Department for Transport, "Copycat"

MVO (very rapidly):

"Pattex. Glues in a second."

Agency	DDB Germany, Düsseldorf
Chief Creative Officer	Amir Kassaei
Executive CD	Eric Schoeffler
Copywriters	Dennis May
	Beathe Ertel
Production	Sprachlabor Audioproduktionen, Düsseldorf
Producers	Eike Steffen
	Petra Hasci
Client	Pattex Super Glue, "The One Second Spot"

SFX (Police radio)

Woman who dispatches the police cars: **"1121, this is 70. Over."**

Police officer (male): **"1121, Maple Street. Vandalism in progress. Two suspects have entered the neighbour's garden and... oh come on..."**

Dispatcher: **"What's happening? Over."**

Officer: **"They're cutting a box hedge into genital shapes. Over."**

Dispatcher: **"Did you say genital shapes? Over."**

Officer (irritated): **"Uhrmm yes, penis. Over."**

VO: **"What are your parents up to when you're away? Keep track with Comviq Prepaid, and call home for just 2.49 a minute."**

SFX (Police radio)

Woman who dispatches the police cars: **"1121, this is 70. Over."**

Police officer (male): **"1121, Maple Street. Party out of control. Over."**

Dispatcher: **"What has happened? Over."**

Officer (troubled): **"The bastards have locked me to a radiator – with my handcuffs. I'm disarmed and undressed. Over."**

SFX: Brief silence...

Dispatcher (surprised): **"Err... Please repeat. Over."**

Officer: **"No. Over."**

VO: **"What are your parents up to when you're away? Keep track with Comviq Prepaid, and call home for just 2.49 a minute."**

Agency	Forsman & Bodenfors, Gothenburg
Production	Flickorna Larsson
Producer	Lotta Wicknertz
Client	Tele2, "Genital Shapes" & "Nude"

(SFX: we hear on-hold music.)

(Warm and friendly female voice:)

"Welcome to the fire department emergency hotline! … We're sorry to inform you that all lines are busy at the moment. In the meantime you may make use of our automated emergency call system. If your house is burning, press «one»! If your house is burning and there are still people inside, press «two»! If your house is burning and you have gas pipes, press «three»! Or simply go online to emergency-service.com to order your personal fire truck! …"

(SFX: the telephone is hung up)

(Male off:)

"Don't let it come to this.
Volunteer at your fire brigade – at firedepartment-dresden.com"

(SFX) Professional kitchen atmosphere

Cook: "...and finally as a topping we cut one radish in thin slices..."

(SFX) (about 35 seconds sound of cutting with a knife on a wooden board)

tack... tack... tack... tack... tack... tack... tack... tack... tack...
tack... tack... tack... tack... tack... tack... tack... tack... tack...
tack... tack... tack... tack... tack... tack... tack... tack... tack...
tack... tack... tack... tack... tack... tack... tack... tack... tack...
tack... tack... tack... tack... tack... tack... tack... tack... tack...
tack... tack... tack... tack... tack... tack... tack... tack... tack...
tack... tack... tack... tack... tack... tack... tack... tack... tack...
tack... tack... tack... tack... tack... tack... tack... tack... tack...
tack... tack... tack... tack... tack... tack... tack... tack... tack...
tack... tack... tack... tack... tack... tack... (fade out)

Off: "Wüsthof. Finest knives for finest cuts. Made in Solingen, Germany."

Agency	Scholz & Friends, Hamburg
Creative Directors	Stefan Setzkorn
	Matthias Schmidt
	Dirk Silz
Copywriter	Bastian Otter
Production	Loft Tonstudios
Producer	Susi Schneider
Client	Dresden Fire Brigade, "On Hold"

Agency	Young & Rubicam, Frankfurt
Creative Director	Deborah Hanusa
Copywriters	Helge Kniess
	Norbert Huebner
	Christian Daul
	Andreas Richter
Production	TonCafé Studios
Producer	Thorsten Rosam
Client	Wüsthof Dreizackwerk, "Little Raddish"

Agency Ogilvy & Mather, Paris
Creative Director Christian Reuilly
Copywriter Edgard Montjean
Art Director Christian Reuilly
Photographer Annie Leibovitz
Client Louis Vuitton

Agency	Lowe London	Agency	Leo Burnett, Milan
Creative Director	Ed Morris	Creative Directors	Enrico Dorizza
Copywriter	George Prest		Sergio Rodriguez
Art Director	Johnny Leathers	Art Director	Alessandro Padalino
Photographer	Nadav Kander	Photographer	Studio Ros
Typographer	Dave Towers	Client	Koleston
Client	John Lewis		

Agency	BBDO, Düsseldorf		Agency	TBWA\Hong Kong
Creative Director	Toygar Bazarkaya		Group CD	Patrick Tom
Art Director	Daniel Aykurt		Executive CD	Mark Ringer
Photographer	Ralf Gellert		Creative Director	Malcolm Costain
Client	Braun Nose Trimmer		Copywriters	Mark Ringer
				Malcolm Costain
			Art Director	Patrick Tom
			Photographer	Nadav Kander
			Client	Adidas

Agency	Taivas, Helsinki	Agency	Armando Testa, Turin
Copywriter	Marku Haapalehto	Creative Directors	Michele Mariani
Art Director	Nestori Brück		German Silva
Photographer	Tuomas Korpi		Ekhi Mendibil
Graphic Design	Nestori Brück		Haitz Mendibil
Client	Oras Cubista	Copywriter	Cristiano Nardò
		Art Director	Andrea Lantelme
		Photographer	Finlay Mackay
		Graphic Design	Laura Sironi
		Client	Lavazza

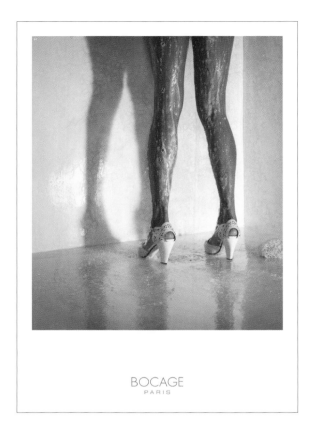

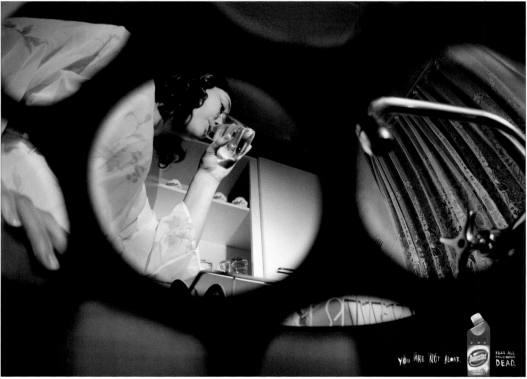

Advertising Photography

Agency	H, Paris		**Agency**	Lowe Bull, Johannesburg
Art Directors	Philippe Boucheron		**Executive CDs**	Rui Alves
	Nicolas Poillot			Matthew Bull
Photographer	Kourtney Roy		**Creative Directors**	Matthew Brink
Client	Bocage			Adam Livesey
			Copywriters	Miguel Nunes
				Andre Vrdoljak
			Art Directors	Miguel Nunes
				Andre Vrdoljak
			Photographer	David Prior
			Client	Domestos

Agency	Åkestam Holst, Stockholm	Agency	Abbott Mead Vickers BBDO, London
Copywriter	Mark Ardelius	Creative Director	Paul Brazier
Art Directors	Andreas Ullenius	Copywriter	Diane Leaver
	Johan Landin	Art Director	Simon Rice
Photographer	Sven Prim	Photographer	Nadav Kander
Client	Pause Ljud & Bild	Client	Pepsi

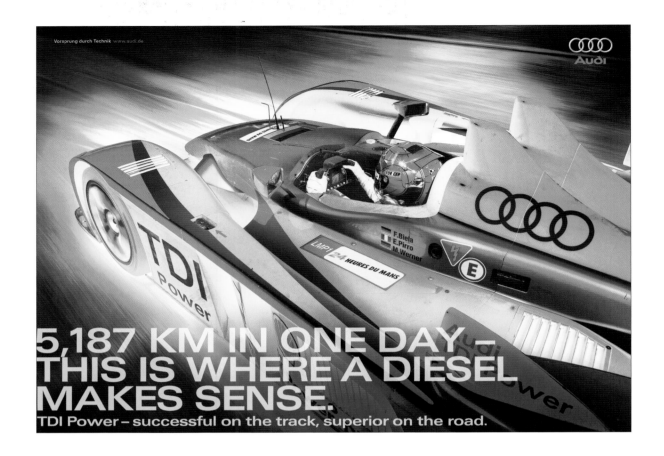

332   Advertising Photography

Agency	Kempertrautmann, Hamburg	Agency	Philipp und Keuntje, Hamburg
Creative Directors	Jens Theil Gerrit Zinke	Creative Directors	Diether Kerner Oliver Ramm
Copywriter	Michael Götz	Copywriters	Daniel Hoffmann
Art Director	Florian Schimmer		Dennis Krumbe
Photographer	Olaf Hauschulz		René Ewert
Client	Audi	Art Directors	Sönke Schmidt
			Rouven Steiman
		Photographer	Jürgen Berderow
		Client	Lamborghini

LUCIANO.CARVARI
-FLORA-AMORE-

Advertising Photography **333**

Agency	Kinograf, Kiev	**Agency**	Scholz & Friends, Hamburg
Creative Director	Lilya Lylyk	**Creative Directors**	Stefan Setzkorn
Copywriters	Konstantin Chernykh		Matthias Schmidt
	Dmitry Marusov		Markus Daubenbuechel
	Alexey Kravtsov		Gunnar Loeser
Art Director	Vitaliy Kokoshko	**Art Directors**	Sascha Dettweiler
Photographer	Yuriy Balan		Christian Doering
Client	Luciano Carvari	**Photographer**	Marius Claudius Wolfram
		Producer	Helen Rudolph
		Client	Siemens IC5, Recipe Cards

Illustration & Graphics

Agency	Young & Rubicam France, Paris
Creative Directors	Les Six
Copywriter	Jean-François Bouchet
Art Director	Jessica Gérard-Huet
Client	Radio Nova

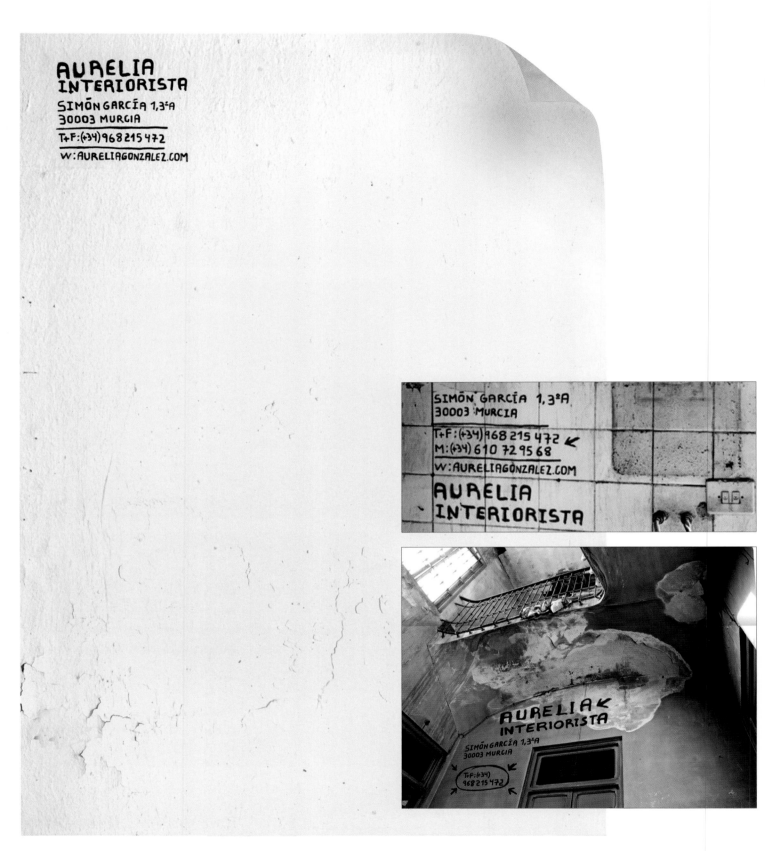

336 **Illustration & Graphics**

Agency	CretaStudio, Murcia
Creative Director	Eduardo del Fraile
Art Director	Eduardo del Fraile
Photographer	Eduardo del Fraile
Client	Aurelia Interiorista, Letterheads & Business Cards

The purpose of the project was to develop a new identity for interior design studio Aurelia. It is common practice in the construction trade to write down contact details on the walls to facilitate communication during a job. The stationery features photographs of places where Aurelia would love to work. The design has helped clients understand the added value of working with such a passionate interior designer. Now potential customers send her photographs of their houses in the hope that she might be interested in them.

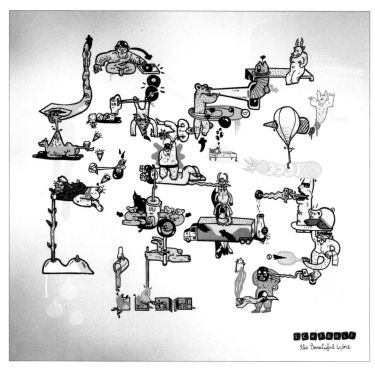

Agency	Jacobson Vellinga Design, Stockholm
Creative Director	John Jacobson
Art Director	John Jacobson
Illustrator	John Jacobson
Clients	Swedish Standards Institute Swedish Institute of Assistive Technology

This important project backed by the Swedish government involved redesigning common public symbols so that more people could understand and interpret them. People with functional impairments of some kind can often have problems in this respect, so the symbols had to be as clear and impactful as possible. The aim was to establish a new Swedish standard for the design and use of pictograms. The Swedish Standards Institute and the Swedish Institute of Assistive Technology led the project, called Design for All.

Agency	Ogilvy & Mather, Paris
Creative Director	Chris Garbutt
Copywriters	Arnaud Vanhelle Benjamin Bregeault, Mihnea Gheorghiu
Art Directors	Antoaneta Metchanova Alex Daff Najin Ha
Illustrators	Am I Collective, Edik, David Ho, Ekta, Dran, Zbiok
Client	Scrabble

Illustration & Graphics

Agency	Arctic Circle, Cape Town	**Agency**	DDB Germany, Berlin
Creative Director	Tyrone Beck	**Chief Creative Officer**	Amir Kassaei
Copywriter	Terri Lategaan	**Executive CDs**	Stefan Schulte
Client	Rock Paper Scissors,		Bert Peulecke
	PR Agency	**Creative Directors**	Ludwig Berndl
			Kristoffer Heilemann
		Art Directors	Marian Grabmayer
			Marcus Intek
		Illustrator	Kirill Chudinskiy
		Client	Volkswagen Polo BlueMotion

Agency   BeetRoot, Thessaloniki
Creative Directors Alexis Nikou
                        Vangelis Liakos
                        Yiannis Haralampopoulos
Art Director   Alexis Nikou
Illustrator   Alexis Nikou
Client   Fena Fashions

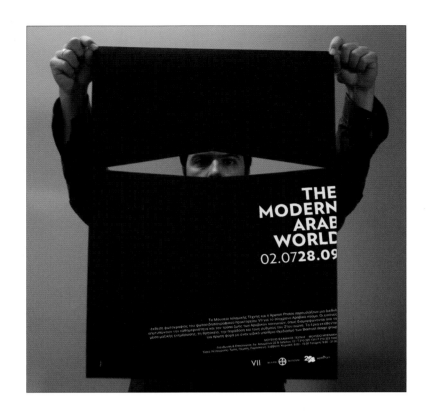

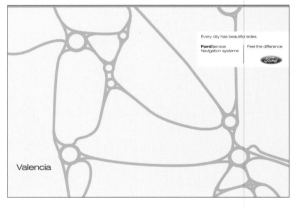

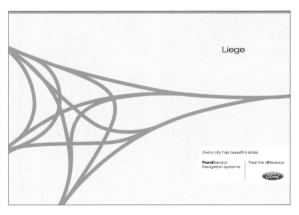

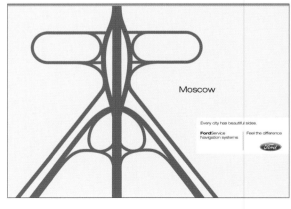

Illustration & Graphics

Agency	BeetRoot, Thessaloniki	**Agency**	Tillmanns, Ogilvy & Mather, Düsseldorf
Creative Director	Yiannis Haralampopoulos	**Creative Directors**	Volker Kuwertz
Art Director	Yiannis Haralampopoulos		Bernd Grellmann
Client	Modern Arab World,	**Copywriter**	Einar Armbruster
	Photography Exhibition	**Art Directors**	Elke Hüsgen
			Barbara Glaeser
			Einar Armbruster
		Illustrators	Elke Hüsgen
			Barbara Glaeser
		Producer	Sarah Kirsch
		Client	Ford Navigation Systems

CHI CHI POTTER
Ink on Paper

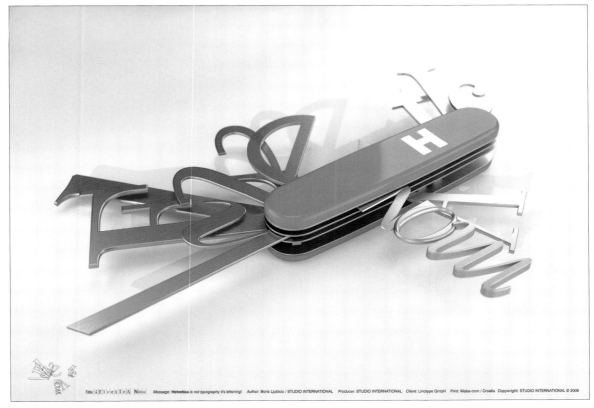

Agency	& Co., Copenhagen	**Agency**	Studio International, Zagreb
Art Director	Sanne Frank	**Creative Director**	Boris Ljubicic
Client	Chi Chi Potter Gallery	**Copywriter**	Boris Ljubicic
		Art Director	Boris Ljubicic
		Illustrator	Igor Ljubicic
		Client	Linotype

Agency	Saatchi & Saatchi, London		**Agency**	DDB, Paris
Creative Directors	Paul Silburn		**Creative Directors**	Alexandre Hervé
	Kate Stanners			Sylvain Thirache
Copywriter	Paul Domenet		**Copywriter**	Matthieu Elkaim
Art Director	Brian Connolly		**Art Director**	Pierrette Diaz
Illustrator	Mike Perry		**Illustrators**	Pierrette Diaz
Typographer	Scott Silvey			Richard N'Go
Client	ChildLine		**Client**	Tiji TV

Agency	Abby Norm, Stockholm
Creative Director	Emil Frid
Copywriter	Kajsa Antonell
Art Director	Emil Frid
Client	Ordning & Reda

Ordning & Reda designs, produces and distributes high quality paper, storage and accessories. The company name means "order & tidiness" in Swedish. The assignment was to create an inspirational brochure for loyal and potential customers. The letters from the logotype are formed into new words that correspond to different parts of the product range. The letters are handmade and photographed on the same cloth that O&R use for their notebooks.

Agency	TBWA\Germany, Berlin
Creative Directors	Stefan Schmidt
	Markus Ewertz
Copywriter	Markus Ewertz
Art Directors	Erik Gonan
	Hendrik Schweder
Illustrator	Gussi Kim
Client	Adidas Football

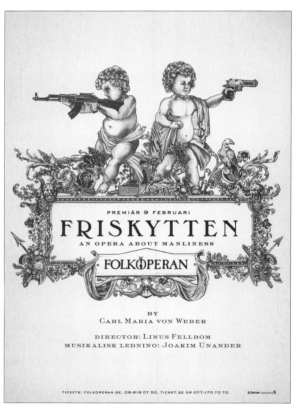

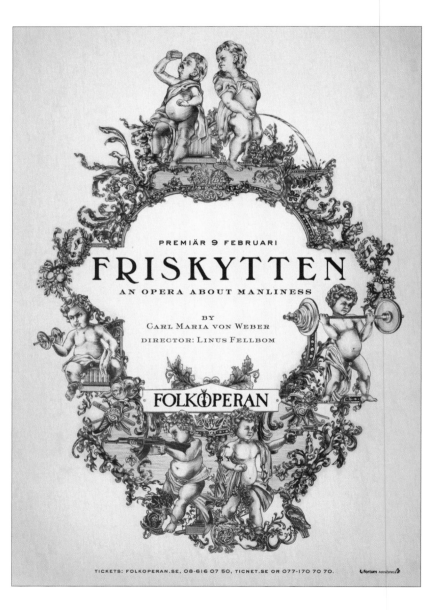

344 **Illustration & Graphics**

Agency	Jung von Matt, Stuttgart	Agency	Lowe Brindfors, Stockholm
Creative Directors	Joachim Silber	Creative Director	Håkan Engler
	Michael Ohanian	Copywriter	Martin Ericson
Copywriters	Lennart Frank	Art Directors	Kalle dos Santos
	Tassilo Gutscher		Petter Lublin
Art Directors	Stefan Roesinger	Illustrators	Emil Bertell
	Dominic Stuebler		Rolle Lindgren
Illustrator	Mark Khaisman	Client	Folkoperan
Client	Tesa Pack Ultra Strong		

Agency	Serviceplan, Munich & Hamburg	Serviceplan is looking for creatives who would give anything for an idea. To back up this claim, the agency constructed 4m x 2.5m recruitment posters out of the "anything" concerned: its art director's entire music collection (1,184 CDs) and its graphic designer's Panini collection (7,482 Panini stickers from all the football world cups since 1970) were featured. The original constructions were displayed in universities and other locations with a response element for potential candidates.
Chief Creative Officer	Alexander Schill	
Creative Directors	Axel Thomsen	
	Maik Kaehler	
	Christoph Nann	
Art Director	Maik Kaehler	
Graphic Design	Roman Becker	
	Amelie Graalfs	
	Patrick Schroer	
	Julia Nowak	
	Jenny Maerkert	
	Ulrike Schumann	
Client	Serviceplan	

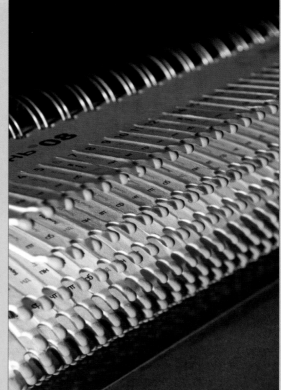

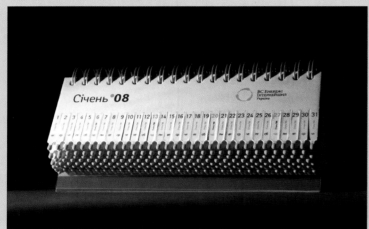

Agency	Yurko Gutsulyak Graphic Design Studio, Kiev	VS Energy International Ukraine is a management company with interests in electric power, hotels, agro-industrial, real estate and banking services. The calendar symbolises the art of managing energy. Called "The Energy Calendar", it contained 365 matches, one for each day of the year.
Creative Director	Yurko Gutsulyak	
Art Director	Yurko Gutsulyak	
Client	VS Energy International Ukraine	

01

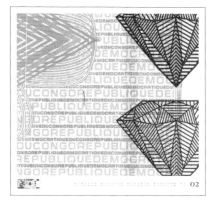
02

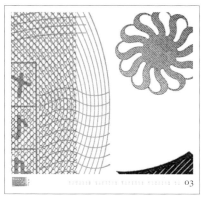
03

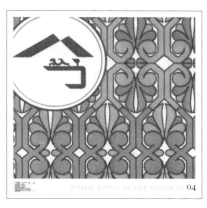
04

05

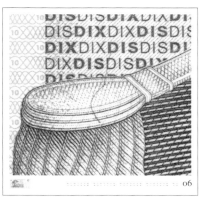
06

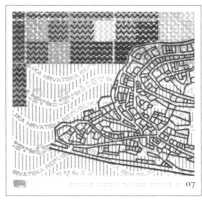
07

08

09

Agency	Euro RSCG, Munich	
Creative Director	Michael Brepohl	
Copywriter	Gerhard Sterr	
Art Directors	Andrea Zeiler	
	Alexandra Spitalny	
Client	Giesecke & Devrient	

Giesecke & Devrient is a technology group specialising in banknote and securities printing. The pictures on the calendar are extreme magnifications of tiny banknote details. Beneath these large images are pockets holding the real banknotes produced by G&D. Only 70 selected clients and business associates of Giesecke & Devrient were the lucky recipients of the calendar.

Agency	Ogilvy, Frankfurt	What's the right way to apply for a job in an advertising or design agency? In this book, prominent German and international creatives from all disciplines give tips and advice to newcomers to the job market. For one thing, have a bit of modesty – it's only advertising. When you go for a job interview, don't spend hours defending your portfolio, causing the interviewer to raise a flag of surrender. And don't stuff your portfolio with "any old crap" just to fill it out. That's the difference between advertising heaven – and hell.
Creative Directors	Helmut Meyer	
	Delle Krause	
Art Director	Helmut Meyer	
Graphic Design	Simon Huke	
Illustrators	Simon Huke	
	Atak	
Production	Thomas Mattner	
Clients	Art Directors Club	
	Germany	

Agency	Bruketa & Zinic, Zagreb	People are the foundation of every successful company. And so every copy of the Adris Annual Report is unique, showing the face of one of its three thousand employees. If you get to know them, you'll get to know Adris.
Creative Directors	Moe Minkara	
	Davor Bruketa	
	Nikola Zinic	
Art Directors	Imelda Ramovic	
	Mirel Hadzijusufovic	
Photographers	Dorijan Kljun	
	Domagoj Kunic	
Client	Adris Group	

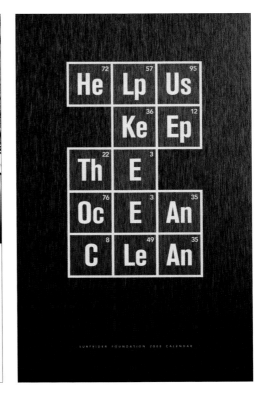

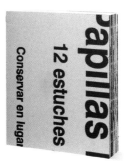

349

Agency	Young & Rubicam, Paris	This calendar for the Surfrider Foundation – surfers against pollution – got its point across by positioning gorgeous bathing beauties on beaches strewn with garbage.
Creative Directors	Les Six	
Copywriters	Gilles Rivollier	
	Louis Carpentier	
Art Directors	Louis Carpentier	
	Gilles Rivollier	
Photographer	Michael Lewis	
Client	Surfrider Foundation	

Agency	CretaStudio, Murcia	This publication is a fundraising initiative that recounts an expedition to bring much needed medical supplies to Mauritania. The covers of the book are made out of the cardboard left over from the packaging of medical products, while inside the pictures capture the harsh reality of life in the country.
Creative Director	Eduardo del Fraile	
Copywriter	Ana Leal	
Art Director	Eduardo del Fraile	
Photographers	Eduardo del Fraile	
	Gabriel Pasamontes	
Clients	AMAMI (NGO)	
	Consejeria de Medio	
	Ambiente de Muria	

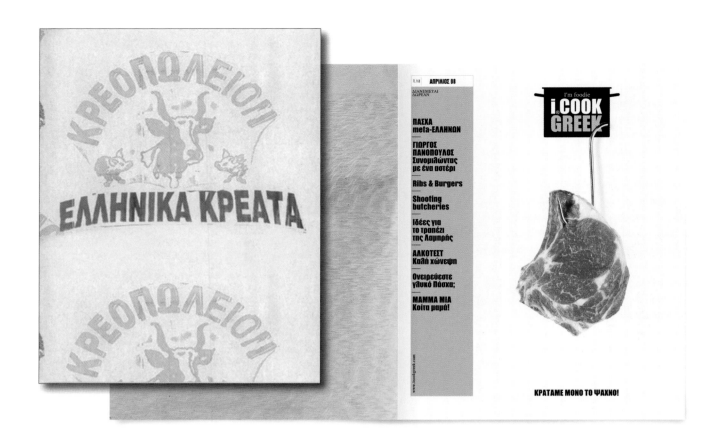

350 **Publications**

Agency	Mouse Graphics, Mellissia	This was a cookery publication called I Cook Greek. While there are many evocative photos inside, the innovative aspects are the covers, which are made from the same paper used to wrap fish or meat in Greek markets.
Creative Director	Gregory Tsaknakis	
Art Director	Yannis Xenakis	
Client	I Cook Greek	

Agency	Nordpol+ Hamburg	The glamorous survivors of car accidents are able to pose almost unscathed with their wrecked vehicles. That's because Renault cars have a five-star safety rating, as this calendar celebrates.
Creative Director	Lars Ruehmann	
Art Director	Bertrand Kirschenhofer	
Photographer	Hans Starck	
Client	Renault	

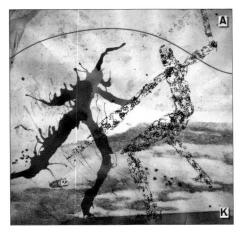

Publications 351

Agency	Kolle Rebbe Werbeagentur (KOREFE), Hamburg
Creative Director	Katrin Oeding
Copywriter	Katharina Trumbach
Art Director	Reginald Wagner
Photographer	Reginald Wagner
Illustrator	Reginald Wagner
Client	Brüder Grimm-Gesellschaft

A radical new interpretation of the brothers Grimm fairy tale "Messengers of Death".

Packaging Design

Agency	Love, Manchester	Silver Cross makes high-chairs, prams, car seats, strollers and other essential furnishings for parents of small children. The packaging idea is based on the insight that kids are often more interested in the boxes than what's inside them. So the Silver Cross boxes can be recycled as children's toys.
Creative Director	Adam Rix	
Copywriter	Simon Griffin	
Art Director	Emma Morton	
Photographer	Ben Wedderburn	
Client	Silver Cross	
	Packaging	

Agency	Lewis Moberly, London	Herbs are as rich in myth and magic as they are in minerals and vitamins. Each pack carries bold tabloid style text, telling you all you may not know about the contents. "Guest" herbs make an exclusive and seasonal appearance with a splash of red in the headline.	Agency	Turner Duckworth, London & San Francisco	This aluminium bottle design embodies Coke's renewed focus on its core brand identity. The classic contour bottle shape features an oversized Coke trademark and nothing more.
Creative Director	Mary Lewis		**Creative Directors**	David Turner	
Copywriter	Mary Lewis			Bruce Duckworth	
Graphic Design	Poppy Stedman		**Graphic Design**	Chris Garvey	
Client	Waitrose		**Client**	Coca-Cola	

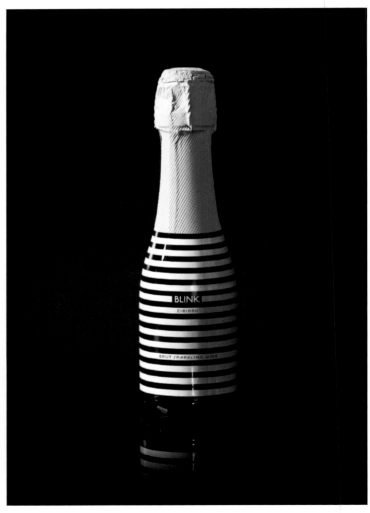

Agency	Noble Graphics Creative Studio, Sofia	Through a small investment in paper bags distributed in stores, pedestrians were turned into free outdoor advertisements for Shumensko beer. The optical illusion of people effortlessly carrying a case of beer in one hand entertained everyone concerned.
Creative Directors	Chavdar Kenarov, Marsel Levi	
Art Director	Joro Kasabov	
Photographer	Atanas Kanchev	
Client	Shumensko Beer	

Agency	BeetRoot, Thessaloniki	Makes your eyes go funny, doesn't it? But it's the perfect packaging for Blink, a brand of Greek sparkling wine. The brief was to create a bottle that would be easily identified in bars and nightclubs.
Creative Director	Yiannis Haralambopoulos	
Art Director	Yiannis Haralambopoulos	
Client	Blink Brut, Sparkling Wine	

Agency	Kolle Rebbe Werbeagentur, Hamburg	Anthony's Garage is called that because Anthony Hammond produces and refines his delicacies in a former tractor factory. The salad oil packaging uses that fact as its inspiration: instead of being contained in bottles, it comes in small oil cans.
Creative Director	Katrin Oeding	
Copywriter	Katharina Trumbach	
Art Directors	Reginald Wagner Lisa Kirchner	
Client	Anthony´s Mini Garage	

Agency	Kolle Rebbe Werbeagentur, Hamburg	Similarly, wine gums from Anthony's Garage take the form of nuts, washers and screws, and look like they come from a DIY display rack.
Creative Director	Katrin Oeding	
Copywriter	Katharina Trumbach	
Art Director	Reginald Wagner	
Client	Anthony´s Mini Garage	

Agency	Comunicación Aldrich, Pamplona	
Creative Director	Alex Viladrich	
Art Director	Andoni Egúzkiza	
Illustrator	Andoni Egúzkiza	
Client	Balthus Wine	

Agency	Blidholm Vagnemark Design, Stockholm
Creative Director	Carin Blidholm Svensson
Art Director	Susanna Nygren Barrett
Client	Stories

The challenge was to create a strong and totally unique café experience from concept and name, to graphic profile, interior design and packaging. Black, white and stainless steel is blended with warm wood, and the old-fashioned café feeling is expressed by things like a board with detachable letters and traditional cups and trays.

Agency	Turner Duckworth, London & San Francisco	Absinthe has a controversial history. It has long been a source of inspiration for artists, but its potency is not to be taken lightly: Le Tourment Vert means literally "The Green Curse". The images that appear in the swirls express this almost mystical quality. The bottle shape was inspired by the water carafes found in cafés throughout France. The secondary labels that carry legally required information were deliberately "un-designed" to adapt to differing regulatory requirements governing the sale of absinthe around the world and can be easily removed.
Creative Directors	David Turner Bruce Duckworth	
Design Director	Sarah Moffat	
Illustrators	John Geary Christopher Garvey	
Graphic Design	Rebecca Williams Britt Hull	
Client	Le Tourment Vert	

Agency	WatersWidgren\TBWA, Stockholm	Vitamin Well's products are sold side-by-side with soft drinks in retail stores as well as in Swedish pharmacies. In order to disrupt conventional soft drink design and reflect the quality of the brand the agency created the clinical look that can be seen on old pharmacy packaging.
Copywriter	Linda Börjesson	
Art Directors	Enis Püpülek Erika Hellström	
Client	Vitamin Well	

Agency	Depot WPF, Moscow	An aged cognac is a quality cognac. Here, the age of the cognac is displayed on the label via a symbolic calendar; a set of 12 marks crossed with a line, each symbol representing one year.
Creative Director	Alexey Fadeyev	
Art Directors	Andrey Gladkov	
	Vadim Briksin	
Client	Mémoire Cognac	

Agency	Tequila\London	The agency wanted to create a brand that celebrated a love of tea in all its forms: My Cup of Tea. And with the client unable to afford traditional advertising, the packaging had to express a distinctive brand personality. The result was a warm and welcoming tone of voice embodied by Pipin, the elephant motif. As well as on packaging, he featured in children's stories launched on the website and as downloadable mp3s.
Creative Director	Cordell Burke	
Copywriter	Tristan Marshall	
Art Director	Ed Shore	
Illustrators	Ed Shore	
	Richard Ardagh	
Client	My Cup of Tea	

Agency	Family Business, Stockholm	The challenge was to stand out in the cluttered trade environment and to stand as the natural choice for those who really want to party. The result was a "disco ball" in the shape of the iconic Absolut bottle. Once the vodka bottle inside is removed, the disco ball can be hung on the ceiling to add glitter to any party.
Creative Director	Mårten Knutsson	
Copywriter	Kalle Söderquist	
Art Director	Fredrik Lindquist	
Photographer	Jens Mortensen	
Client	Absolut Vodka	

Agency	Family Business, Stockholm	The objective here was to celebrate the 30th anniversary of the Pride flag, and make room for pride-related discussions in bars, as well as supermarkets. Absolut collaborated with the designer of the original Pride flag, Gilbert Baker, to create packaging that could not be misunderstood. This was supported by a stunning cocktail book in which all the cocktails were arranged by colour!
Creative Director	Mårten Knutsson	
Copywriters	Mårten Knutsson	
	Fredrik Skärheden	
	Bo Madestrand	
	Gilbert Baker	
Art Director	Jesper Klarin	
Photographer	Erik Hagman	
Client	Absolut Vodka	

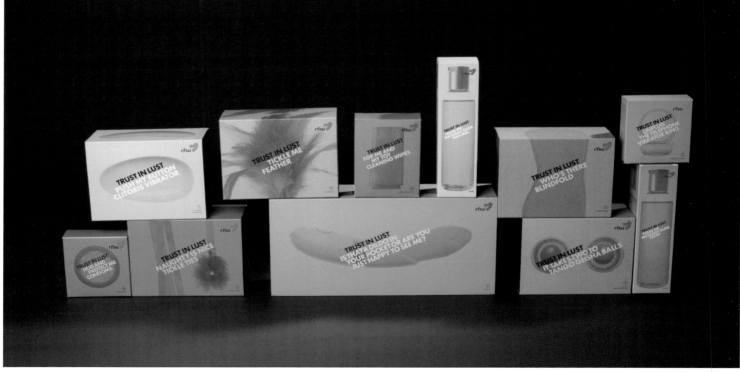

Agency	Bruketa & Zinic, Zagreb	People don't tend to drink fruit wines because they don't know enough about them. The idea was to introduce the concept of fruit wines. That's why the label with the product information is on the front of the bottle rather than on the back. The text forms an illustration in the shape of the corresponding fruit.	
Creative Directors	Tonka Lujanac Davor Bruketa Nikola Zinic		
Copywriters	Sandi Paris Tonka Lujanac		
Art Director	Tonka Lujanac		
Photographer	Domagoj Kunic		
Typographer	Nikola Djurek		
Client	Incanto		

Agency	King, Stockholm
Creative Director	Frank Hollingworth
Copywriter	Emma Zetterholm
Art Director	Helena Redman Bielke
Client	RFSU, "Trust in Lust" Sex Toys

The packaging for these sex toys was designed to be accessible in stores while also provoking curiosity and excitement.

Agency	Demner, Merlicek & Bergmann, Vienna
Creative Director	Franz Merlicek
Art Director	Felix Broscheit
Graphic Design	Felix Broscheit
Client	Stiegl, Limited Edition Beers

Stiegl, the top-quality Austrian brewery, regularly produces limited edition beers for connoisseurs. Sold only at the company-owned shop and at hand picked restaurants, these delicacies are not only characterised by their exceptional taste, but the aesthetic design of their labels.

Agency	Illan Advertising Group, St.Petersburg
Creative Director	Vladimir Fedoseev
Copywriter	Vladimir Fedoseev
Art Director	Vladimir Fedoseev
Illustrator	Vladimir Fedoseev
Client	Vegestory

The client planned to launch about 50 varieties of unusual preserved vegetables. The agency's solution was "vegetable stories", which featured on the labels and described what was inside in an entertaining manner. Since the products are packed in glass jars, no vegetables appear on the labels.

ALL THE MOVEMENTS YOU ARE ABOUT TO SEE ARE CONTROLLED BY SOUND AND MUSIC. SO CHANGE SONGS, UPLOAD YOUR OWN MUSIC, PLAY ON YOUR KEYBOARD OR SING INTO THE MICROPHONE.

362   **Websites (Durables)**

Agency	Forsman & Bodenfors, Gothenburg
Production	Chamdin/Stohr, Stockholm
	Kokokaka, Gothenburg
Director	Amir Chamdin
DOP	Gösta Reiland
Client	Ikea,
	"Come into the Closet.
	Let's Dance"

This is a campaign to promote Ikea's wardrobe solutions. Ikea wanted to show their huge range of wardrobe styles and all the smart features inside. So the website shows five different people – with five different wardrobes – doing five very weird dances. All their movements are controlled by music. Users can change the songs, upload their own music, play on their computer keyboard or sing into the microphone. The characters on the site have no choice but to dance along…

Agencies	OgilvyOne Worldwide, Paris
	Ogilvy Interactive, Paris
Creative Director	Frederic Bonn
Copywriters	Rosecrans Baldwin
	Virginie Achard
Art Directors	Lang Teav
	Cedric Aceres
	Thomas Legrand
Photographers	Annie Leibovitz
	Frédéric Guelaff
Flash	Sami Meziani
Client	Louis Vuitton,
	"Journeys with Coppola"

Travel has been at the heart of Louis Vuitton for more than 150 years. As part of Ogilvy's campaign to reconnect the brand with its core values, the agency created "Journeys" within louisvuitton.com. In this version, Francis Ford Coppola describes San Francisco, his favorite city, with eight short films. A camera truck drove around the city for a week recording interviews with key San Francisco personalities to bring Coppola's city to life.

Agencies	OgilvyOne Worldwide
	Ogilvy Interactive, Paris
Creative Director	Frederic Bonn
Copywriters	Rosecrans Baldwin
	Virginie Achard
Art Directors	Lang Teav
	Cedric Aceres
	Thomas Legrand
Photographers	Annie Leibovitz
	Frédéric Guelaff
Flash	Sami Meziani
Client	Louis Vuitton, "Journeys with Keith Richards"

For Keith Richards' "Journey", Ogilvy illustrated his stories about London with eight short movies set in the city. 16-millimeter film captured the city's gritty spirit, while an original score and ambient sound allowed visitors to discover Keith's birthplace, then and now. It's a journey straight to the heart of the city, personalized by the star.

Agencies	OgilvyOne Worldwide
	Ogilvy Interactive, Paris
Creative Director	Frederic Bonn
Copywriters	Rosecrans Baldwin
	Virginie Achard
Art Directors	Lang Teav
	Cedric Aceres,
	Thomas Legrand
Photographers	Annie Leibovitz
	Frédéric Guelaff
Flash	Sami Meziani
Client	Louis Vuitton, "Journeys with Gorbachev"

Mikhail Gorbachev guides visitors to the Louis Vuitton site around his favorite city, Moscow. Via original photography, interviews with Moscow citizens, ambient sound and a commissioned score, we discover the different faces of modern Russia.

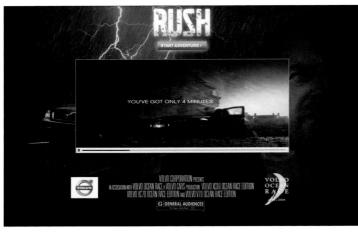

Agency	Euro RSCG 4D, Amsterdam
Creative Directors	Bram de Rooij
	Martijn Sengers
Copywriter	Bram de Rooij
Art Director	Martijn Sengers
Designer	Antonio Costa
Project Manager	Sabine Marleen Haverkamp
Producer	Nicole Siers
Technical Director	Bob Elbersen
Production	Annex Films, London Lbi, Gothenburg
Client	Volvo, "Rush - an Interactive Adventure"

We meet four members of a lifeboat rescue crew who've just received an emergency call. They have four minutes to reach their lifeboat, driving in their Volvo Ocean Race Edition vehicles. Things go wrong and the user needs to help them out. From a split-screen overview showing each crew-member's narrative, the user zooms in on any of the four members and can control the narrative.

 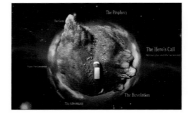 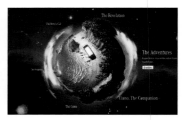

364   Websites (Durables)

Agency	DDB Germany, Hamburg
Chief Creative Officer	Hartmut Kozok
Creative Director	Thomas Bober
Copywriter	Jan Hertel
Art Directors	Torben Cording
	Rainer Deutschmann
Programmers	Sebastian Fiedler
	Gregory Jacob
	Michael Niestedt
Client	Volkswagen Golf GT Sport, "The Chase Goes On"

The Golf GT Sport is the official "getaway car" in the spy movie "The Bourne Ultimatum". In this online game, users get to join in the espionage fun as they help a top assassin locate the car and deliver it to the meeting point – while obviously discovering all the vehicle's features.

Agency	Syzygy, Bad Homburg
Creative Directors	Dirk Ollmann
	Daniel Richau
Copywriter	Dorothee Zoll
Art Directors	Alexander Meinhardt
	Wolfgang Schröder
	Christina Metzler
	Thorsten Binder
Programming	Leonardo Paredes
	Christian Nowak
Clients	Mercedes-Benz & Disney, "A Web Wide World"

This world is not enough when Mercedes-Benz and Disney collaborate. Therefore the agency created a new and better world as an online communication platform for the Mercedes Viano and Disney's movie "The Chronicles of Narnia Prince Caspian". On a 3-D globe the user experiences fantastic adventures while travelling with the Viano. Whatever he does, he is always in the best place for heroes – a world where adventures lurk behind every corner.

Agency	These Days, Antwerp
Creative Director	Sam De Volder
Copywriter	Raf De Smet
Art Directors	Valentijn Destoop
	Jeroen Goossens
Designer	Valentijn Destoop
Production	Creacon
Client	Pioneer Kuro,
	"Kuro Experience"

The Pioneer flat screen TV range is called Kuro, which means "black" in Japanese. Navigate using an interactive black cube to see how Kuro's intense black delivers a sharper picture, intense colours and optimal viewing no matter what the time of day. The strength of 3D audio is also discussed – and there's an expert on hand to guide you through all the features.

Agency	Lowe Brindfors,
	Stockholm
Creative Director	Magnus Wretblad
Copywriter	Henrik Haeger
Art Directors	Tim Scheibel
	Jakob Swedenborg
Production	Alphabetical Order
	Acne Film
Production Manager	Helena Wård
Producer	Espen Bekkebråten
Graphic Design	Joakim Norman
Client	Saab, "The Turbo
	Gene Test"

This entertaining site enables users to uncover their hidden "turbo gene" and determine which of the Saab turbo range is right for them. Answer a series of easy questions – about your favourite historical figure, your media preferences and the kinds of roads you usually drive on – and the site matches you with your ideal car.

Agencies	McCann-Erickson
	Belgium, Hoeilaart &
	Antwerp
Creative Director	Michael Thuy
Copywriters	Frank Van Venrooij
	Madelieve Timmermans
Art Directors	Greg Pin
	Gilles Deketelaere
Client	Harley-Davidson,
	"Your Perfect
	Harley-Davidson
	Weekend"

An interactive game puts you in the saddle of a Harley-Davidson. Get on the iconic motorcycle and head to the terrain of your choice. The site gives you lots of choices along the way, from the picnic you take with you to what you're going to wear. But the main purpose of the site is to encourage users to discover the joy of the open road – Harley-Davidson style.

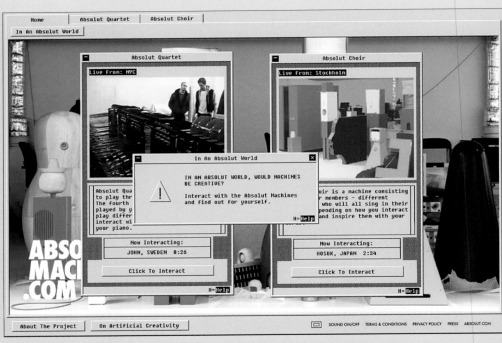

Agencies	Great Works, Stockholm	Designers	Fredrik Karlsson
	Frankenstein, Stockholm		Mathias Päres
	TBWA\Paris	Project Mgrs	Charlotta Rydholm
Creative Directors	Ted Persson		Kaj Bouic
	Mathias Päres		Cilla Winbladh
	Pontus Frankenstein		Christelle Delarue
	Sébastien Vacherot	Production Mgrs	Linn Tornérhielm
Copywriter	Mathias Päres		Jocke Wissing
Art Directors	Mathias Päres	Production	Fredrik Karlsson
	Pontus Frankenstein		Ola Löfgren
Photographers	Erik Hagman		David Andersson
	Sesse Lind	Client	Absolut Vodka,
Technical Director	Micke Emtinger		"Absolut Machines"

In an Absolut world, machines would be creative. This was the insight that led the agency to collaborate with two cutting edge design teams Dan Paluska and Jeff Lieberman of MIT and Sweden's Teenage Engineering. Both teams were challenged to build "creative machines" with which users could interact over the internet. Teenage Engineering came up with the Absolut Choir – which used artificial intelligence and voice synthesizing technology – while Paluska and Lieberman delivered a mechanical orchestra. Using their computers, visitors to the site could "play" the machines.

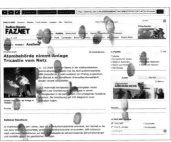

Agency	Abbott Mead Vickers BBDO, London
Art Director	Tim Vance
Copywriter	Paul Knott
Production	iChameleon Group
Client	Guinness, "Tipping Point"

The Guinness "Tipping Point" commercial was about a community coming together to create the world's most ambitious domino run. The agency cut the ad into segments and scattered it across the internet, creating a treasure trail of puzzles for users to follow. The reward for solving each puzzle was the next segment of the commercial, with solid gold dominoes awaiting those who could put it together first. Tens of thousands rose to the challenge.

Agency	Nordpol+ Hamburg
Creative Directors	Ingo Fritz
	Lars Ruehmann
Copywriters	Ingmar Bartels
	Klaudija Sabo
Art Directors	Dominik Anweiler
	Mark Hoefler
	Claudius Gerstner
Programmers	Felix Geisendörfer
	Christoph Tavan
	David Zuelke
Client	Open-trace.de, "Open Trace / Fingerprints"

This complex project drew attention to the fact that the German government wants to collect information on private internet use. Although the legislation has been blocked, the threat remains. The operation worked with a banner ad that turned mouse clicks into fingerprints. Immediately after landing on the banner, when users clicked anywhere else on the page, they left a fingerprint behind. This led to a website that showed them how the government could easily collect data about their browsing habits – and build up a detailed profile of them.

Agencies	JWT Paris	
	Grouek, Paris	
Creative Directors	Ghislain de Villoutreys	
	Olivier Courtemanche	
Copywriter	Thierry Brioul	
Producer	Jean-François	
	Casamayou	
Client	Nestlé Extreme	

Ever wanted to direct your own movie? Now you can, with this amazing website set up by Nestlé Extreme. The site provides high-quality film sequences that users can edit into any form they like. They can also write dialogue and choose the soundtrack. Then they can share their masterpiece with other users, who can vote on it. The winner was projected in a cinema on the Champs Elysées.

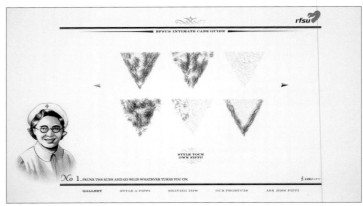

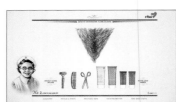

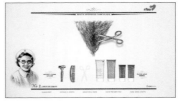

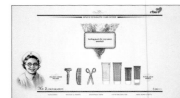

Agencies	MediaFront, Oslo
	Kitchen Leo Burnett, Oslo
Copywriter	Bendik Romstad
Art Directors	Anne Gravingen
	Mathias Friis
Designers	Sverre Stabel
	Christian Ruud
Client	Fretex, "See My Dress"

This interactive site promotes the Salvation Army's surprisingly hip second-hand clothing shop. Make a series of decisions to see your vintage dress displayed on the screen – then visit the shop to pick up one just like it. Charity is the new fashion.

Agency	Åkestam Holst, Stockholm
Creative Director	Paul Collins
Copywriter	Hanna Björk
Art Directors	Andreas Ullenius
	Paul Collins
Project Leader	Jerker Winther
Production	Dallas, Stockholm
Producer	Lina Drot
Client	RFSU, The Swedish Association for Sexual Education, "Miss Fifi"

An online campaign helped launch new intimate hygiene products. This was done through a campaign site (shavethepussy. com) where users could win a shaving kit via an interactive shaving game. After shaving and grooming their "fiffi" they would be awarded points from Miss Fifi herself. But users would only receive full points if they used the products in the right order e.g., first the shaving gel, then the shave, style and trim, followed by a cooling balm.

Agency	Scholz & Friends Interactive, Hamburg
Creative Director	Mario Gamper
Copywriter	Kathrin Schmitz
Art Director	Patricia Stolz
Photographer	Joerg Klaus
Flash	Fabian Aumiller
Graphic Design	Annika Stierl
Illustrator	Knut Weber
Client	Berlin Philharmonic Orchestra, "Chello Challenge"

There are one million ways of getting the right tone from a cello. Will you pick one of the right ones? This promotional site for the Berlin Philharmonic Orchestra puts you in the place of a cello player. Yes, it's you versus Camille Saint Saëns!

Agency	Great Works, Stockholm
Creative Directors	Ted Persson
	Fredrik Carlström
Copywriter	Deborah Moss
Art Directors	Jacob Åström
	Jakob Nielsen
Illustrator	Ola Persson
Production	Jocke Wissing
Flash	Carlos Ulloa.
Client	Absolut Vodka, "In an Absolut World"

The site invites all sorts of visionaries, from big name celebrities to consumers, to come up with their own vision of a perfect world. If the vision is interesting enough Absolut will try and make it a reality. All visions – both realised and unrealised – are gathered on the website for people to vote and comment on.

Agency	Storåkers McCann, Stockholm
Copywriters	Christian Heinig
	Hanna Belander
Art Directors	Ola von Bahr
	Henric Almquist
Production	B-Reel
Client	Magnum Ice Cream, "Magnum Manor"

This amusing site took users on a tour of Magnum spokeswoman Eva Longoria's imaginary house: Magnum Manor. Within, they met her three helpers, a gardener, a butler and a spiritual guru. But because this is a Magnum production, these characters offered the users various temptations.

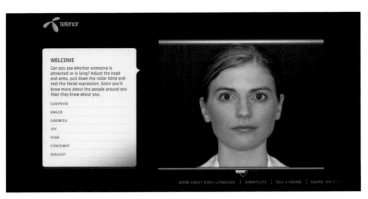

Agency	Garbergs Reklambyrå, Stockholm
Copywriters	Henning Wijkmark
	Johan van der Schoot
Art Directors	Malin von Werder
	Johan Wilde
Web Directors	Carl Bock
	Bjarne Melin
Producers	Jessica Thorelius
	Simon Hernadi
Graphic Design	Jonas Bäckman
	Beatrice Sztanska
Flash	David Wahlgren
	Magnus Svensson
Client	Telenor, "Body Communication"

Telenor is all about communication. This site enables users to discover the secrets of "body talk". Click on gestures or expressions and find out what they mean. Soon you'll be able to decipher even the subtlest gestures in order to determine what the person in front of you really feels – and what they are trying to hide.

Agency	BETC Euro RSCG, Paris
Creative Directors	Jacques Jolly
	Christophe Clapier
Copywriters	Adrien Heron
	Ivan Beczkowski
Art Director	Pierre Marly
Designer	Silvere Marechal
Client	Disneyland Paris, "Tower of Terror"

An interactive game takes users on a tour of the haunted Hollywood Tower Hotel. Explore the hotel, solve mysteries and experience a fraction of the fear that lies in store when you ride the new attraction at Disneyland Paris: The Tower of Terror.

Agency	Farfar, Stockholm
Production	Colony, Stockholm
Director	Henrik Gyllenskiold
Producer	Mats Sandin
Client	Nokia N82, "The World is my Canvas"

To promote the Nokia N82 and its integrated GPS, the site introduced wacky artist Stavros to the world. In turn, he gave the world: Position Art. This new art form is all about tracking your positions through your GPS; plan your design, find a good spot, switch on your mobile's tracking application, and "walk" your art. The concept was explained by Stavros, who became the face of the campaign.

Agency	DDB, Milan
Executive CD	Vicky Gitto
Creative Director	Giuseppe la Spada
Client	Mono No Aware "Spread Your Voice"

The Japanese musician Ryuichi Sakamoto is the main name behind this amazingly attractive site. Ostensibly it is the "Stop Rokkasho" project, drawing attention to the radioactive contamination that is occurring at a nuclear fuel reprocessing plant in the village of Rokkasho in Japan. But it is also a collection of music downloads, interactive digital artworks and digital film experiments. You can also buy activist T-shirts by Japanese graphic designers.

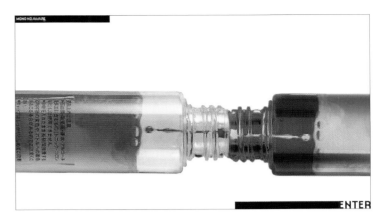

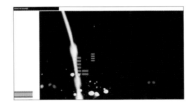

Agency	Hyperhappen, London
Art Director	Simeon Rose
Designer	Jakob Nyland
Planner	Brad Fairhead
Production	North Kingdom, Skellefteå
Producer	Ingrid Thorpe
Client	Cadbury Dairy Milk, "Glass and a Half Full Productions"

Everybody loved Cadbury's "Gorilla" and "Truck" ads. The site extends the faintly surreal world of these spots, taking us inside a richly imagined Cadbury factory. We see the gorilla's "lair", meet some friendly Cadbury cows, get to design our own truck and meet the parrot who is apparently the factory boss! It's a glass and a half full of fun.

Agency	North Kingdom, Skellefteå
Creative Director	David Eriksson
Copywriter	Roger Stighäll
Art Director	Robert Lindström
Photographer	Dreamfield
Illustrators	Kenny Lindström
	Anton Eriksson
Designers	Mikael Forsgren
	Mathias Lindgren
	Daniel Wallström
Client	Coca-Cola Zero, "Coke Zero Game"

Users are put in the shoes of the game's hero, Tim, as he starts a really bad day. His girlfriend has left him and he's missed out on tickets to the UEFA Euro 2008 soccer tournament. But when he spends his last few pennies on a bottle of Coke Zero, his luck begins to change. Join Tim as he meets beautiful women, is escorted to a football stadium, and tries his luck at getting into the VIP area in time for the match.

372   **Websites (Business to Business)**

Agency	Blackbeltmonkey, Hamburg
Creative Directors	Mike John Otto
	Oliver Bentz
Copywriter	Oliver Bentz
Art Director	Mike John Otto
Photographer	Verena Knemeyer
Flash	Nikolai Bockholt
Client	Blackbeltmonkey

This is a creative site for a creative agency. Hear about the agency's credo, watch the work, discover the profiles of employees and meet the Blackbeltmonkey himself in this stylish space.

Agencies	Leo Burnett, Chicago & Toronto
Creative Directors	Peter Gomes Shirley Ward-Taggart Judy John
Copywriters	Greg Shortall Len Preskow
Illustrator	Dan Turner
Client	Leo Burnett Global Website

This giant global agency's website is unexpectedly whimsical, with its jaunty background music and entertaining interactive options. All the objects associated with the Burnett brand are present and correct: the big black pencils Leo always used, the apples he placed on the reception desk to welcome visitors (just as the agency does today) and a cartoonish silhouette of the man himself. Eschewing easy hipness, the site captures Leo Burnett's positioning as a creative yet accessible agency.

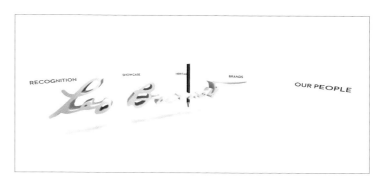

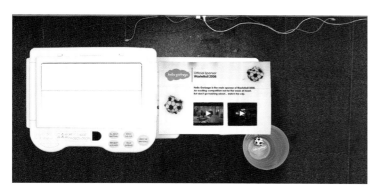

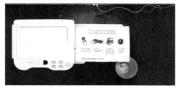 

Agency	Fitzroy Amsterdam
Client	Hello Garbage, "Wasteball in the Office"

Hello Garbage is a waste disposal service for big and small businesses. Its website makes a game out of garbage. As it says, you can throw paper away – or you can make a game out of it! The site shows you how to play the new sport of Wasteball. Print out the wasteball template (basically, it's a bit of paper that you screw up), form a team and get prepared to win prizes of beer and stuff. Rubbish has never been so much fun.

Agencies	Starring, Stockholm LBi Starring Stockholm
Creative Director	Fredrik Lundgren
Copywriter	Mia Robertsson
Art Director	Jörgen Jörälv
Client	Trygg-Hansa, "The Company"

This insurance company has come up with an interactive solution to enable you to find out what kind of cover you need. Play the online game – which involves movie clips and lots of fun objects – to create a virtual version of your business, before finally being given a quote.

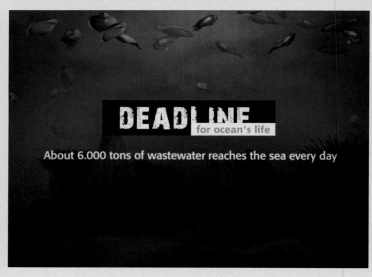

DEADLINE for ocean's life

About 6.000 tons of wastewater reaches the sea every day

Agency	Serviceplan, Munich & Hamburg	Yaqu Pacha is an organisation that helps conserve South American aquatic
Creative Director	Danusch Mahmoudi	mammals, its name means "water world"
Copywriter	Nina Thiel	in the language of the Quitchua Indians.
Art Directors	Christian Sommer Ivana Cevra	The Oceanic Screensaver, with its colourful underwater world, was offered for free.
Graphic Design	Christian Sommer Ivana Cevra	A couple of days after the download, however, the underwater application starts
Programmer	Daniel Ernle	to change: the ecosystem begins to fail due
Client	Yaqu Pacha, "Oceanic Screensaver"	to pollution, the water turns murky and fish start to die. On the sixth day one can read the call for action: "Save the ocean before it's too late!"

Agency	Serviceplan, Munich & Hamburg
Creative Director	Danusch Mahmoudi
Copywriter	Peggy Jürges
Art Director	Axinja Werner
Graphic Design	Anke Buchta
	Tobias Mayer
Screen Design	Anke Buchta
	Tobias Mayer
Programmer	Ret Lauterbach
Client	Fromms Condoms, "Dare to Touch"

Contraception is always a matter of trust. This prompted Fromms to demonstrate their condom's reliability – with a banner apparently made of latex. Since Fromms condoms are more durable than those of their competitors, once users have clicked on the ad the banner stretches with their exertions, with no danger of tearing.

Agency	DDB, Hamburg
Creative Director	Justin Landon
Copywriters	Katja Behnke
	Jan Hertel
	Mareike Woischke
Art Directors	Andrea Schlaffer
	Frederike Eichmann
	Stephanie Schramm
	Till Heumann
Illustrator	Kay Tennemann
Programmers	Svenja Schürmann
	Daniel Knobloch
Client	Nike +, "Miles"

The brief was to increase awareness and the number of users of the Nike+ website. The agency gave birth to Miles, a unique widget who acts as your personal trainer. He lives on your desktop, encourages you to run and comes with interactive tools such as a weather forecast, running news and an integrated RSS Reader. Thanks to Nike+, Miles is directly connected to your running shoes. He knows which days you run and tracks your goals.

Agency	Wieden+Kennedy, Amsterdam
Creative Directors	Edu Pou
	Joakim Borgstrom
	Mark Bernath
	Eric Quennoy
Copywriter	Patrick Almaguer
Art Director	David Stadtmüller
Production	Grupo W
Photographer	Santiago Barreiro
3D Artist	Eugenio Garcia
Animation	Fransisco Romahn
Client	Bad Company

These banner ads refer to the video game Bad Company, in which a disaffected army unit goes off the rails in search of girls and gold. In each animated banner, the soldiers attack a neighbouring ad to grab the cash or the pretty girl. The provocative humour of the banners captures the atmosphere of the game and appeals to its target audience.

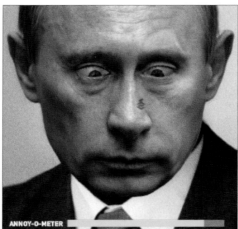

376   **Online Ads**

Agency	DDB Germany, Hamburg
Executive CD	Martin Drust
Art Directors	Christos Zarampoukas
	Kathleen Standke
Programmers	Frithjof Millies
	René Schapka
IT-Management	Detlef Niemann-Bode
	Florian Liss
Client	Ikea Austria, "Blinds"

Click on the website of your favourite newspaper and it appears to be printed on Venetian blinds. When you scroll down in an attempt to escape, you actually pull up the blind. Underneath is revealed an ad for Ikea: the Lindmon blind is only €49.45.

Agency	Contrapunto, Madrid
Creative Directors	Antonio Montero
	Carlos Jorge
	Félix del Valle
Copywriter	Félix del Valle
Art Director	Carlos Jorge
Production	Cocoe
Client	Amnesty International, "Putin" & "Hu Jintao"

These little ads allow the user to annoy abusive world leaders by using the mouse to control what looks like a tiny fly. A buzzing noise accompanies its movement as you try to send the "annoy-o-meter" off the scale. When you succeed, the fly is revealed to be the Amnesty International logo – a fly in the ointment to leaders who don't respect basic freedoms.

KNOW WHAT TO DO WHEN
CARDIAC ARREST STRIKES.

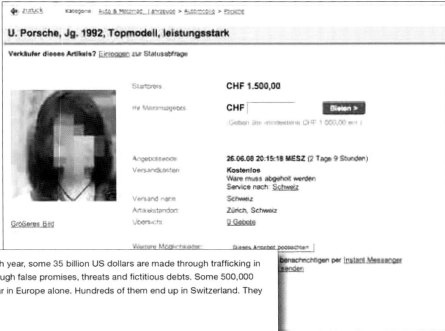

Those who trade in women make bigger profits than car dealers: each year, some 35 billion US dollars are made through trafficking in human beings. The women are blackmailed and kept dependent through false promises, threats and fictitious debts. Some 500,000 women and children fall victim to the booming sex industry every year in Europe alone. Hundreds of them end up in Switzerland. They need greater protection and more rights.

Buying a woman is an easy matter.
And it's an easy matter to do something against it too:

IT'S NOT HAPPENING HERE. BUT IT
IS HAPPENING NOW. amnesty international

Add your signature at www.amnesty.ch

Agency Publicis, Amsterdam
Creative Directors Marcel Hartog
Jeroen van Zwam
Copywriter Katelijne Kenter
Art Director Hans Bolleurs
Designers Jeroen Hessing
Patrick Tang
Dave Fransen
Producer Elsbeth Zandvoort
Director Tom Sijmons
Editor F. Rodriguez Bouzas
Client Dutch
Heart Foundation

On a website, an ad features a middle-aged man who is selling cheap loans. Suddenly, he clutches his chest and collapses. The occupants of two other banner ads then spring into action. A guy from an ad for a gym climbs down and tries to jolt the man's heart back into life. And a woman from a mobile phone company ad calls an ambulance. She then hops down with a defibrillator before the ambulance arrives. Could you be as helpful as these two? If not, you need training from the Dutch Heart Foundation.

Agency Walker, Zurich
Creative Director Pius Walker
Copywriter Martin Arnold
Art Director Nik Hodel
Client Amnesty International,
"Stop Slavery/
e-Bay Attack"

Trafficking in human lives has taken on proportions greater than slavery. Every year, an estimated 2.5 million people are victims of this crime, 80 per cent of them women. Today, virtually anyone can buy a woman. Amnesty International drew attention to this appalling fact by placing ads for women within e-Bay auction sites. Men looking for cars were suddenly confronted with pictures of women for sale. A pop-up then asked them to help stop this violation of human rights.

Online Films

Agency	Abstract Groove, Milan
Creative Director	Luigi Pane
Designers	Vichie Chinaglia
	Vito D'Ambrosio
	Luigi Pane,
	Luca Siano
	Valentina Vicini
DOP	Luca Fantini
Director	Luigi Pane
Producers	Giada Risso
	Mauro Mastronicola
Client	Diesel Kid, "Explorers of the Past and Future"

In this beautifully imagined film – a combination of live action and animation – Diesel Kids search for hidden treasure on a mysterious planet of snow and ice. Their journey combines vintage Arctic expeditions with Jules Verne's space adventures. After voyaging with mechanical balloons, sleighs pulled by unicorns and antiquated rockets, the kids use crystal keys to open a secret cavern. But they will not emerge intact!

Agency	Openhere, Antwerp
Creative Director	Stijn Gansemans
Copywriter	Sam De Vriendt
Art Director	Bart Gielen
Client	Microsoft, "Inspiration Anyone?"

In 2008 Microsoft produced a humorous viral about an advertiser, Brad, who'd been dumped by his consumer, Claire. This is the sequel. After a buzz-provoking trailer, the film was released online. At the office, Brad asks his CEO, Simon for help. The response is a "massive TV campaign" to "blitz through the soft tissue of all our consumers". Meanwhile, all Claire wants is some "interaction". If Brad gets to know her better, she'll introduce him to her friends. Finally, with the help of Jerry, his creative director, Brad realises that he's going to have to go online.

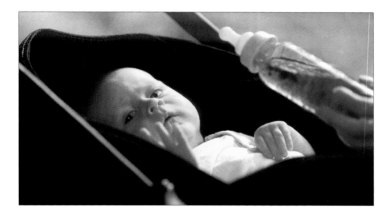

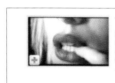

Online Films   **379**

Agency	Meteorite, London
Creative Director	Dan Douglass
Copywriter	Dan Douglass
Art Director	Gavin MacKinnon-Little
Digital Director	Marcus Hadfield, Harry Scotting
Producer	
Client	World Vision, "Would You?"

A mother lovingly watches her children playing in a paddling pool as she looks out of the kitchen window while doing the dishes. The water runs pure and clear. Suddenly, though, it takes on a distinctly muddy hue. Soon the contents of the pool, the spray from the sprinkler and even the water the mother puts in a baby's bottle are dirty and worm-ridden. Every day, 1.1 million people have to wash with and drink dirty water. World Vision can't live with that fact. Can you?

Agency	Saatchi & Saatchi, Frankfurt
Creative Directors	Anne Petri Mathias Henkel
Copywriter	Mathias Henkel
Art Director	Anna-Marina Pirsch
Director	Sven Stausberg
Client	Amnesty International, "The Trojan Girl"

The preview picture of a YouTube film often convinces users to click on it. But the still is not picked entirely at random – it always comes from the exact middle of the film. Amnesty International used this knowledge to sneak an image of a sexy blonde chick onto the YouTube menu. But in fact her pouting lips only appear for a couple of seconds in the middle of a serious speech by a member of Amnesty International, who just lifts the image into the frame at the appropriate moment.

Agency	Scholz & Friends, Berlin
Creative Directors	Oliver Handlos
	Wolf Schneider
	Matthias Spaetgens
Copywriter	Edgar Linscheid
Art Director	Sara Viera
Graphic Design	Kathrin Wetzel
Client	Amnesty International, "Crazy-Leaders"

It's those crazy leaders again! George Bush practises origami, Vladimir Putin makes balloon animals and Mahmoud Ahmadine-jad demonstrates speed knitting to an appreciative crowd. In real life, of course, these leaders are even nuttier than they appear here. Join Amnesty International to protest against their madness.

380   **Online Films**

Agency	Wieden+Kennedy, Amsterdam
Creative Directors	Mark Bernath
	Eric Quennoy
	Jorge Calleja
Copywriter	Gregg Clampffer
Art Director	Christiano Abrahao
Producers	Corey Bartha
	Olivier Klonhammer
Client	EA Sports, "The Street is Moving"

Gamers had criticised previous versions of the FIFA Street series for their lack of in-novative skills and tricks. To reverse this perception the agency invited gamers to experience the amazing new moves in FIFA Street 3 via a viral video. The film shows a group of kids combining acrobat-ics and soccer on the pitch, in the street, in car parks and finally on rooftops – which is when the cops show up to warn them to cut it out.

| Agency | Farfar, Stockholm |
| Client | Nokia N-Gage, "Get Out and Play" |

Mobile gaming should be fun and easy going. To convey that feeling the agency created a web campaign with stop motion versions of classic computer games. Video game themed home-made stop motion films are popular on YouTube. Unfortu-nately, they cannot be played - only watched. That is, until now. For the N-Gage brand re-launch the agency created the first stop motion film that is actually a game you can play. The game integrates seamlessly into a film story titled: "Get Out and Play".

Agency	Rainey Kelly Campbell Roalfe/Y&R, London	Former Monty Python Terry Jones narrates in this BBC "mockumentary" about the arctic. He introduces us to a colony of penguins with a special skill: they can fly. Sure enough, after a short, waddling run-up the penguins take majestically to the sky and migrate to the rainforests of South America. Missed something interesting on the BBC? Thanks to its new digital service, you needn't. Watch BBC shows from the past week, on your computer.
Creative Director	Mark Roalfe	
Copywriter	Paul Silburn	
Production	Red Bee Media, London	
Director	Vince Squibb	
Producer	Sarah Caddy	
Client	BBC iPlayer, "Penguins"	

Agency	JWT Spain, Barcelona	What would happen if two of the most thrilling filmmakers of all time, Alfred Hitchcock and Martin Scorsese, got together? That's exactly what Freixenet achieved to promote this sparkling wine. Scorsese explains that three pages of an unmade Hitchcock film have been found and that he proposes to shoot them. We then see the results: a mini thriller full of references to the master's works, including the music of Bernard Hermann. It's all about finding the key to a box containing a very special bottle of Reserva.
Creative Directors	Alex Martinez	
	Carles Puig	
	Rory Lambert	
Copywriter	Ted Griffin	
Production	RSA Films, New York	
Director	Martin Scorsese	
DOP	Harris Savides	
Editor	Thelma Schoonmaker	
Client	Freixenet	
	Carta Nevada Reserva, "The Key to Reserva"	

Agency	Ogilvy, Amsterdam	A squadron of bombers converges on Burma. Their bomb bays open and a million objects rain down. But these are not bombs – they are flowers, their petals opening as they spin gracefully to earth. This is the world's message to the people of Burma. They have endured 40 years of brutal tyranny and fought back with nothing but peaceful protests. Surely they deserve our support?
Creative Director	Carl Le Blond	
Copywriter	Carl Le Blond	
Art Director	Carl le Blond	
Production	Shilo, New York	
Director	André Stringer	
Producers	Tracy Chandler	
	Brenda Bentz	
	van den Berg	
Client	Noneofusarefree.org, "Support Burma"	

Agency	TBWA\Germany, Berlin		Martin Sulzbach
Creative Directors	Stefan Schmidt	**Illustrators/Flash**	Jue Zhang
	Dirk Henkelmann		Pinja Korhonen
	Philip Borchardt		Eduardo Maluf de Campos
Copywriters	Djamila Rabenstein	**Media Prod. Mgr**	Katrin Dettmann
	Frederick Kober	**Producers**	Johannes von Liebenstein
	Vesna Koselj		Johann-Georg Hofer
	Matthäus Frost		von Lobenstein
	Martin Sulzbach	**Digital Producer**	Patrick Vater
Art Directors	Djamila Rabenstein	**Project Managers**	Tanja Kurr
	Frederick Kober,		Julia Fiesselmann
	Ramona Stöcker	**Client**	Absolut Vodka,
	Matthäus Frost		"In an Absolut World"

In the real world, only Absolut vodka delivers perfection. But what would an Absolut world look like? The agency used every available medium to express its idea of paradise. Banner ads and catalogues given away in bars promoted products like "the perfect handwriting pen" or "the sweet dreams pillow". Press ads and posters suggested that "one swallow makes a summer" and "all good things never come to an end". Poetic graffiti was scratched in perfect calligraphy on subway windows, and viral ads featured a washing machine that folds your shirts. A "spam" chain letter promised eternal happiness if users deleted it immediately. And even packaging became part of the campaign…in an Absolut world.

NO PAIN
A LOT OF GAIN

IN AN ABSOLUT WORLD

Von: ABSOLUT
Betreff: Chain mail
Datum: 16. September 2008 10:06:55 MESZ
An: Anne Doering

IF YOU FORWARD THIS MESSAGE TO 10 OF YOUR FRIENDS GREAT
MISFORTUNE WILL OVERTAKE YOU. IF YOU DELETE IT IMMEDIA-
TELY YOU WILL GAIN, LOVE, MONEY AND INFINITE WISDOM!!!!!
++++++++IN AN ABSOLUT WORLD___THE ABSOLUT VODKA++++++++
IF YOU FORWARD THIS MESSAGE TO 10 OF YOUR FRIENDS GREAT
MISFORTUNE WILL OVERTAKE YOU. IF YOU DELETE IT IMMEDIA-
TELY YOU WILL GAIN, LOVE, MONEY AND INFINITE WISDOM!!!!!
++++++++IN AN ABSOLUT WORLD___THE ABSOLUT VODKA++++++++
IF YOU FORWARD THIS MESSAGE TO 10 OF YOUR FRIENDS GREAT

AUSSEN HUI.
INNEN HUI.

IN AN ABSOLUT WORLD

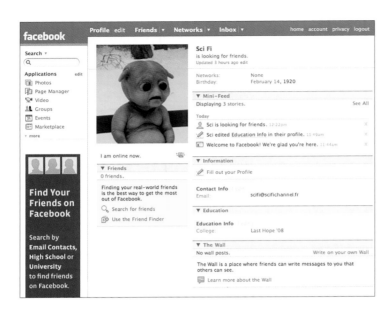

384 **Integrated Campaigns**

Agency	BETC Euro RSCG, Paris		
Creative Directors	Stéphane Xiberras Valérie Levy-Harrar		
Copywriters	Arnaud Assouline Guillaume Boulay		
Art Directors	Benjamin Le Breton Nicolas Casanova		
Director	Reynald Gresset		
Client	Sci-Fi Channel, "Adopt Sci-Fi"		

Sci-Fi Channel in France wanted to attract a wider audience beyond science fiction fans. In January 2008, through mock news reports and its website, it launched a competition challenging viewers to find 10 extraterrestrial kids abandoned all over France. As the little statuettes were recovered one by one, the media followed the story. Clues led to the whereabouts of the last missing child: a website showing a tear-jerking ad about an alien child left in a human orphanage. This was also on TV and in cinemas. An interactive online game supported the ads.

Agencies	Serviceplan, Hamburg Plan.Net, Hamburg
Chief CO	Alexander Schill
Creative Directors	Maik Kaehler Christoph Nann Axel Thomsen Friedrich von Zitzewitz Daniel Koennecke
Art Directors	Amelie Graalfs, Till Diestel Roman Becker Andreas Lexa
Client	Unicef, "ProAging"

In the west, anti-aging is a big thing. But in Africa, many kids don't get the chance to grow old. That's why Unicef adopted a policy of promoting "pro-aging" products. It packaged items like pure water, serum or mosquito nets as if they were expensive cosmetics. The strategy was expressed via viral ads, a website and press and poster work. There were interesting ambient media executions – such as branding soap dispensers in public toilets – and free samples of the "products" were placed in pharmacies.

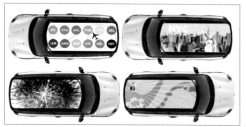

Agency	Farfar, Stockholm		The Swedish underwear brand placed its site in the hands of web wizards Farfar, with the result that they knocked it down and started from scratch. The new site is an irony-laden maze of entertainment. You can see Björn in slick 70s action and ask him a few questions. You can also meet the brand's wacky new management team, whose boss is a leggy blonde and whose distribution specialist drives a fork-lift in her underwear. And then you can discover the brand's missions: to provide love for all, send old underpants to "war mongers" and to harass the paparazzi.
Production	Colony, Stockholm		
Producer	Mats Sundin		
Client	Björn Borg Underwear		

Agency	Kreativekonzeption, Berlin		The ultimate small car, Mini embarked on a campaign under the slogan "Creative use of space". It kicked off with a 10-day music and cultural festival on the roof of a New York skyscraper. This drew attention to the online community Mini Space, where visitors could take part in creative projects. The website's background was a blank canvas that users filled with their own designs. These fed back into the campaign as posters, flyers, or designs for the roofs of promotional Minis. And of course the campaign was referenced on other social networking sites like Facebook and Flickr.
Creative Director	Alexander Diehl		
Copywriter	Fabian Blume		
Art Directors	Antonio Ferreira		
	Sascha Burk		
	Fabienne Meyer		
Client	Mini Cooper, "Creative Use of Space"		

WATCH YOUR OWN HEART ATTACK

SUNDAY AUG 10TH 9:17PM ITV1

The most important two minutes of TV you'll ever see

2minutes.org.uk

British Heart Foundation

386   **Integrated Campaigns**

Agency	Grey, London
Creative Directors	Jon Williams
Copywriter	Joanna Perry
Art Director	Damon Troth
Illustrators	Mark Cakebread
	Paul Reddington
Client	British Heart Foundation, "Watch Your Own Heart Attack"

Too many people die of heart attacks because they don't spot the early symptoms. The British Heart Foundation asked Grey London to warn people about those symptoms. The agency created a national event. Posters and print ads told everyone in Britain, "Watch your own heart attack, August 10, 9:17pm". The BHF also spread the message with TV and radio interviews and web commentary. Celebrities backed up the call and thousands of people signed up to receive reminders by SMS. Finally, 6.5 million people joined in to watch the TV ad on Britain's leading commercial channel.

Agency	Contrapunto, Madrid
Creative Directors	Antonio Montero
	Carlos Jorge
	Félix del Valle
Copywriter	Felix del Valle
Art Director	Carlos Jorge
Client	Amnesty International, "The Power of Your Voice"

Amnesty International never receives state funding – it relies entirely on its members. To attract new ones, it launched a micro-site as a hub for a multimedia campaign. A TV spot literally put words in the mouths of leaders with troubling human rights records. Print ads did the same thing, in the form of speech bubbles. Posters encouraged passersby to add their own comments to empty speech bubbles. A fake radio interview featured a woman whose voice could "stop bullets". And all this led to the site, where ordinary people verbally encouraged users to become members of Amnesty.

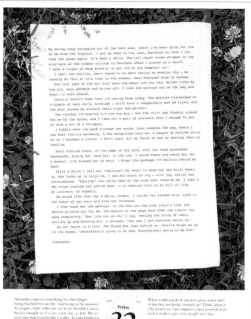

Join us in creating a new day.

Buy your seconds of the new day at cancerfonden.se

We will defeat cancer. Join us!

Cancerfonden
The Swedish Cancer Society

JCDecaux

LOUIS VUITTON

Agencies	WatersWidgren\TBWA, Stockholm
	Starring, Stockholm
Creative Director	Fredrik Lundgren
Copywriters	Johan Nilsson
	Mia Robertsson
	Alexander Stutterheim
Art Directors	Patrick Waters
	Jörgen Jörälv
Designer	Erika Hellström
Production Mgr	Sofia Widman
Client	Cancerfonden, "A New Day!"

Some of us take life for granted. That is certainly not the case for cancer sufferers. In order to raise money for the Swedish Cancer Society, an extra day was created: July 32. Print ads led to a website where visitors could buy a few seconds of the new day. They were also asked to describe what they would do with the extra time. Their names and notes were displayed on the site. At the end of the campaign, participants were asked to return and describe a "bonus day" of their summer. The results were life affirming.

Agency	Ogilvy & Mather, Paris
Creative Directors	Christian Reuilly
	Frederic Bonn
Copywriters	Edgard Montjean
	Rosecrans Baldwin
Art Director	Lang Teav
Photographers	Annie Leibovitz
	Andrew Durhan
Web Director	Frédéric Guelaff
Producer	Laure Bayle
Film Director	Bruno Aveillan
Client	Louis Vuitton, "Core Values"

As a maker of luxury luggage since the 19th century, Louis Vuitton has travel at the heart of its brand. The campaign expanded this into the idea of individual journeys. The print campaign shot by Annie Leibovitz features personalities whose lives have been remarkable journeys, including Keith Richards, Sir Sean Connery, Francis Ford Coppola and his daughter Sofia. A dedicated website allows them to share some of their favourite journeys through rich visual and audio experiences. Finally, a 90-second film restates travel as a process of self-discovery.

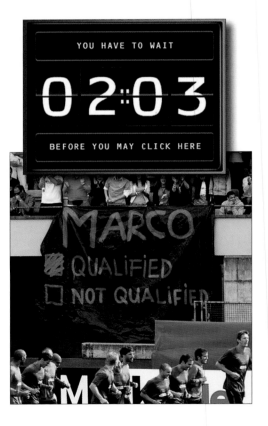

Agency	Forsman & Bodenfors, Gothenburg	**Agency**	Publicis, Amsterdam
Photographer	Erik Undéhn	**Creative Directors**	Marcel Hartog
Production	Perfect Fools, Stockholm		Jeroen van Zwam
	MFL, Stockholm		Massimo van der Plas
Director	Johan Skog		Joep de Kort
Producer	Lolo Uggla	**Producer**	Manon Langelaar
Client	AMF Pension, "MMS"	**Illustrators**	Bart ter Haar
			Janneke Koning
		Designers	Simone Keyzer
		Client	Royal Dutch Army, "Who Can Handle the Army?"

AMF Pension wanted to make the idea of a pension important for younger people by encouraging them to think about the future. Via mobile phone or internet, participants could send photos of themselves to a website, where they would be "aged" so they could see what they would look like at 70. The campaign embraced films, billboards, internet banners and the website. During one month 322,946 photos were submitted. The goal had been 50,000.

The Dutch Army did not just want recruits – it wanted the right recruits! So it ran a campaign around the idea of "qualified or not qualified". TV ads set the tone: a feeble kid who can't open a jar of mayonnaise – not qualified. A kid who defiantly uses a pedestrian crossing even though a white van is speeding illegally towards it – qualified. The campaign was extended to a website and even bus shelters (waiting in the rain outside the shelter? – qualified). The phrase found its way into popular culture, appearing on T-shirts and quoted by TV shows – and even by other ads.

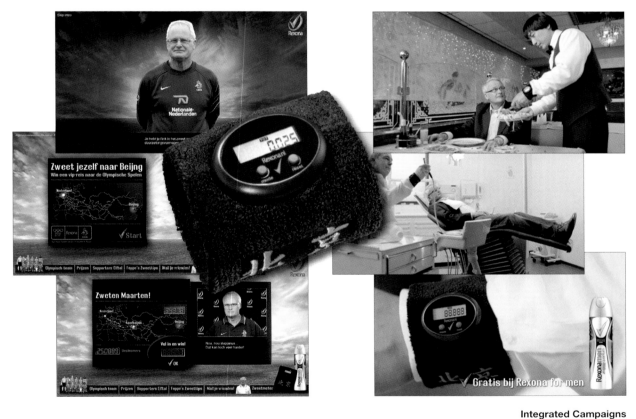

Agency	Dubois Meets Fugger, Antwerp		**Agency**	Lemz, Amsterdam
Creative Director	Peter Foubert		**Creative Director**	Peter de Lange
Copywriters	Bart Uytdenhouwen		**Copywriter**	Mark van der Werff
	Öznur Karaca		**Art Director**	Fleur Westerbeek
	Nuran Karaca		**Production**	Us Media, Amsterdam
Art Director	Caroline Vermaerken		**Director**	Jeroen Annokkeé
Account Manager	Stephanie Adriaansen			(Czar)
Client	European		**Client**	Rexona for Men,
	Social Foundation,			"Road to Beijing"
	"180"			

In Flanders, one out of 50 people are long-term unemployed. Many of them are women. The brief was to reach and empower them. First, the agency created a self-help book. But how to promote it? Instead of running ads, the agency wrote a genuinely gripping TV series in ten episodes. It features "Gina", a desperate housewife who finds salvation through the book. At the end of each dramatic episode, viewers find out that they can get the book from the local council. The series was supported by TV trailers and a multimedia campaign, including a site.

Rexona is an excellent antiperspirant – but how much do men really sweat any more? They spend all day sitting at computers. So to celebrate the Beijing Olympic Games, Rexona created the "Sweat-o-meter", a wristband that measures your movements and thus your perspiration potential. The agency, in partnership with the Dutch Olympic Football team, promoted its invention with TV ads and through the press. Wearers who "sweated" the most won a VIP trip to Beijing.

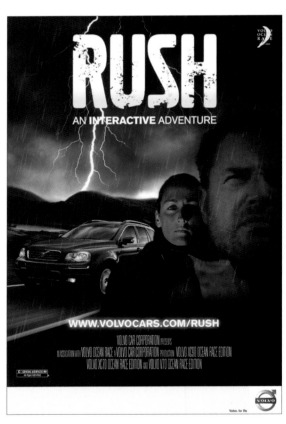

Agency	Change Integrated, Warsaw	The brief was to launch a new hangover remedy on the Polish market. The agency decided that Spectab had originally been a "secret" cure created by a KGB scientist named Colonel Onovalov. His biography was planted on credible sites online – such as Wikipedia – free of charge. Viral ads of Onolov's "experiments" were placed on YouTube. Better still, a fake statue of Onolov was erected in the city's main square, generating huge media buzz. A website now keeps the legend alive.
Creative Directors	Jakub Korolczuk Ryszard Sroka Rafal Gorski	
Copywriter	Franciszek Toeplitz	
Art Director	Adam Szczepocki	
Designer	Adam Szczepocki	
Client	Spectab, "Onovalov's Statue"	

Agencies	Euro RSCG 4D, Amsterdam Arnold, Boston Nitro, London	The challenge was to establish a connection between boats and cars to promote Volvo's sponsorship of the Ocean Race event. The key was a lifeboat rescue crew. On the Volvo Cars website the visitor meets four members of the crew racing to reach the lifeboat. The user needs to help them out. The campaign for this interactive adventure included a movie-like trailer. Dealerships were provided with poster material and a stand-alone DVD version of the adventure. This same story was consistently told in other media such as TV, POS and print.
Executive CD	Paul Shearer	
Creative Directors	Bram de Rooij Martijn Sengers	
Copywriter	Bram de Rooij	
Art Director	Martijn Sengers	
Designer	Antonio Costa	
Client	Volvo Cars, "Rush - an Interactive Adventure"	

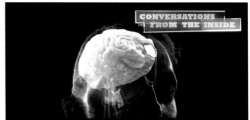

Agency	Wieden+Kennedy, Amsterdam	In order to convince young European women to embrace sport, Nike created a limited edition coffee table book containing 22 illustrated stories of sporting achievement. The collection was developed into art exhibitions across Europe. Five of the stories became animated films on the web. Along with banners, these drove women to nikewomen.com. Here they would find sports clothing, training regimes, and digital versions of the remaining stories. Social networking sites were also used.
Executive CDs	John Norman Jeff Kling	
Creative Directors	Eric Quennoy Mark Bernath	
Copywriter	Betsy Decker	
Art Directors	Anders Stake Craig Williams, Ayse Altinok	
Producers	Corey Bartha Cat Reynolds	
Client	Nike Women	

Agency	Wieden+Kennedy, Amsterdam	Videogame maker EA Sports wanted to stage the biggest, most exciting football videogame event ever. It did this by bringing real footballers, regular sports gamers and fans together to play a soccer video game – live in a stadium. Pre-launch banners and emails directed people to the FIFA 09 website, where short films featured real fans predicting the result of the matches. At launch, four-minute films of the matches premiered on the site, with shorter versions for TV. Print and outdoor ads showcased the energy and excitement of the events.
Executive CDs	John Norman Jeff Kling	
Creative Directors	Edu Pou Joakim Borgstrom	
Copywriter	Carlo Cavallone	
Art Director	Alvaro Sotomayor	
Producers	Corey Bartha Neil Henry Kimia Farshizad Jamie Kim	
Client	EA Sports, "FIFA 09"	

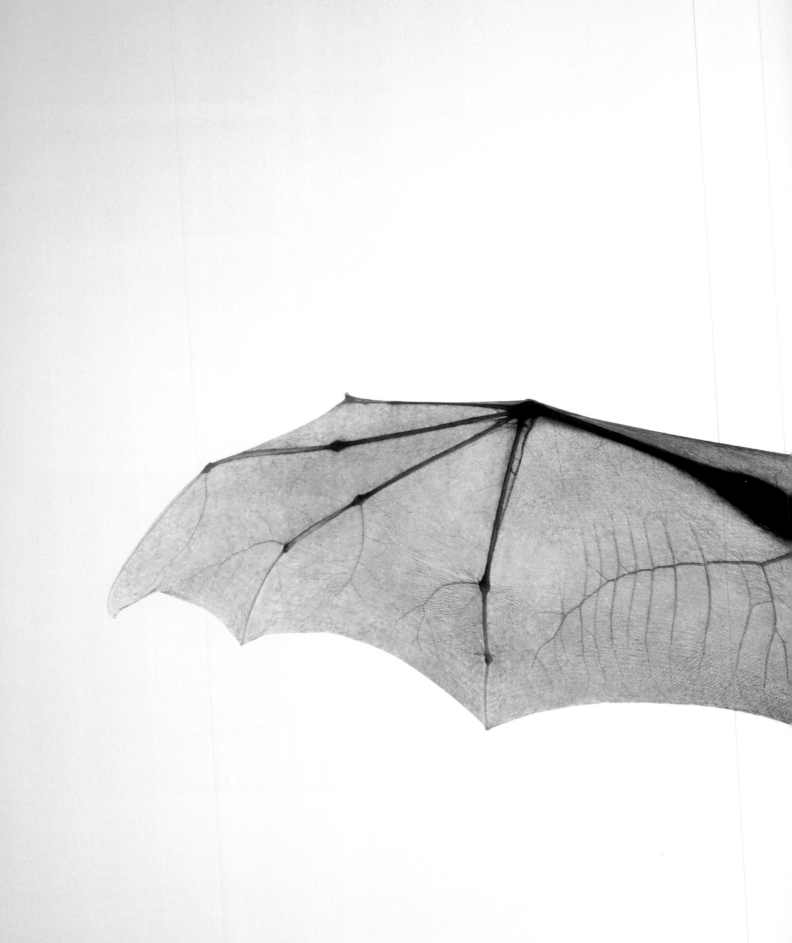

ABBOTT MEAD VICKERS BBDO, London 30, 48, 61, 250, 271, 307, 331, 367
ABBY NORM, Stockholm 343
ABD EL-SALAM Kai 310, 322
ABRAHAO Christiano 380
ABSOLUT VODKA 46, 50, 52, 282, 359, 366, 369, 382
ABSTRACT GROOVE, Milan 378
ABSUDOVA Lilia 165
ABU GHAZELEH Rami 282
ACADEMY FILMS, London 134
ACÇÃO ANIMAL 116
ACE 153
ACERES Cedric 363
ACHARD Virginie 322
ACHTERBERG Jaikko 297
ACIKTAN Ozan 244
ACKERUP Andreas 70
ACKROYD Heather 304
ACNE DIGITAL, Stockholm 365
ACNE FILM, Stockholm 365
ACTION GROUP FOR WORLD SOLIDARITY 124
ADAM & EVE, London 288
ADAM Thomas 311
ADAMSKY, Stockholm 70
ADAMSSON Anna 32
ADELFIO Marco 274
ADENA 312
ADIDAS 311, 318, 328, 343
ADMCOM, Bologna 291
ADNER Josephine 266
ADRIAANSEN Stephanie 389
ADRIS GROUP 348
ADVICO YOUNG & RUBICAM, Zurich 133, 233, 235
AEGEAN AIRLINES 74
AEMMER Juerg 308
AERTS Peter 63, 205, 221, 222
A-FILM, Tallinn 253
AGAINST ALL ODDS, Sausalito 54
AGIANOGLOU Despoina 41
AGLAVE Milind 37
AGOSTO, Barcelona 209
AGUILAR Pedro 103
AHLENIUS Anton 317
ÅHLÉNS 90, 91
AHLGREN Hans 29
AHLGREN Karin 290
AIDES 113
AIG INSURANCE 281
AIR FRANCE 77
AIYAR Kartik 157
AKAMA STUDIO 34
AKBANK JAZZ FESTIVAL 244
AKBAS Yasar 83
ÅKERSTEDT Magnus 100
ÅKERSTEN TRIUMF Malin 129
AKESSON Samuel 134
ÅKESTAM Göran 316
ÅKESTAM HOLST, Stockholm 87, 175, 285, 287, 316, 331, 368
AKIN Asligul 139
AKITA FILM, Milan 233
AKOGLU ERGULEN Idil 83
ALAIN WILDLIFE PARK 254
AL ARABIYA 233
ALBERS Hans 67
ALBERT Damien 97
ALBERT Thierry 97, 183
ALEKSEEVA Tatyana 165
ALENDAHL Peter 125
ALEXANDER Jo 289
ALFRED KRIESLER 283
ALI Ali 140, 264, 271
ALLAN GRAY INVESTMENTS 98
ALLEGRINI Muriel 64, 69
ALLISON John 49
ALLWARDT Benjamin 268
ALM Niklas 129
ALMAGUER Patrick 54, 375
ALMEIDA Gonçalo 131
ALMQUIST Henric 70, 155, 369
ALPHABETICAL ORDER, Stockholm 365
ALTINOK Ayse 391
ALTINOK Sezay 184
ALTMANN Olivier 51, 64, 69, 72, 119, 150, 151, 183, 186
ÁLVAREZ Javier 242
ALVES Rui 330
ALZEN-SANMARTIN Marjorieth 67
AM I COLLECTIVE 249, 337
AMAMi 349
AMENTA Aspasia 210
AMF PENSION 99, 100, 388
AMICHAY Gideon 27, 72, 93, 299
AMMANATH Manoj 31, 240
AMMERLAND DAIRIES 43
AMNESTY INTERNATIONAL 108, 109, 127, 129, 130, 131, 310, 376, 377, 379, 380, 386
AMP COMMUNICATIONS, London 288
AN Adrian 185
ANAHORY Diogo 108, 112, 131
ANDERSSON David 366
ANDERSSON Finn 174
ANDERSSON Magnus 251
ANDERSSON Mimmi 76, 279
ANDRÉ Philippe 69
ANÉER Lars 234
ANNEX FILMS, London 364
ANNOKKEÉ Jeroen 389
ANR BBDO SWEDEN, Gothenburg & Stockholm 285
ANSPACH Mario 225
ANTHONY'S MINI GARAGE 355
ANTÓN Rafa 242
ANTONELL Kajsa 343
ANTTILA Sami 259, 266

ANWEILER Dominik 367
APERS Olivier 292
APOLLINARIS 60
APOLLO 176
ARABI Souheil 60
ARAMIS Frederico 207
ARCTIC CIRCLE, Cape Town 338
ARDAGH Richard 358
ARDELIUS Mark 87, 285, 331
ARIEL 157
ARMANDO TESTA, Turin 63, 329
ARMBRUSTER Einar 340
ARNDT Kerstin 208
ARNOLD Martin 377
ARNOLD, Boston 390
AROMA COFFEE 60
ART DIRECTORS CLUB GERMANY 348
ARTAMONOVA Daria 136
ARTHUR Aaron 60
ARTOIS 47
ARVE Viktor 88, 89, 296
ASCHER Clemens 82
ASCHHEIM Yoram 27, 93
ASHKOL Daniel 293
ASHLEY Michael 101
ASICS SHOES 196
ASKIM Thomas 66
ASPIRIN CARDIO 174
ASPIRIN EFFECT 179
ASSOR Denis 51
ASSOULINE Arnaud 232, 237, 384
ASTORGA Alberto 209
ASTORGUE Eric 212
ÅSTRÖM Jacob 369
ASVESTA Eleni 247
ATAK 315
ATAMAN FIRAT Ebru 244
AUDI 209, 332
AUMILLER Fabian 369
AURELIA INTERIORISTA 336
AUTERI Lilli 49
AUZANNET Cedric 90
AVDEEVA Arina 26
AVEILLAN Bruno 387
AVI STUDIO, Bratislava 101
AXE 315
AXELL Ylva 68
AYKURT Daniel 178, 328
AZEMARD Francis 78
AZMY George 264
BAARZ Danny 93, 154
BABINET Rémi 212
BABU Sukesh 305
BACCELLI Cristina 33
BACH Claudia 208
BÄCKMAN Jonas 370
BACON, Copenhagen 49, 58, 68, 209
BAD COMPANY 375
BAD SODEN RIDING SCHOOL 255
BADIA Jaume 209
BAETTIG Johan 316
BAGNOLI Riccardo 39, 189
BAHAR Shirley 299
BAIKER Ralph 146
BAJER Eva 290
BAKER Dean 101
BAKER Gilbert 359
BAKERKIN Ilya 166, 260
BAKERY FILMS, Hamburg 208
BALABONIN Sergei 136
BALALÓ 156
BALAN Yuriy 333
BALDWIN Rosecrans 363, 387
BALKAN CAPITAL MANAGEMENT 104
BALLANCE Feargal 200
BALLESTER Alphée 56
BALTHUS WINE 356
BAR Guy 31, 156
BARADOY Nikolai 67
BARBERO Joaquín 179
BARBIER Patrick 64
BARCELO Didier 69
BÁRCENA Julio 137
BARHAINSKI Andreas 290
BARILLA 29
BARLUET Bill 184
BARNES James 304
BARNES Nicky 132
BARREIRO Santiago 375
BARRET Christian 168
BARRY Ted 52
BARTELS Ingmar 367
BARTHA Corey 380, 391
BARTLEY Laurie 190
BAR-YOCHAI Eran 31
BASCHINSKI Patrick 301
BATES PANGULF, Dubai 254
BATTAGLIA Roberto 184, 186, 189, 233
BAUR Georg 239
BAUTZER Phil 205
BAVARIA BEER 44
BAVARIAN MINISTRY OF SOCIAL AFFAIRS 110
BAYER 157
BAYLE Laure 387
BAZ Yasmina 295
BAZARKAYA Toygar 39, 59, 171, 178, 179, 180, 181, 201, 211, 280, 288, 313, 328
BAZING Jan 39
BBC 232, 381
BBDO GERMANY, Stuttgart 239
BBDO, Düsseldorf 39, 59, 171, 178, 179, 180, 181, 201, 210, 211, 280, 288, 313, 328
BBH, London 184
BDDP & FILS, Paris 125, 129

BEARDEN Keith 144
BEATE UHSE 231
BEATO Luca 186, 189
BEAUMONT Phil 55
BEAUREGARD Xavier 34
BECK Ahmad 60
BECK Maren 43
BECK Tyrone 338
BECKER Roman 345, 384
BECZKOWSKI Ivan 370
BEDERNA Laszlo 69
BEDESCHI FILM, Milan 22
BEERLING Dennis 276
BEETROOT, Thessaloniki 339, 340, 354
BEGO 275
BEHAEGHEL Vincent 123
BEHNAM Reza 119
BEHNKE Katja 375
BEIMDIECK Maik 130
BEKKEBRÅTEN Espen 365
BELANDER Hanna 70, 155, 248, 369
BELL Nick 37
BELLINI Sofia 317
BELLON Damien 183
BELTRAMI Carla 233
BEN DOR Ido 45, 47
BENGTSSON Bisse 90
BENSON Jonathan 167, 305
BENT Gordan 205
BENTZ Oliver 372
BENTZ VAN DEN BERG Brenda 381
BERDEROW Jürgen 332
BERENDS Joost 300
BERGENDAHL Peter 285
BERGENGREN Ola 78
BERGER Lisa 310
BERGMAN Daniel 56
BERLANDER Elisabeth 76, 279
BERLIN PHILHARMONIC ORCHESTRA 369
BERLITZ 269
BERNATH Mark 182, 184, 375, 380, 391
BERNDL Ludwig 219, 338
BERTELL Emil 344
BERTELLI Bruno 49
BERTH Tom 63, 221, 222
BERTHAT Jocelyn 123
BERTHER Daniela 86
BETC EURO RSCG, Paris 212, 232, 236, 237, 292, 370, 384
BETHKE Wiebke 215
BETTI Alessandro 48
BEZERRA Marco 311
BIANCO 198
BIC 196
BIEBACH Wolfgang 86
BIENFUSS Helmut 288
BIG FISH FILMPRODUKTION, Berlin 102
BIJL Jeroen 62
BILBAY Tugbay 153
BINDER Thorsten 364
BINEFA Alfredo 209
BINYILDIZ Ergin 153
BIRKNER Florian 133
BITDEFENDER 273
BITNAR Natalie 86
BIVV 121
BJÖRK Hanna 175, 316, 368
BJORN BORG 385
BLACK & DECKER 258
BLACKBELTMONKEY, Hamburg 372
BLAHO Radim 101
BLANKENHORN Nicolas 154
BLIDHOLM SVENSSON Carin 356
BLIDHOLM VAGNEMARK DESIGN, Stockholm 356
BLINK BRUT 354
BLOMKVIST Mitte 155
BLOODBUSTER 245
BLUME Fabian 385
BLUNIER Charles 169, 308
BMW 227
BOASE Hannah 86
BOBER Thomas 290, 364
BOBST Christian 233, 235
BOCAGE 196, 330
BOCCASSINI Cristiana 49
BOCK Carl 370
BOCKHOLT Nikolai 372
BODIN Frank 169, 246, 302, 308
BODINI Davide 173
BOECKLER Claudia 306, 307
BOEDEKER Daniel 262, 302
BOISSINOT Julien 52
BOLDSEN Thomas 138, 253
BOLGER Briana 128
BOLLAND Philip 219
BOLLEURS Hans 377
BOMTEMPO José 108, 112, 131
BONAVIA Fulvio 215
BOND Fredrik 46, 164, 166
BOND Mike 48
BONKERS, Amsterdam 44
BONN Frederic 363, 387
BONSE Damian 98
BONVINI Ada 49
BOO PRODUCTIONS, Athens 74
BORCHARDT Philip 46, 282
BORGSTROM Joakim 375, 391
BORIS BECKER & CO 247
BÖRJESSON Linda 357
BORKER Lars 197
BORN Monica 175, 287
BOSCH 143

BOSCHMAN Laurens 270
BOSE 139
BOSMA Arno 103, 267
BOTAN Adrian 62
BOUADJERA Sophian 225
BOUCHERON Philippe 330
BOUCHET Jean-François 334
BOUGOURD Simon 174
BOUIC Kaj 366
BOULAY Guillaume 384
BOUYGUES TELECOM 66
BOVILL Chris 49
BOWEN Don 294
BOWERS Dave 275
BOYERO Dani 56
BPG, Kuwait City 60
BRAAM Sanne 286, 297
BRADLEY Yvette 288
BRAGA Emerson 112, 131
BRAINWAVES, Munich 110
BRANDCOM MIDDLE EAST, Dubai 31, 240
BRANDT 144
B-RAPPU, Helsinki 248
BRATKOV Boris 104
BRAUN 178, 181, 328
BRAZIER Paul 30, 48, 61, 250, 271, 307, 331
BREDENBERG Aslak 174
B-REEL 369
BREGEAULT Benjamin 249, 337
BREIT Holger 303
BREPOHL Michael 347
BREUER Kerstin 154
BRIKSIN Vadim 358
BRIM Richard 123, 323
BRINK Matthew 330
BRIOUL Thierry 368
BRITISH HEART FOUNDATION 110, 386
BRÖNNIMANN Peter 321
BROSCHEIT Felix 361
BROVELLI Fabrice 212, 292
BROWN Ross 192
BROWNINGHILL Adam 265
BRÜCK Nestori 329
BRÜDER GRIMM-GESELLSCHAFT 351
BRUECKNER Mathias 82
BRUHNS Konstanze 171
BRUKETA & ZINIC, Zagreb 348, 360
BRUKETA Davor 348, 360
BRUSH Neil 174
BRYAN Rupert 305
BRYDE Petter 247
BRYLCREEM 166
BÜCHELER Julia 303
BUCHTA Anke 375
BUCK Peter 294
BUDGEN Frank 132
BUDUKEVIČIŪTĖ Asta 295
BUDWEISER 49
BUEHLER Isabelle 246, 302
BUISSET Nicolas 142
BUJUPI Bes 318
BULL Matthew 330
BULTHUIS Dieuwer 293
BUNGALOW25, Madrid 320
BURCHELL Rafe-Jon 48
BURGER KING 25
BURIEZ Thierry 161
BURK Sascha 385
BURKE Cordell 358
BURLEY Jon 123, 289, 304, 319, 323
BURMEISTER Nina 208
BURTON Tim 199
BUSCH Alexander 180
BUSTAN EGGS 31
BUTTER Tiina 174
BÜYÜKDOGANAY Tolga 33
BYRNE Noel 46
CABRAL Izabella 207
CABRAL Juan 132, 134, 251, 319
CACIOLI Leandro 211
CADBURY'S DAIRY MILK 371
CADDY Sarah 232, 381
CAFE NOIR 58
CAHILL Patrick 102, 202, 312
CAKEBREAD Mark 386
CALADO Nuno 108
CALDAS Gustavo 103
CALDAS NAYA, Barcelona 103
CALLEGARI BERVILLE GREY, Paris 39, 90, 159
CALLEJA Jorge 380
CALLINGAARD Fredrik 69
CAMBRIDGE CENTER 263
CAMENSULI Olivier 64, 69, 150, 186
CAMP DAVID, Stockholm 32, 111
CAMPBELL Sally 134
CAMPBELL-SALMON Zeno 202
CAMPORA Stefano 215, 245
CANAL+ 232
CANCERFONDEN 387
CANON 134, 138
CAPANESCU Razvan 273
CAPORN Olly 217
CAPPARONI Ascanio 22
CAREY Darragh 248
CARIBONI Tomaso 184
CARLIN Kristoffer 66, 67
CARLSBERG 49, 58, 305
CARLSSON Niclas 80, 81
CARLSTRÖM Fredrik 369
CAROLAN Onagh 48
CARP Klaudia 155
CARPARK 77
CARPENTER Wendy 58
CARPENTIER Louis 117, 349

CARTA NEVADA RESERVA 381
CASAMAYOU Jean-François 368
CASANOVA Isidro 76
CASANOVA Nicolas 384
CASINI Alessia 22
CASTELLANO Pablo 211
CASUELA Manuel 306
CATANA Nadja 289
CATHOLIC CHURCH 298, 303
CATSKY Claude 169, 308
CATTLEMASTER 259
CAVALLONE Carlo 391
CAVIAR, Brussels 102, 300
CAYENNE, Vienna 298
CECCHI Andrea 22
CEDERBERG Mia 155
CENTRAAL BEHEER INSURANCE 101, 293
CERKEZ Robert 58
CEVRA Ivana 374
CFP EUROPE 270
CHALDECOTT Axel 101, 304
CHALKLEY Yvonne 307
CHAMBERS Richard 164, 202
CHAMDIN Amir 362
CHAMDIN/STOHR, Stockholm 362
CHAMIZO Mariluz 136
CHAN Albert S. 124
CHANDLER Tracy 381
CHANEY Richard 248
CHANGE INTEGRATED, Warsaw 390
CHAPI 220
CHARHON Sylvie 199
CHARLESWORTH Jo 49, 134
CHARLESWORTH Tim 164
CHAUVIN Nicolas 190
CHÁVARRI Jaime 312
CHEIL COMMUNICATIONS GERMANY, Schwalbach
    Im Taunus 53, 255
CHEIL RUSSIA, Moscow 136
CHEN Bey-Bey 247
CHERNYKH Konstantin 333
CHESNE Julien 220
CHEUNG Stanley 167, 305
CHI CHI POTTER GALLERY 341
CHIFFLOT Guillaume-Ulrich 125, 129
CHILDLINE 342
CHIMBUROV Ivan 166, 260
CHINAGLIA Vichie 378
CHIUMINO Thierry 57
CHMEL Jozef 101
CHMIL Lessly 90
CHOICES CLINIC 121
CHRYSLER JEEP 208, 214, 215
CHUBB Candice 49
CHUDINSKIY Kirill 338
CIGNONI Giorgio 189, 233
CINTI Maurizio 291
CIORITA Ela 62
CITROËN 217
CITY OF HOPE 282
CLAMPFFER Gregg 380
CLAPIER Christophe 370
CLARK Neil 252
CLARK Steven 109
CLAUDIUS Wolfram Marius 333
CLAVERIE Faustin 144, 229
CLEARBLUE 174
CLÉMENT Bruno 161
CLIFTON Toby 305
CLINET Baptiste 56
CLM BBDO, Paris 225, 241
CLORMANN Lorenz 105
COBBLESTONE FILMPRODUKTION, Hamburg 247
COCA-COLA 54, 58, 88, 353, 371
COCOE 376
COFFEECOMPANY 313
COFFRE Christophe 220
COJOCARU Daniel 118
COLIN Emmanuel 145
COLLIENNE Gregor 221
COLLINS Paul 175, 368
COLLSTRUP Claus 53, 70, 253
COLONNESE Pablo 56, 76
COLONY, Stockholm 108, 370, 385
COMRAD, Amsterdam 231
COMUNICACIÓN ALDRICH, Pamplona 356
COMVIQ 68
CONDÉ NAST 229
CONESA Eva 77, 175, 226
CONNOLLY Brian 342
CONROY Isobel 194
CONSEJERIA DE MEDIO AMBIENTE DE MURIA 349
CONTO BARRIERS 122
CONTRAPUNTO, Madrid 131, 210, 211, 312, 376,
    386
COOP BANK 105
COPIC Svetlana 263
CORBIS 206, 272
CORDING Torben 364
CORNARA Guido 173, 177
CORNELISSEN Martin 101, 293
CORPS Daryl 126
CORREMANS Wim 28
CORY Ran 93
COSA, Paris 292
COSGROVE Adrian 205
COSMOFON 67
COSTA Antonio 364, 390
COSTAIN Malcolm 328
COURADJUT Olivier 236
COURTEMANCHE Olivier 34, 368
COVO Asaf 72
CPT COUVERT 263

CRAFT HELMETS 226
CRAIGEN Jeremy 23, 94, 95, 96, 97, 200, 202
CRAMER Julia 196
CRASTE Marc 48
CREACON 365
CREAM, Athens 112
CRESPO Felipe 77, 175, 226
CRÉATIVE SYNDICATE 51
CRETASTUDIO, Murcia 336, 349
CROSBIE Julie 58
CUBELLS Elena 77
CUENCA David 171
CULLEN Jonathon 48
CULLEN Vicky 202
CULLINAN Tom 256
CZAR 389
D'ADDA, LORENZINI, VIGORELLI, BBDO, Milan 259
DAFF Alex 249, 337
DAGIEL Wojtek 243
DAGLI Ilker 83
DAGNELL Erik 309
DAGO, Moscow 166
DAHAN Olivier 109
DAHLBERG Fredrik 234
DAHLQVIST Andreas 88, 89, 296
DALDRY Graham 172, 174
DALENIUS Anders 108
DALIN Carl 32
DALLAS, Stockholm 368
DALL'OLIO Manuel 291
DAMLE Kedar 37, 282
DAMPKRING COFFEE HOUSE 62
DAN Adela 62
DANIELS James 163
DANILOFF Dimitri 123, 176
DANISH PARKINSON'S DISEASE ASSOCIATION 321
DANK 148
DAOU Mazen 60
DARFEUILLE Martin 241
DARKOFILMS, Munich 110
DARMON MILANO 186
DAUBENBUECHEL Markus 333
DAUBERT Hélène 69
DAUL Christian 325
DAUM Jens 170
DAVIDSSON Victor 111
DAWSON Neil 164
DAYIOS Aris 74
DDB GERMANY, Berlin 149, 171, 199, 204, 207, 219,
    222, 290, 301, 310, 320, 322, 338
DDB GERMANY, Düsseldorf 149, 162, 168, 204, 223,
    226, 230, 269, 324
DDB GERMANY, Hamburg 67, 364, 375, 376
DDB WORLDWIDE 290
DDB&CO., Istanbul 114, 148
DDB, Amsterdam 101, 203, 286, 293, 297
DDB, Barcelona 36, 202, 209
DDB, Brussels 63, 205, 221, 222
DDB, Budapest 127
DDB, Johannesburg 144
DDB, London 23, 94, 95, 96, 97, 164, 200, 202, 218
DDB, Milan 156, 221, 371
DDB, Paris 66, 144, 224, 229, 342
DDB, Stockholm 88, 89, 296
DDB, Warsaw 29
DE BACKER Dylan 203
DE BOISMENU Geoffroy 72
DE DIOS Iván 312
DE FRANCE Fernando 136
DE GERMON Ghislaine 83, 88
DE KORT Joep 388
DE LANGE Peter 389
DE LAUW Michel 113, 267
DE LIGT Francis 232
DE MAUPEOU Anne 190, 234
DE MONTFERRAND Pauline 56, 191
De Ranadip 281
DE ROCKER Geert 63, 221, 222
DE ROOIJ Bram 364, 390
DE SMET Raf 365
DE VALCK Sebastien 102, 291
DE VILLIERS Francois 48, 94
DE VILLOUTREYS Ghislain 34, 368
DE VOLDER Sam 365
DE VOLKSKRANT 231
DE VOS Isabelle 205
DE VRIENDT Sam 379
DE WIT Niels 101, 286, 297
DEACON Philip 304
DEBOEY Yves-Eric 151
DECAIX Patrick 306
DECEUSTER Philippe 300
DECKER Betsy 182, 391
DEGRYSE Mathieu 151
DEKETELAERE Gilles 365
DEL FRAILE Eduardo 336, 349
DEL GOBBO Luissandro 39, 159
DEL VALLE Félix 131, 210, 376, 386
DELARUE Christelle 366
DELEIER Kurt 102
DELI PICTURES, Hamburg 208
DELSAUX Cédric 79, 236
DEMIDOVA Natalia 136
DEMNER, MERLICEK & BERGMANN, Vienna 33,
    84, 361
DEMUYNCK Koen 266
DENNEY Richard 96, 218
DEPARTMENT FOR TRANSPORT 123
DEPOT WPF, Moscow 358
DERDIYOK Sebahat 321
DERRON & KUHN 133
DESOWSKI Michal 29
DESTOOP Valentijn 365

DETTMANN Katrin 382
DETTWEILER Sascha 333
DEUTSCHE BAHN 76
DEUTSCHE POST 71
DEUTSCHMANN Rainer 364
DEVK INSURANCE 102
DHKD 114
DHL 267
D'HONT Caroline 178
DIADERMINE 171
DIAZ Pierrette 342
DIE TIERFREUNDE 118
DIEHL Alexander 385
DIESEL 190, 378
DIESTEL Till 317, 384
DÍEZ MUNTANE Luis 179
DIMETTO Thomas 234
DIMITROV Filip 67
DIMITROV Martin 104
DINAMO REKLAMEBYRÅ, Oslo 25
DISNEYLAND PARIS 370
DIVER Mike 103
DIXON Vincent 119
DJENDER Wacyl 234
DJUICE 66
DJUREK Nikola 360
DODD Spencer 101, 111
DODONI ICE CREAM 41
DOERING Christian 333
DOHNAL Bohumil 246
DOLORMIN 180
DOM & NIC 49
DOMEN Dirk 102, 284, 291
DOMENET Paul 342
DOMESTOS 330
DON 255
DONG Allen 157
DORIZZA Enrico 22, 174, 327
DOS SANTOS Kalle 283, 317, 344
DOSHIRAK NOODLES 26
DOUGLASS Dan 379
DOULEURS SANS FRONTIERES 109, 127
DOWNING Michael 212
DRAFTFCB DEUTSCHLAND, Hamburg 225
DRAFTFCB KOBZA, Vienna 114, 283
DRAFTFCB, Cape Town 48
DRAFTFCB, Stockholm 108
DRAKALSKI Dusan 67
DRAN 337
DRANE Suki 110
DREAMFIELD 371
DREIER Till 106
DRESDEN FIRE BRIGADE 325
DRESSLER Jan 154
DRIESANG Sascha 67
DRIESEN Tim 300
DROT Lina 368
DROUOT Cyril 176
DRU Christophe 75
DRUST Martin 376
DSCR 123
DÜBER Susanne 93, 154
DUBOIS Fabrice 69, 151
DUBOIS MEETS FUGGER, Antwerp 389
DUBRUQUE Joseph 56
DUCHNIEWSKA Zuza 29
DUCKWORTH Bruce 353, 357
DUERUEMOGLU Mert 179
DUMAS Patrice 224
DUMITRESCU Alexandru 62
DUPIN Pierre-Antoine 117
DUPONT Nathalie 232
DURACELL 179
DURAND Emmanuelle 56
DUREX 179
DURHAN Andrew 387
DUTCH HEART FOUNDATION 377
DUVAL Fabien 125
DUVAL GUILLAUME, Antwerp 102, 284, 291
DVORECKY Juraj 246
DYE Kirsty 218
DYHRING Malene 209
DZENDROVSKII Taras 66
EA SPORTS 380, 391
EALES Peter-John 256
EBAY 292
EBENWALDNER Marc 146
EBERBACH Kerstin 301
ECKSTEIN Axel 246, 302
ECO-SYSTÉMES 117
EDIK 337
EGÜZKIZA Andoni 356
EICHLER Stephan 171
EICHMANN Frederike 375
EICHNER Kay 82
EIGNER Wolfgang 69
EISENWAGEN Andreas 69
EKBERG Pär M 100
EKELUND Sofia 155
EKSTRÖM Pontus 90, 91
EKTA 249, 337
EL KHATIB 281
EL SHERIF Magd 228
ELBERSEN Bob 364
ELERS Alexander 90, 91, 169
ELFENBEIN Nadine 43
ELFERS Christine 275
ELKAIM Matthieu 342
ELKJAER Anna-Marie 321
ELLERT Caroline 278
ELLES Julia 187, 207
ELMASOGLU Adnan 244
ELSTERMANN Rainer 170
ELUNG-JENSEN Mikkel 53, 70

ELY Adrian 165
EMTINGER Micke 366
EN VOUGE 169
ENCHEV Vasil 104
ENDRESEN Ole 40
ENERGIZER 144
ENEROTH Jan 76, 279
ENGBERG Therese 111
ENGLER Håkan 91, 283, 317, 344
ENGLUND Andreas 108
ENSLIN-LOHMANN Berend 53, 255
ENTSPANNTFILM, Berlin 262
ERCAN Taner 118
ERICSON Martin 283, 344
ERICSTAM Jesper 100
ERIKSEN HILLBLOM Tove 88
ERIKSSON Anton 371
ERIKSSON David 371
ERIKSSON Peter 155
ERIKSSON Ulrika 317
ERK Glenn 225
ERMOLI Sara 33
ERNLE Daniel 374
EROL Gokhan 139
ERONN Jesper 108
ERSTE LIEBE FILMPRODUKTION, Hamburg 67
ERTEL Beathe 324
ESDAR Maren 269
ESER Caglar 114
ESSLIN Alex 112
ESTERMANN Karin 43
EU 106
EURO RSCG 4D, Amsterdam 364, 390
EURO RSCG GROUP SWITZERLAND, Zurich 169,
    246, 302, 308
EURO RSCG SOUTH AFRICA, Johannesburg 163
EURO RSCG SPAIN, Madrid 77, 175, 226
EURO RSCG, Amsterdam 270
EURO RSCG, Athens 210
EURO RSCG, London 55, 217
EURO RSCG, Munich 344
EUROPEAN SOCIAL FOUNDATION 389
EUROSTAR 75, 78, 79
EVANGELICAL CHURCH 280
EVIAN 55
EVSTAFIEV Igor 159
EWALD Daniela 294, 303
EWERT René 332
EWERTZ Markus 311, 318, 343
EXCLUSIVE ESCAPES 83
EYE DREAM 51
EZRA Igal 156
FABELLA Arnoldfelix 282
FABRICIUS Thomas 58
FACE TO FACE, Dubai 281
FADEYEV Alexey 358
FAIRBANKS Mark 30, 307
FAIRHEAD Brad 371
FAKTA 314
FALK Pia-Maria 91
FALLON, London 49, 132, 134, 251, 319
FAMILY BUSINESS, Stockholm 359
FANTEFILM, Oslo 246
FANTINI Luca 378
FARBER Alex 260
FARFAR, Stockholm 370, 380, 385
FARQUHAR Sophie 46
FARRA Caroline 295
FARSHIZAD Kimia 391
FASHION OUTLET ZURICH 89
FAULDS Paul 289, 319
FAULHABER Nina 290, 310
FAVRE Romin 190
FEDERAL MINISTRY FOR THE ENVIRONMENT 116
FEDORENKO Tatiana 128
FEDOSEEV Vladimir 361
FEDRIGO Silva 291
FELIX KETCHUP 33
FELOT Sandrine 145
FELTEN-GEISINGER Petra 76
FENA 339
FENSKE Roderick 106
FENTON Richard 56
FERNANDES Rodrigo 127
FERNANDEZ Iván 220
FERNANDEZ MARENGO Flora 166
FERNET BRANCA 53
FERREIRA Antonio 385
FHV BBDO, Amstelveen 35, 62
FIAT 227, 289, 293, 303, 319
FICHARD Vincent 265
FICHTEBERG Gilles 225, 241
FIEDLER Sebastian 364
FIESSELMANN Julia 382
FILM MAGICA, Helsinki 174
FILMMASTER, Milan 49
FIRMINGER Richard 46
FISCHER David 262, 302
FISCHER Teja 102
FISHER Daniel 123, 323
FITZROY, Amsterdam 373
FIVE THREE DOUBLE NINETY FILMPRODUCTIONS,
    Hamburg 202
FJØSNE Einar 40
FLEMMING Holly 127
FLICKORNA LARSSON 324
FLINTHAM Richard 132, 134, 251, 319
FLODELL FILM, Stockholm 100
FLX, Stockholm 68
FOCUS MAGAZINE 348
FOERSCHLER Ariane 313
FOERSTERLING Stephan 197
FOKUS 234
FOLKOPERAN 283, 317, 344

FONDATION ABBÉ PIERRE 129
FONFERRIER Marianne 83, 88
FORAKER Brett 110
FORD 340
FORD Joseph 24
FOREST STEWARDSHIP COUNCIL 119
FORGAN Mark 192
FORSGREN Mikael 371
FORSLING Fredrik 29
FORSMAN & BODENFORS, Gothenburg 68, 71, 99, 100, 111, 146, 240, 324, 362, 388
FORTUNE PROMOSEVEN, Dubai 140, 264, 265, 271
FOUAD Mohamed 228
FOUBERT Peter 389
FOURNIER Vincent 161
FOURNON Jean-François 173, 177
FOX TELEVISION 320
FP7, Doha 32, 135, 157
FRANCE24 234
FRANK Jonas 155, 248
FRANK Lennart 119, 162, 344
FRANK Sanne 341
FRANK Solène 212
FRANKEL Johnnie 174
FRANKENSTEIN Pontus 366
FRANKENSTEIN, Stockholm 366
FRANSEN Dave 377
FRED & FARID, Paris 56, 191
FREDDY 184, 189
FREELANCERPORTAL.CH 286
FREIXENET 381
FREMBGEN Simon 162
FRENDBERG Mattias 76, 279
FRENKLER Ekki 158
FRETTON Howard 157
FREY Hendrik 187
FREYLAND Heiko 162, 204, 223, 269
FRIBERG Daniel Lars 296
FRID Emil 343
FRIEDLAND Liora 48
FRIEDMAN Caz 48, 98
FRIENDLY FIRE COMMUNICATIONS, Vienna 193
FRIIS Mathias 368
FRISKIES 32
FRITSCH Sonja 115
FRITZ Ingo 367
FRIXE Michael 162
FROMMS CONDOMS 375
FROST Matthäus 46, 382
FRUSCELLA Alessandro 259
FUERER Alexander 169, 302
FUNERAL.EU 103
FUNK 199
FURBY Jay 65
FURIA 264
FURMAN Adam 323
FÜRST Mathis 247
GABISON Elad 45, 47
GABRIEL Nancy 64
GABRIELS Alex 28
GAJIC Nemanja 246
GAL Amit 93
GALLARDO Hugo 156
GALLÉ Alban 176
GALLIFA Joan 36
GALMARD Eric 196
GALOVIC Dejan 246
GÁLVEZ Julio 320
GAMER Philippe 109
GAMPER Mario 369
GANSEMANS Stijn 379
GAP FILMS, Munich 86
GARBERGS REKLAMBYRÅ, Stockholm 290, 370
GARBUTT Chris 249, 337
GARCÍA CADAFALCH Mario 179
GARCIA Eugenio 375
GARCIA Nathalie 274
GARCIA Raul 202
GAREIS Sven 239
GARMASTAN 295
GARNIER Maxence 57
GARVEY Chris 353
GARVEY Christopher 357
GASSER FRANKFURTERS 33
GAUBE Thimothée 220
GAULTIER Gabriel 75, 78, 79, 238
GAYAN Nacho 209
GAYRAUD Pascale 69, 151
GEARY John 357
GEBHARDT René 149
GEHRKE Peter 169
GEISENDÖRFER Felix 367
GELLER NESSIS LEO BURNETT, Tel Aviv 42
GELLERT Ralf 178, 328
GENTIS Steffen 210
GEORGIOU Fotis 112
GÉRARD-HUET Jessica 334
GERKEMA Sikko 286, 297
GERKEN Kai 93, 154
GERMAN Alexei 136
GERMAN FOUNDATION FOR MONUMENT PROTECTION 279
GERMEAU Benoît 267
GERRITSEN Willem 231
GERSHFELD Michail 260
GERSHON Geva 45, 47
GERSTNER Claudius 367
GESIERICH Andreas 283
GESSAT Soeren 302, 309
GESSULAT Karsten 303
GHEORGHIU Mihnea 249, 337
GHISO Federico 189, 233
GIANOLLI Xavier 232

GIBLIN & JAMES 29
GIELEN Bart 379
GIESECKE & DEVRIENT 347
GILLETTE 180
GINÉS Guillermo 136, 137, 141
GIRARD Olivier 173
GITAM BBDO, Tel-Aviv 31, 156
GITTO Vicky 156, 221, 371
GJOKOVIK Marko 67
GKK DIALOGGROUP, Frankfurt 309
GLABUS Jen 48
GLADKOV Andrey 358
GLAESER Barbara 340
GLAGE Tibor 202
GLAWION Joachim 114
GODETZ Manuel 193
GOEPFRICH Annika 253
GOETZ Marian 199
GOLAN Tzur 72, 93, 299
GOLDSTAR BEER 45, 47
GOMES Peter 373
GONAN Erik 311, 343
GOODING Emma 134
GOOSSENS Jeroen 365
GORDON Nick 134
GORSKI Rafal 390
GOSS, Gothenburg 76, 279
GOSSAGE Lucy 134
GÖTEBORGS-POSTEN 240
GOTHENBURG HOMELESS AID 279
GOTHENBURG SYMPHONY ORCHESTRA 252
GOTSHAL Tim 142
GOTTLIEBSEN Rasmus 107, 314, 315
GOTTSCHALCK Silke 306
GÖTZ Marian 310, 322
GÖTZ Michael 231, 297, 332
GOUBY Marc 120, 151
GOVENDER Prenneven 144
GQ MAGAZINE 229
GRAALFS Amelie 345, 384
GRABARZ & PARTNER, Hamburg 102, 118, 144, 202, 203, 206, 207, 312
GRABMAYER Marian 338
GRACEY Michael 86
GRAF Jennifer 255
GRAFL Bernhard 263
GRAMM WERBEAGENTUR, Düsseldorf 209
GRAND CRU WINE 53
GRANDT Oliver 145
GRASS Martin 102, 202
GRASSL Andreas 110
GRAVINGEN Anne 368
GRAY Greg 48, 208
GREAT WORKS, Stockholm 366, 369
GREEN Andy 216
GREEN David 232, 292
GREEN Howard 73
GREENPEACE 114, 308
GREGOIRE Pascal 142
GRELLMANN Bernd 340
GRESSET Reynald 232, 384
GREY WORLDWIDE, Dubai 65, 134, 138
GREY, Beirut 233
GREY, Brussels 145
GREY, Istanbul 153
GREY, London 110, 386
GREY, Moscow 159
GREY, Stockholm 266
GRICHOIS Mathieu 90
GRIFFIN Simon 352
GRIFFIN Ted 381
GRIGORE ANTIPA NATURAL HISTORY MUSEUM 299
GRIMSTAD Lars Joachim 246
GROB Marco 169
GROSSECOSSMANN Uwe 306
GROUEK, Paris 368
GROUSSET Matt 202
GROUSSET Sebastian 202
GRUJARD Antoine 220
GRÜNDLING Kristian 209
GRUNDNER Matthias 278
GRUPO W 375
GSW WORLDWIDE, Columbus 276
GUELAFF Frédéric 363, 387
GUERASSIMOV Dimitri 190, 234
GUGLIELMONI Paolo 22
GUHL Tabea 321
GUILLEMANT Charles 72
GUINET Sébastien 120
GUINNESS 46, 48, 52, 367
GUNES Erol 227
GURPINAR Ilkay 26, 227
GUTSCHER Tassilo 162, 344
GUTSULYAK Yurko 346
GUZMÁN Alvaro 312
GYFTOULA Yola 74
GYLLENSKIOLD Henrik 370
H FILMS, Milan 184
H, Paris 196, 330
HA Najin 249, 337
HAAPALEHTO Marku 329
HAARS Joana 82
HAASE Alexander 76, 124
HADDAD Chafic 37, 185, 192, 281, 282
HADFIELD Marcus 379
HADZIJUSUFOVIC Mirel 348
HAEGER Henrik 365
HAEUSERMANN Dirk 143, 197
HAEUSSLER Michael 289
HAGELSTEN Henrik 25

HAGMAN Erik 359, 366
HAGWALL BRUCKNER Hedvig 90, 91, 169
HAHNE Patrick 210
HAIDER Rosa 33
HAILS Suzanne 73
HAKTANIR Guven 83
HALD Søren 70
HALL Graeme 23, 94, 202
HALVARSSON Henrik 91
HAMDALLA Mohamed 228
HAMILTON Rory 48
HANDLOS Oliver 108, 262, 302, 309, 380
HANEBECK Timm 143
HÄNEL Johann Sebastian 311
HANKE Sascha 143
HANSAPLAST 176
HANSEN Alexander 197
HANSEN Jesper 107, 314, 315
HANTSON Geoffrey 102, 284, 291
HANUSA Deborah 325
HARALAMPOPOULOS Yiannis 339, 340, 354
HARBECK Jan 71, 102, 196, 220
HARBECK Matthias 152, 176, 227, 247, 258
HARDIECK Sebastian 59, 210, 280, 288
HARLEY-DAVIDSON 365
HARRIMAN David 83, 183
HARRIS Brent 184
HARRISON Dylan 200
HARRY MELLSTRÖM Ted 296
HARTMANN Rob 233, 235
HARTOG Marcel 276, 377, 388
HARVEY Dan 304
HARVEY NICHOLS 94, 95, 96, 97
HASCI Petra 324
HASHEMI Adam 49, 58
HASHMI Anna 46
HASKELL Lawrence 47
HASLEHURST Simon 288
HASSAN Hadi 34
HASSETT Ben 97
HATZY Nadja 225
HAUCH Julia 262, 302
HAUSCHULZ Olaf 332
HAUSER Tom 278
HAVERKAMP Sabine Marleen 364
HAVLICEK Nina 84
HECKEL Yona 206
HEFFELS Guido 93, 154
HEGDE Prasanna 254
HEI REKLAMEBYRÅ, Oslo 67
HEIGHES Dan 208
HEILEMANN Kristoffer 219, 338
HEIMAT, Berlin 93, 154
HEINEKEN 49, 51
HEINEL Fabian 67
HEINEN 257
HEINIG Christian 369
HEINZ 27, 28
HEINZE Gunnar 311
HEINZE Ramona 294, 303
HEINZEL Andreas 306, 307
HELBIG Silvio 196
HELLGE Sebastian 208
HELLO GARBAGE 373
HELLSTRÖM Erika 357, 387
HENDERSON Dave 96, 218
HENING Christian 155
HENKEL Mathias 310, 379
HENKELMANN Dirk 46, 282
HENNERMANN Felix 25
HENNIGER VON WALLERSBRUNN Ulf 293, 294, 303
HENRY Alexandre 161
HENRY Neil 58, 391
HENRY Olivier 66
HERBRICH Thomas 259
HERMAN Jonathan 44
HERNADI Simon 370
HERNÁNDEZ Bernardo 136, 137
HERNÁNDEZ Clara 312
HERNANDEZ Eduardo 56
HERNGREN Felix 68
HERON Adrien 370
HERSEKLI Dide 153
HERTEL Jan 364, 375
HERVÉ Alexandre 66, 144, 224, 229, 342
HESSING Jeroen 377
HESSLER Eva 84
HEUEL Ralf 102, 118, 144, 202, 203, 206, 207, 312
HEUMANN Till 305
HEUMANN Wolf 143, 197
HEYE & PARTNER, Unterhaching 86
HEYN Nina 108
HICKS Johannes 199, 290, 310
HIEMANN Anna 118
HIETALA Jere 270
HIETALAHTI Olli 77
HIGBY Simon 88, 89, 296
HILLAND Thomas 58
HILLENIUS Diederick 44, 231
HILLER Jost 288
HILTL 86, 92
HIMMELSPACH Christian 170
HINCKLEY Mark 84
HINKE Lasse 188
HIRT Kristin 220
HITCHHIKER FILMS, Bratislava 246
HJALMAR Björn 155
HLA, London 134
HLADKY Milan 246
HLAVAC Ivo 176
HO David 204, 337
HODEL Nik 377
HOEFLER Mark 367
HOELTSCHI Serge 86, 321

HOENTSCHKE Ingo 181
HOFBECK Thomas 301
HOFER Johann-Georg 382
HOFFMAN Thomas 58
HOFFMANN Andreas 102
HOFFMANN Daniel 217, 308, 332
HOFFMANN Kai 171
HOFFMANN Thomas 49, 191, 198
HOFMANN Fredrik 170
HÖGLIN Marie 287
HOHEISEL Folko 202
HOHMANN Till 305
HOHNDORF Julian 220
HOLDEN Eric 199
HOLLAND Tobias 170
HOLLANDER Nicolas 220
HOLLANDER Ton 201, 210, 211, 313
HOLLE Niels 116, 180, 193, 214, 215
HOLLINGWORTH Frank 80, 81, 90, 91, 169, 360
HOLMBERG Helena 87, 316
HOLST Jesper 287
HOLST Ran 46, 166, 184
HOLTHE Lars 316
HOLUBOVA Katerina 122
HOLZER Felix 38, 158
HOLZHAUSEN Kristine 149, 168, 226, 230
HOME OFFICE 111
HOOPER Justin 217
HOPE Lottie 54
HOPKINSON Lindsey 153
HOPPE Jessica 71
HORNBACH 93, 154
HÖRNSTRÖM Lars 266
HORVATH Klemens 193
HORVATH Norbert 193
HOUPLAIN Cédric 125
HOUSE OF PROSE 240
HOVART Arnold 267
HOVDA LUNDE Helene 40
HSBC 101, 304
HUBER Helmut 152
HUEBNER Norbert 325
HUESMANN Bernd 176
HUKE Simon 348
HULL Britt 357
HÜMMELS Yona 35
HUNGRY MAN, London 106
HUNTER Bern 48
HUNTER Mark 55, 217
HURENTOURS 82
HÜSGEN Elke 340
HUSSEY Dingus 30
HUT WEBER 185
HUVART Lars 141, 301
HYGEN Christian 66
HYNES Jason 46
HYPERHAPPEN, London 371
I COOK GREEK 350
ICHAMELEON GROUP 367
ICHEDEF Gamze 227
ICHI 191
IFF Vanessa 144
IKEA 142, 144, 146, 149, 278, 301, 322, 362, 376
ILIESCU Mihai 299
ILLAN ADVERTISING GROUP, St. Petersburg 361
IMMISCH Gunnar 25
IMPACT/BBDO, Riyadh 60
IMPULSE 166
INCANTO 360
INDEPENDENT, London 200
INDERBITZIN Eduardo 206
INDIO FILMS, Madrid 56, 76
INLINGUA 268, 269
INTEK Marcus 338
INTERNATIONAL FESTIVAL OF THEATRE SCHOOLS 246
INTERNATIONAL ORGANIZATION FOR MIGRATION 128
INTERONE WORLDWIDE, Munich 306
IPOD 139
IPSEN 276
IRÈNE, Paris 232
IRISH INTERNATIONAL BBDO, Dublin 46, 48, 52
ISAACS Jelani 231
ISABETTINI Ingo 322
ISBERG Axel 91
ISKEN Marc 310
ISMAILI Fisnik 318
IWC SCHAFFHAUSEN 197
JÄÄSKELÄINEN Jussi 204, 222, 320
JACOB Gregory 364
JACOBS Jan 194
JACOBSON John 337
JACOBSON VELLINGA DESIGN, Stockholm 337
JAKOBI Julia 278
JAMES Taylor 153
JANI Peter 263
JANNEAU Pierre 58
JANNON Eric 190, 234
JANSEN Robbert 62
JANSSEN Sven 170
JANSSON Silas 321
JARL Per Erik 66
JAZZ RADIO 243
JEAN James 113
JITZMARK Robert 154
JOISCHMID FILMPRODUKTION, Berlin 196
JOBSINTOWN.DE 262, 302
JOCHUM Armin 239
JOHANNES LEONARDO, New York 194
JOHANSEN Martin 70, 155
JOHANSSON Katarina 285
JOHN Judy 373
JOHN LEWIS 85, 86, 327

JOHNSON Rosita 285
JOLLY Jacques 370
JONES Cris 167
JONES Matthew 265
JONGENELEN Stef 35
JONSGÅRDEN Tomas 100
JOPPEN Jürgen 196
JÖRÄLV Jörgen 373, 387
JORGE Carlos 131, 210, 376, 386
JOSEFSSON Fredrik 316
JOSHUA Justin 256
JOYE Tom 178
JUENGER Nico 187
JUERGENS Nele 108
JUICY FRUIT TROPIKIWI 39
JUNCTION 11, London 275, 276
JUNG VON MATT, Berlin 71, 102, 170, 196, 220, 289
JUNG VON MATT, Hamburg 143, 196, 197, 216, 278, 298
JUNG VON MATT, Stockholm 251
JUNG VON MATT, Stuttgart 119, 162, 344
JUNGHANNS Stephan 253
JÜRGES Peggy 375
JUROK Imke 185
JWT ITALIA, Milan 49
JWT RUSSIA, Moscow 166, 260
JWT SPAIN, Barcelona 381
JWT, Dubai 37, 185, 192, 281, 282
JWT, London 36, 37, 101, 304
JWT, New York 101
JWT, Paris 34, 368
JWT, Tunis 197
KACAR Suleyman 83
KACENKA Peter 139
KAEHLER Maik 317, 345, 384
KAFADAR Engin 153
KAGAWA HOLM Cliff 321
KAINZ Sebastian 84
KALLMEYER Julia 310
KAMBAYASHI Yuka 101
KAMERAD Marcus, Düsseldorf 310
KANAAN Marwan 104
KANCHEV Atanas 354
KANDER Nadav 61, 85, 327, 328, 331
KANELAKI Vicky 247
KAPLAN Emre 227
KAPLAN Micheal 164
KAPOOR Dinesh 101
KARACA Nuran 389
KARACA Öznur 389
KARAKASOGLU Volkan 26, 148
KARAKASOGLU Zeynep 114
KARASEK Jonas 139
KARBASSIOUN David 184
KÄRKKÄINEN Heikki 174
KARLSSON Fredrik 366
KARLSSONS 155
KARPOVA Vera 26
KASABOV Joro 354
KASPAR Marcus 67
KASSAEI Amir 149, 162, 168, 171, 199, 204, 207, 219, 222, 223, 226, 230, 269, 290, 301, 310, 320, 322, 324, 338
KAUFMANN Sebastian 82
KAUNECKAS Tomas 295
KAY Ben 126
KEFF Darren 36, 304
KEHL Fedja 312
KELDA SOUP 32
KELLOGG'S 22
KEMPERTRAUTMANN, Hamburg 231, 297, 332
KENAROV Chavdar 354
KENNEDY Devin 98
KENNEDY Roger 157, 173
KENNY Helen 164
KENO 246
KENTER Katelijne 377
KERBER Christian 144
KERNER Diether 217, 308, 332
KERNSPECKT Björn 149
KEYZER Simone 388
KHAIRALLAH Ghassan 233
KHAISMAN Mark 162, 344
KHALIFA Hesham 110
KHAN Khurram 31
KHARMA Hisham 216, 298
KHOURY Celine 295
KHOURY Rania 233
KIDDER Blake 54
KILLI Lars 122
KIM Gussi 318, 343
KIM Jamie 391
KIMPEL Stephen 301
KINCH Ida 315
KING JAMES, Cape Town 98
KING STUDIO 91
KING, Helsinki 77
KING, Stockholm 80, 81, 90, 91, 169, 360
KINOGRAF, Kiev 333
KIRCHNER Lisa 355
KIRNER Fabian 204
KIRSCH Sarah 340
KIRSCHENHOFER Bertrand 350
KISSELEV Vassiliy 136
KITCHEN LEO BURNETT, Oslo 66, 368
KITKAT 34, 37
KITTEL Marc-Philipp 170
KITTEL Michael 162, 204
KITZING Florian 289
KIZILAY Cevdet 244
KLARIN Jesper 359
KLASEN Sven 201
KLAUS Joerg 369

KLAVER Stijn 121, 178
KLEFFNER Sonja 179
KLEIN Michael 246
KLEINMAN Danny 174
KLESSIG Daniel 108
KLEVENHAGEN Karolin 311
KLING Jeff 182, 184, 391
KLINGBEIL Fabian 202
KLJUN Dorijan 348
KLOHK Sven 130
KLONHAMMER Olivier 380
KLOPPERS Karen 98, 256
KLUBNIKIN Pavel 128
KLUMAN Sophie 48
KLUSZCZYNSKA Iwona 243
K-LYNN 192
KNEIPFERAVIČIUS Marius 295
KNEMEYER Verena 372
KNIESS Helge 325
KNOBLOCH Daniel 375
KNOPF Thomas 280
KNOTT Paul 367
KNOWLES Tim 119
KNSK WERBEAGENTUR, Hamburg 116, 180, 193, 208, 214, 215
KNUTSSON Mårten 359
KÖBBEL Uwe 209
KOBER Frederick 50, 282, 382
KOCH Christopher 180
KOCH Michael 280
KOCHBA Geva 72, 93, 299
KODAK 141
KOENNECKE Daniel 317, 384
KOK Saskia 44, 184
KOKKEN Guy 121
KOKOKAKA, Gothenburg 362
KOKOSHKO Vitaliy 333
KOKSAL Arzu 244
KOLESTON 295, 327
KOLIGIANNIS Nicholas 41
KOLLE REBBE WERBEAGENTUR, Hamburg 130, 268, 269, 351, 355
KOLOS Sergey 66
KOMATSU 291
KONIETZKO Joe 366
KONING Janneke 388
KOOPERATIVA INSURANCE 101
KOREN Merav 42
KORHONEN Pinja 382
KORINE Harmony 49
KOROLCZUK Jakub 390
KORPI Tuomas 329
KORPIALA Olli 248
KOSELJ Vesna 382
KOSINA Hannes 193
KOSKINEN Timo 77
KOSLIK Matthias 222
KOSOVO INDEPENDENCE 318
KOSTOPOULOS Kostas 41
KOTLINSKI Łukasz 243
KOTULEK Michal 122
KOTWICA Petri 248
KOULOURES Elias 280
KOUTSKY Dusan 130
KOZOK Hartmut 280
KRANEFELD Stefan 180
KRANTZ Torbjörn 87, 175, 285, 287
KRAUSE Delle 348
KRAUSE Martin 225
KRAUTER Michael 76
KRAVTSOV Alexey 333
KREATIVEKONZEPTION, Berlin 385
KRETZER Roman 309
KRINK Tim 116, 180, 193, 214, 215
KRISHNA Dv Hari 37, 282
KROEBER Florian 306, 307
KRUEGER Fabian 59
KRUG Hermann 220
KRÜGER Nathalie 116
KRUMBE Dennis 332
KRUMKAMP Lena 92
KRUSHEVA Tsanka 104
KRZESLACK Johannes 187
KUDASHKIN Mikhail 26
KUIJPERS Joris 203
KUNIC Domagoj 348, 360
KUNSEMUELLER Caroline 288
KUNTZE Sascha 305
KURECKOVA Katarina 101
KURR Tanja 46, 318, 382
KUWERTZ Volker 340
KWIK-FIT 218
KYDD Peter 32
KYRATSOULI Kallina 74
LA CHOSE, Paris 142
LA PAC, Paris 88, 229
LA REDOUTE 88
LA SPADA Giuseppe 371
LABBE Jeff 184
LABORATORIVM 62
LACOURT Laurie 142
LAGERHOLM & CO. 296
LAGES Graziela 90, 91
LAMBERT Carol 248
LAMBERT Rory 381
LAMBORGHINI 217, 332
LAND ROVER 216
LANDIN Johan 87, 331
LANDMARK Anke 262
LANDON Justin 375
LANGELAAR Manon 388
LANGLEY TRAVEL 76
LANGSETH Tove 91, 317

LANTELME Andrea 63, 329
LANTHIMOS Giorgos 74
LANZ Danielle 86, 89, 92, 105, 261, 286
LANZON Carlos 209
LAPORTE Laurent 225
LAPSHIN Oleg 159
LARIONOVA Olga 166
LARSSON Albin 76, 279
LARSSON Emil 155
LARSSON Håkan 285
LARSSON VON REYBEKIEL Max 251
LASS Torsten 82
LATEGAAN Terri 338
LATERNA MAGICA, Düsseldorf 209
LAUNE Jouko 77
LAURENT Mathias 57
LAURENT Romain 90
LAURSEN Morten 191
LAUTERBACH Ret 375
LAUTHIER Nicolas 56
LAVAZZA 63, 329
LAVOIX Juliette 56, 191
LAVOLA Minna 270
LAWRENCE David 47
LAWSON Martin 289
LBI STARRING, Stockholm 373
LBI, Gothenburg 364
LE BLOND Carl 267, 381
LE BRETON Benjamin 232, 237, 384
LE SPOT, Athens 247
LE TOURMENT VERT 357
LEAGAS DELANEY ITALIA, Rome 215, 245
LEAGAS DELANEY, Hamburg 145
LEAHY Dennis 275
LEAL Ana 349
LEATHERS Johnny 85, 86, 327
LEAVER Diane 61, 271, 331
LEBLANC-BONTEMPS Jean-Noel 199
LECOQ Stéphane 109, 127
LEDWIGE Ringan 64
LEE Films, Madrid 220
LEE Kevin 158
LEENDERTSE Stefan 284
LEEP SCHOOL OF HAIR 168
LEFEBVRE Jean-Paul 28, 267
LEG, Paris 75, 78, 79, 238
LEGER Rolf 269
LEGRAND Thomas 363
LEHNINGER Sandra 298
LEHTINEN Mikko 66
LEIBOVITZ Annie 326, 363, 387
LEICA 308
LEICK Stefan 187
LEKORCHI Yasin 129
LEMOIGNE Jean-Yves 241
LEMOINE Yoanne 225
LEMZ, Amsterdam 389
LENOR 159
LENZ Stefan 115
LEO BURNETT & TARGET, Bucharest 299
LEO BURNETT UKRAINE, Kiev 128
LEO BURNETT WORLDWIDE 373
LEO BURNETT, Beirut 295
LEO BURNETT, Brussels 28, 267
LEO BURNETT, Cairo 228
LEO BURNETT, Chicago 373
LEO BURNETT, Frankfurt 293, 294, 303, 306, 307
LEO BURNETT, London 123, 289, 304, 319, 323
LEO BURNETT, Milan 22, 174, 327
LEO BURNETT, Moscow 26
LEO BURNETT, Toronto 373
LEONARDO Johannes 194
LERNER Eric 58
LEROUX Benoît 24, 160
LES SIX 117, 120, 192, 334, 349
LES TÉLÉCRÉATEURS, Paris 69, 142, 212
LESSING Gareth 144
LEUBE Jan 146
LEVANDER Aron 91, 125
LEVI Marsel 354
LEVI Yoram 27
LEVI'S 184
LEVY-HARRAR Valérie 384
LEWIS Mary 353
LEWIS Michael 349
LEWIS MOBERLY, London 353
LEXA Andreas 384
LIAKOS Vangelis 339
LIBANO-FRANÇAISE BANK 104
LIEDMEIER Ronald 181
LIFSHITZ Anne 182
LIGA DIREITOS DOS ANIMAIS 116
LIM Adrian 216
LIMA Pedro 116
LIME 304
LIMES, Berlin 311
LIND Sesse 366
LINDA ZLOK FASHIONS 193
LINDE Lotta 87, 316
LINDE Nicolas 196
LINDEMANN Arno 278
LINDGREN Mathias 371
LINDGREN Rolle 344
LINDQUIST Fredrik 359
LINDSTRÖM Kenny 371
LINDSTRÖM Robert 371
LINEVELDT Marc 140, 264, 265, 271
LINOTYPE 341
LINSCHEID Edgar 108, 146, 380
LINTON Grant 31
LISS Florian 376
LITHO NIEMANN + STEGGEMANN 163, 257
LITTLE Bryan 220

LIVESEY Adam 330
LJUBICIC Boris 341
LJUBICIC Igor 341
LKXA YOUTH BANK 103
LOCK Sam 174
LOCK Samantha 172
LOESER Gunnar 92, 333
LÖFGREN Ola 366
LOFT TONSTUDIOS 325
LOFTUS Steve 172
LOHMANN Marius 220
LOIBL Sandra 152
LONNING Lis 25
LOPES André 112, 131
LOPEZ Fran 141
LOPEZ Philippe 123
LORENZ Ritter 130
LORENZINI Luca 173
LORÉS Xavier 179
LOTTMANN Julia 309
LOTTO 248
LOUIS VUITTON 326, 363, 387
LOVE Clayton 274
LOVE, Manchester 352
LOVRINIC Darko 110
LOWE BRINDFORS, Stockholm 91, 125, 283, 317, 344, 365
LOWE BULL, Johannesburg 330
LOWE STRATÉUS, Paris 123
LOWE, London 47, 85, 86, 208, 327
LUBARS David 180
LUBLIN Petter 283, 317, 344
LUCET Patrice 72
LUCIANO CARVARI 333
LUCK LOTTERY 247
LUDWIG Florian 269
LUJÁN Javier 211
LUJANAC Tonka 360
LUKAS Bernhard 278
LUNAR BBDO, London 126
LUNDGREN Fredrik 373, 387
LUNDGREN Martin 89, 296
LUNDQUIST Pelle 125
LUNDY Emma 208
LUPARELLI Claudio 39
LUPO Thomas 119
LUTHER Tina 118
LYKOURESIS Stelios 74
LYLYK Lilya 333
LYNGNERN Magne 246
LYON Scott 202
M&M'S 35
MAAS Torsten 89, 92
MAASS Francisca 185
MAC Andy 277
MAC Flávio 108
MACKAY Doug 282
MACKAY Finlay 63, 329
MacKINNON-LITTLE Gavin 379
MACLAGAN Mungo 101
MADESTRAND Bo 359
MAERKERT Jenny 345
MAGAD Nassar 140
MAGICTOUCH 318
MAGIN Stefan 309
MAGLITE 145
MAGNUM ICE CREAM 369
MAHMOUD Areej 295
MAHMOUDI Danusch 374, 375
MAINFRAME PRODUCTION, Zagreb 67
MAKAREM Rania 192
MAKINEN Tommy 231, 248
MALCOLM Tony 123, 304, 323
MALLIARD Daniel 167
MALUF DE CAMPOS Eduardo 382
MANARCHY Dennis 276
MAÑAS Diego 76
MANDELBAUM Jaime 140, 255, 271
MANDT-MERCK Marietta 317
MANKOVSKY Tomas 134
MANMOHAN Vidya 134, 138
MANN ZEMMER Shiri 42
MANNILA Erkko 231, 248, 270
MANPOWER 266
MANWARING Guy 233
MANZ Jochen 171
MARA Luka 234
MARAN Valentina 215
MARCEL, Paris 190, 234
MARCUS Pierre 64, 69
MARCUSSEN Sebastian 247
MARDISALU Margit 270
MARECHAL Silvere 370
MARIANI Michele 63, 329
MARIE CURIE ACTIONS 106
MARK Henning 108
MARKENFILM, Berlin 108
MARKENFILM, Hamburg 210
MARKENFILM, Zurich 233
MARKOM LEO BURNETT, Istanbul 83
MÅRLIND Måns 111
MARLY Pierre 370
MARMITE 23
MARRONI Patrizia 38
MARSEILLE Kathrin 53
MARSHALL Tristan 358
MARSTRAND Mads 69
MARTENS Ernesto 203
MARTIJN Sengers 390
MARTIN David 90
MARTIN Greg 36

MARTIN Victor 175
MARTINEZ Alex 381
MARTINEZ Raquel 76
MART'YAKHIN Sergey 26
MARUSOV Dmitry 333
MASCHKE Michael M. 310
MASTRONICOLA Mauro 378
MATHIOT Julie 229
MATHON Antoine 129
MATTAR Gabriel 199, 207, 219
MATTEL 253
MATTINGLY Matthew 194
MATTNER Thomas 348
MAUSON Sascha 92
MAY Dennis 149, 168, 207, 226, 230, 324
MAYER Tobias 375
McANNANEY Andy 307
McCANN ERICKSON ISRAEL, Tel Aviv 45, 47
McCANN ERICKSON POLSKA, Warsaw 243
McCANN ERICKSON, Bucharest 62
McCANN ERICKSON, Lisbon 108, 112, 131
McCANN ERICKSON, Madrid 56, 76, 179
McCANN ERICKSON, Paris 199
McCANN ERICKSON, Prague 122, 130
McCANN ERICKSON BELGIUM, Hoeilaart & Antwerp 365
McCARTHY Ciaran 248
McCLELLAND Patrick 47, 208
McCRACKEN Heather 101
McDONALD'S 29, 86, 88, 89, 296
McGINLEY Ryan 191
McKENNA Mike 36
McKENZIE Selena 251, 319
McKINSEY & COMPANY 261
McLEOD Andy 218
MEARS Eben 48
MEBIUS Arthur 217
MEBUCAIINE 178
MECKING Jens 322
MEDAL OF HONOR 135
MEDIA CONSULTA, Berlin 106
MEDIAFRONT, Oslo 368
MEDINA TURGUL DDB, Istanbul 139
MEDROWS Firas 281
MEEK Nick 73
MÉGROUS Sophie 229
MEHRWALD Marco 25, 323
MEINHARDT Alexander 364
MEISTER CAMERA 308
MELDGAARD Morten 188
MELIN Bjarne 370
MELLA Sylvaine 56
MELLSTRÖM Ted Harry 89, 296
MELODY TUNES 228
MEMAC OGILVY & MATHER, Beirut 121
MÉMOIRE COGNAC 358
MENARD Isabelle 232
MENDIBIL Ekhi 63, 329
MENDIBIL Haitz 63, 329
MENDIVIL Ander 56
MENHALL Dalia 121
MERCATOR INSURANCE 102
MERCEDES-BENZ 201, 216, 220, 225, 298, 364
MERLICEK Franz 361
MERTENS Melanie 145
MERZ Klaus 181
MESSAGER Pierre-Louis 88, 161
METCHANOVA Antoaneta 249, 337
METEORITE, London 379
METRA FILMS, Moscow 136
METRO 241
METRO DE MADRID 76
METZLER Christina 364
MEUTHEN Markus 179
MEYER Fabienne 385
MEYER Helmut 124, 348
MEYER Olivia 56
MEYLER Phillip 36, 304
MEZIANI Sami 363
MFL, Stockholm 388
MICHALIK Rasto 101
MICHAUX TERRIER Agathe 66
MICROSOFT 379
MIDDELINK Gersom 184
MIETZ Jamie 208
MIGROS 321
MILK AGENCY, Vilnius 295
MILLER Alisdair 65, 134, 138
MILLIES Frithjof 376
MINDER Stefan 89
MINI 306, 385
MINIVEGAS 229
MINKARA Moe 348
MINKEN Tomas 231
MIR 160, 161
MISEREOR 130
MISSING 289
MISTER HIDE, Paris 144
MISTER KRISTER, Stockholm 108
MITCHELL Ian 319
MITSUBISHI 213
MITTUN-KJOS Thomas 67
MOCK Andreas 143
MODERN ARAB WORLD 340
MODERNA MUSEUM 248
MOE Eivind 40, 246, 247
MOFFAT Sarah 357
MOHR Moritz 247
MÖMAX 84
MOMENTUM, Prague 130
MOMMERTZ Christian 76, 115
MONCEAU Benoit 90
MOÑINO Vicky 202, 209
MONO NO AWARE 371

MONSARRO Marta 36
MONSTER COMMERCIALS, Oslo 40, 247
MONTERO Antonio 131, 210, 211, 312, 376, 386
MONTGOMERY Randall 275
MONTILLA Rafa 209
MONTJEAN Edgard 326, 387
MOORE Guy 123, 304, 323
MOORE Toby 251, 319
MORAES Tico 213
MOREIRA Andre 208
MORENO Luis Felipe 56
MORENO Toni 209
MORGAN & MORELL 138
MORGANKANE, Stockholm 317
MORIA Arno 142
MORIC Miro 38, 158
MORINA Jeton 318
MORO Monica 56, 76
MORRIS Ed 47, 85, 86, 327
MORRIS Simon 47
MORTENSEN Jens 359
MORTIER Jens 300
MORTIERBRIGADE, Brussels 300
MORTON Emma 352
MOSCHONAS Manos 74, 247
MOSELEY Al 54, 58
MOSS Deborah 369
MOSTAFA Shereen 228
MOTHER, London 46
MOURAD Leslie 121
MOUSE GRAPHICS, Mellissia 350
MOUSLY David 71, 102, 196, 220
MOUTAUD Cédric 79
MOUZANNAR Bechara 295
MOVE IT MEDIA 311
MOYNIHAN Muiris 52
MOYSE Peter 185
MPH, London 305
MRAZ Jakub 130
MSTF PARTNERS, Lisbon 116, 213, 272
MTHAMBO Themba 48
MTV 239
MUCK Michael 177
MUELLER Lothar 141
MUELLER Matias 179
MUELLER Volker 294, 303
MUELLER Wolfgang 306
MÜLLER Ingo 268
MÜLLER Markus 93, 154
MÜLLER-FLEISCHER Kurt 116, 214, 215
MÜLLER-LIERHEIM Pei-Jen 158
MÜNCHEN TICKET 323
MUNNE Luis 175
MUNNS Garry 289, 319
MUNTEANU Stefan 299
MURELLI Manuela 22
MURGRABIA Lukasz 243
MURPHY Al 23
MURPHY Colin 205
MURRAY Rachel 248
MURRO Noam 200
MUSEUM OF CHILDHOOD 250
MUSEUM OF COMMUNISM 255
MUSIC FOR LIFE 300
MUSKEN Ole 25
MUSTAFA Sabina 240
MUW/SAATCHI & SAATCHI, Bratislava 101
MY CUP OF TEA 358
NACHTIGALL Petra 38
NAGEL Jörg 308
NAGERNAUFT Bernd 323
NAGY Dezsó 127
NAJARIAN Rodrigue 121
NANJA Dinny 234
NANN Christoph 317, 345, 384
NANOU Evelyn 247
NARDÒ Cristiano 63, 329
NAUSCH Kerrin 293, 294, 303, 306, 307
NAVILLE Bernard 79
NESCAFÉ 62
NESTEA 56
NESTLÉ EXTREME 368
NEUHAUS Hazel 256
NEUMANN Christopher 59
NEVIANS Mathieu 66
NEW MOMENT NEW IDEAS COMPANY Y&R, Belgrade 195, 263
NEW MOMENT NEW IDEAS COMPANY Y&R, Skopje 67
NEXUS PRODUCTIONS, London 194
N'GO Richard 342
NGUYEN Duc 59
NICHOLSON Mike 250
NICOLA FINETTI 185
NIELSEN Jakob 369
NIEMANN Nic 262
NIEMANN-BODE Detlef 376
NIEMINEN Yrjo 248
NIENTIEDT Tobias 306
NIESTEDT Michael 364
NIETO Luis 182
NIKE 182, 184, 375, 391
NIKOL 156
NIKOU Alexis 339
NILSSON Johan 387
NILSSON Mattias 129
NITRO, London 390
NJUGUNA Antony 158
NOBLE GRAPHICS STUDIO, Sofia 354
NOËL Rémi 199
NOK OUT ICE CREAM 42
NOKIA 370, 380
NOLTING Ralf 118, 203, 207
NOMIS 194

NONEOFUSAREFREE.ORG 381
NORCUTT Mark 37, 304
NORDISKA KOMPANIET 91
NORDPOL+ HAMBURG 350, 367
NORMAN Joakim 365
NORMAN John 54, 58, 182, 184, 391
NORRLANDS GULD 7
NORTH KINGDOM, Skellefteå 371
NOWAK Christian 364
NOWAK Julia 345
NOWAK Olivia 204, 222
NUGENT Richard 254
NUNES Miguel 330
NUNEZ Fabien 125
NUSSBAUM Jan Steffen 309
NYCOMED 274
NYGREN BARRETT Susanna 356
NYKKE & KOKKI 92
NYLAND Jakob 371
OBAID Javed 31
OBRANT ANDREASSON Ola 168
OCEAN CARE 118
OEDING Katrin 351, 355
OELKERS Oliver 110
OGILVY & MATHER, Copenhagen 53, 70, 138, 253
OGILVY & MATHER, Paris 57, 249, 326, 337, 387
OGILVY GROUP UKRAINE, Kiev 66
OGILVY INTERACTIVE, Paris 363
OGILVY KOSOVO, Pristina 318
OGILVY, Amsterdam 103, 267, 381
OGILVY, Cape Town 208
OGILVY, Dubai 305
OGILVY, Frankfurt 76, 115, 118, 124, 141, 253, 279, 301, 348
OGILVYONE WORLDWIDE, Frankfurt 280
OGILVYONE WORLDWIDE, Paris 363
OH Shin 25
OHANIAN Michael 119, 162, 344
OHLSSON Lena 157
OJHA Rajaram 254
OLAY 165, 167
OLIVER Isahac 202
OLIVER Sam 200, 218
OLLMANN Dirk 364
OLSSON ADAMSKY Petrus 81
OLYMPIA 192
OMETITA Dragos 273
ONFILM, Zurich 86
ONUK Banu 244
OPAP 247
OPEL 208
OPEN BAKERY 25
OPENHERE, Antwerp 379
OPEN-TRACE.DE 367
OPPLYSNINGEN 67
OPPMANN Simon 118, 279
ORANGE 64, 69, 72
ORANGINA 56
ORAS CUBISTA 329
ORB Stefan 152
ORDNING & REDA 343
ORGANIC DELIVERY COMPANY 30
ORIAN Matan 156
OROVERDE FOUNDATION 115
ORQUIN Xavi 226
ORSINI Stella 184
OSBOURNE Mark 217
OSCARSSON Patrik 296
OSEM'S KETCHUP 31
OSSAMA Hany 228
ÖSTBERG Tommy 252
ÖSTRÖM Stefan 316
OSVALD Rebecka 290
OSWALD David 322
OTRIVIN 173
OTT Jan Hendrick 171
OTTEN Torben 239
OTTER Bastian 325
OTTO Mike John 372
OUCHIIAN Djik 102, 202
OUI FM 238
OUTSIDER, London 202
OWENS DDB, Dublin 205
PACK Florian 102
PACKER Richard 200
PACREAU Josselin 120
PADALINO Alessandro 327
PADAN Eyal 299
PAEPS Marc 28
PAKULL Thomas 25, 323
PALAVIDIS Manos 210
PALING WALTERS, London 277
PALLANT John 173, 177
PALMER Chris 110, 172
PALMER Matt 55
PALMER Oliver 227, 247, 258
PALOMAKI Aleksi 231
PALTEMAA Henri 204
PALYEKAR Anil 240
PANAGIARI Matina 210
PANAIT Cezar 273
PANCALDI Massimiliano 291
PANE Luigi 378
PANNESE Luca 173
PANOV Oleg 159
PAPATHEODOROU Kostas 112
PAPOULIAS George 210
PARADOX, Oslo 66, 67
PAREDES Leonardo 364
PAREDES Nico 155
PARENT Benjamin 142
PÄRES Mathias 366
PARIS Sandi 360

PARISH Isabella 58
PARK PRODUCTION, Moscow 260
PARKER 199
PARKER Grant 95
PARKER John 177
PARR Adrian 277
PARTIZAN, London 36, 58, 86
PARTL Patrik 283
PASAMONTES Gabriel 349
PASSION PICTURES, London 54
PASTOR Montse 136, 137, 141
PATANKAR Kalpesh 32, 135
PATEL Shishir 200, 218
PATEMAN Paul 250
PATERSON Michael 107, 314, 315
PATIL Makarand 157
PATNI Tejal 37, 185
PATNI Tina 192
PATRAMANIS Harry 247
PATTEX 156, 162, 163, 324
PATZNER Henning 196, 202, 206
PÄTZOLD Patricia 118, 203, 207
PAULI Andreas 293, 294, 303, 306, 307
PAULIK Vlasto 101
PAULIN Carl-Johan 316
PAUSE LJUD & BILD 87, 331
PAY Egil 246
PEARSE Simon 208
PECHLIVANIDIS Nikos 41
PEDERSEN Per 107, 314, 315
PEDIGREE 24
PENICAUD Pierre 51
PENICAUT Alban 109, 127
PENNINGS Serge 109
PENSE Jacques 211
PENZO Sergio 216, 298
PEPE Federico 184, 189
PEPSI 59, 61, 331
PEQUEÑO Julita 242
PERARNAUD Edouard 241
PEREZ David 36
PÉREZ-SOLERO Pablo 320
PERFECT FOOLS, Stockholm 388
PERRIER 57
PERRONET- MILLER Karena 96
PERRY Joanna 110, 386
PERRY Mike 342
PERRY Rob 173
PERSSON Ola 369
PERSSON Ted 366, 369
PERSSON Thomas 168
PETERSEN Rasmus 188
PETERSEN Sascha 268
PETRI Anne 310, 379
PEUGEOT 212, 226, 315
PEULECKE Bert 149, 171, 199, 204, 207, 219, 222, 290, 310, 320, 322, 338
PFARR Bjoern 25
PFUND Julia 152
PHILIPP UND KEUNTJE, Hamburg 217, 308, 332
PHILIPS 164
PICKERING Clive 208
PICKMANN Anatolij 146
PIEBENGA Piebe 103
PIHL Alexander 89, 296
PIHL Johan 234
PIKASSO 295
PIN Greg 365
PINGUET Hugues 292
PINTAUDE Giovanni 127
PIONEER Kuro 365
PIONEER PRODUCTIONS, Buenos Aires 98
PIONEER, Budapest 69
PIRÁMIDE, Madrid 136
PIRSCH Anna-Marina 310, 379
PITKÄNEN Pasi 77
PLAN.NET, Hamburg 317, 384
PLATINUM 127
PLAYGROUND 316
PLOJ Michael 306
PLUECKHAHN Michael 59
PLUMET Hervé 150, 151
POILLOT Nicolas 330
POLARGUARD 193
POLAT Karpat 114, 148
PONTACQ Nicolas 52
POPLE Rebecca 110
POPP Martin 124
PORST Soeren 278
PORT Lisa 208
PORTE Dominique 144
PORTIUS Jan 43, 257, 275
PORTUGUESE LEAGUE AGAINST AIDS 112
POSTEN 285, 287
POTTER Claudi 144
POTTHIÉ SPERRY Florence 144
POU Edu 375, 391
POWELL Carol 48
POZANTZIS Thanassis 41
PRADHAN Prasad 134
PRALONG Franck 109
PREMIÉRE HEURE, Paris 220
PREMUTICO Leo 194
PRESKOW Len 373
PRESSMAN Nadav 27
PREST George 85, 86, 327
PRIEST Ben 288
PRIM Sven 87, 331
PRINGLES 39
PRIOR David 330
PROCHAZKA David 130
PROKOPETZ Felicitas 298

PROPACH Jan 204
PROTEFIX 170
PRZEPIORSKA-KOTLINSKA Iza 243
PSL SWISS MILK PRODUCERS 43
PSYOP, New York 48, 56
PTT, Istanbul 244
PUBLICIS CONSEIL, Paris 51, 64, 69, 72, 119, 150, 151, 183, 186
PUBLICIS EAD, Sofia 258
PUBLICIS GROUP AUSTRIA, Vienna 69
PUBLICIS HEALTHCARE, Amsterdam 276
PUBLICIS QMP, Dublin 248
PUBLICIS ROMANIA, Bucharest 273
PUBLICIS YORUM, Istanbul 244
PUBLICIS, Amsterdam 276, 377, 388
PUBLICIS, Frankfurt 187
PUBLICIS, Helsinki 259, 266
PUBLICIS, Stockholm 129
PUERTAS Gonzalo 136, 141
PUIG Carles 381
PUIG Mireia 103
PÜPÜLEK Enis 357
PURDIE James 305
PURVIS Ivo 116
QUAD, Paris 232
QUEER-TRAVEL.DE 82
QUENNOY Eric 182, 184, 375, 380, 391
QUERCUS 108
QUEST Tim 73
QUIKSILVER 188
QUIN Laurence 37, 304
QUINTANA Raquel 242
QUINTERO Cadmo 67
RABBIT @ BONKERS, New York 184
RABENSTEIN Djamila 50, 282, 382
RACHEL Philippe 192
RADICAL MEDIA, Berlin 220
RADIO CONTACT 267
RAILLARD Thomas 56
RAINEY KELLY CAMPBELL ROALFE/Y&R, London 216, 232, 381
RAJU Sunil 240
RAMBRIDGE Chris 289, 319
RAMM Oliver 217, 308, 332
RAMOVIC Imelda 348
RAMS Bartek 66
RAMSEY Russell 36, 37, 304
RAPETTI Ermenegildo 174
RAPIRA 166
RAPOSO Leandro 56, 76, 179
RATTIGAN Simon 134
RATTLING STICK, London 64, 174, 218
RAUFMANN Hendrik 322
RAUN SOFAS 147
RAUSCHER Tabea 262, 302
RAVENSBURGER 309
RAY Gordon 208
RAYMENT Richard 275, 276
RBK, Stockholm 234
REBBOT Guillaume 142
RECHTACEK Wulf 204, 301
RECKEWEG Lena 230
RECUENCO Eugenio 159
RED BEE MEDIA, London 232, 381
REDDINGTON Paul 386
REDMAN BIELKE Helena 360
REES Barney 169
REFORMA ADVERTISING, Sofia 104
REGAN Noah 23, 94, 202
REICHERT Arnulf 309
REICHL-SCHEBESTA Gerda 263
REIDENBACH Felix 227
REILAND Gösta 362
REINHARDT Michael 39
REISENBÜCHLER Arno 114
REISS Alexander 162, 204, 223, 269
REISSINGER Michael 208
REMUZAT Fred 109
RENAULT 350
RENDAL Kimble 233
RENDEL Thomas 268
RENKEL Harald 318
REPO Olli 270
REPSOL 220
RESTYLANE 169
REUILLY Christian 326, 387
REUTERSKIÖLD Patrik 155
REVELL Giles 95
REXHAUSEN Jan 196, 216, 298
REXONA 389
REYNOLDS 197
REYNOLDS Cat 182, 391
REYS Olaf 180, 181
RFSU 175, 360, 368
RICE Simon 61, 271, 331
RICHARD Stéphane 78, 238
RICHARDS Samantha 55
RICHAU Daniel 364
RICHTER Andreas 325
RICHTER Ralf 253
RIISER Andreas 66, 67
RINALDO Daniel 29
RINGER Mark 328
RIPOSA 302
RISSO Giada 378
RITTENBRUCH Markus 226, 230
RIVOLLIER Gilles 349
RIX Adam 352
ROALFE Mark 216, 232, 381
ROBBE Arnout 276
ROBERTSSON Mia 373, 387
ROBIN WOOD 297
ROBINSON Stuart 165
ROCA DE VIÑALS José Maria 202

ROCHOW Silke 210
ROCK PAPER SCISSORS 338
ROCKY ADVERTISING, Helsinki 174
RODEN Ralph 281
RODRIGUEZ BOUZAS Francisco 377
RODRÍGUEZ Carolina 137
RODRIGUEZ Sergio 22, 174, 327
RODRÍGUEZ Vicente 136, 137
ROE Ger 243
ROEMMELT Peter 118, 279
ROESINGER Stefan 162, 344
ROGUE, London 307
RÖLL Anke 301
ROMAHN Fransisco 375
ROMAN Torsten 309
ROMENSKY Eugeny 166
ROMEYKO Jason 69
ROMSTAD Bendik 368
RÖNNBÄCK AF LULEÅ Ulf 234
ROSAM Thorsten 325
ROSE Annika 143
ROSE Keith 98, 256
ROSE Simeon 371
ROSENBERGER Kirsten 76
ROSENGREN Josefine 108
ROSENKAMP Fred 276
ROSSELLI Stefano 215, 245
ROSSI GUIDO Alberto 158
ROTEM Judy 42
ROWEN SPEAKERS 133
ROY Kourtney 330
ROYAL DUTCH ARMY 388
ROYAL MAIL 271
ROYER Frédéric 64, 69, 150, 186
ROYER Jean-Christophe 212
ROZZI Pino 184, 186, 189, 233
RSA FILMS, New York 381
RSA, London 110
RUCKI Jérome 220
RUCKWIED Christopher 220
RUDOLPH Helen 333
RUEBENIAN Peter 179
RUEHMANN Lars 350, 367
RUF LANZ WERBEAGENTUR, Zurich 86, 89, 92, 105, 261, 286
RUF Markus 86, 89, 92, 105, 261, 286
RUGGIERI Eustachio 245
RUNNERS POINT 196
RUOLA Eka 270
RUSSELL Mike 37
RUSSO Fabrizio 33
RÜTHEMANN Andreas 43, 163, 257, 275
RUUD Christian 368
RUUD Thorbjørn 247
RUZICKA Daniel 255
RYDHOLM Charlotta 366
SAAB 215, 365
SAATCHI & SAAATCHI RUSSIA, Moscow 165
SAATCHI & SAATCHI EUROPE 69
SAATCHI & SAATCHI SIMKO, Geneva 173, 177
SAATCHI & SAATCHI, Beirut 104
SAATCHI & SAATCHI, Brussels 121, 178
SAATCHI & SAATCHI, Copenhagen 188, 321
SAATCHI & SAATCHI, Frankfurt 177, 310, 379
SAATCHI & SAATCHI, London 73, 157, 167, 305, 342
SAATCHI & SAATCHI, Milan 173, 177
SAATCHI & SAATCHI, Paris 220
SABINA STOBRAWE 309
SABO Klaudija 367
SACCO Jean-Francois 225, 241
SADAKANE Gen 171
SÆTHER Henrik 25
SÆTRE Gry 66
SAHBAZ Gokce 153
SAIEGH Santiago 242
SAIZ Peru 141
SAKAN Dragan 195, 263
SALGADO Manolo 226
SALVADOR-D 260
SALVAGGIO Giovanni 177
SALZMANN Eva 130
SAMAAN Tarek 282
SAMARITANS 126, 307
SAMMALISTO Vesa 77
SAMSUNG 136
SÁNCHEZ Juan 136, 137, 141
SANDERSON Ella 86
SANDIN Mats 370
SANDS Mike 281
SANITERPEN 159
SANROMA Bernat 36
SANTAISABEL Guillermo 312
SANTANA Jonathan 113
SASOL 256
SATTEN Eric 29
SAVANNA 48
SAVE THE CHILDREN 125
SAVIC Slavisa 195
SAVIDES Harris 381
SAWARD Adam 307
SAX Jo 205
SCALABRE Aurélie 224
SCHAFFARCZYK Till 141
SCHAPKA René 376
SCHEIBEL Tim 365
SCHEMMANN Frank 180
SCHILDT Claudia 216, 298
SCHILL Alexander 185, 247, 317, 345, 384
SCHILLING Nele 210
SCHIMMER Florian 231, 297, 332
SCHINDLER Heribert 145
SCHIPPER Sebastian 220
SCHLAEFLE Marcel 92, 261

SCHLAFFER Andrea 375
SCHMERBERG Ralf 154
SCHMID Thomas 193
SCHMIDT Christiane 225
SCHMIDT Heiko 92
SCHMIDT Jesper 147, 198, 209
SCHMIDT Matthias 92, 170, 325. 333
SCHMIDT Sönke 217, 308, 332
SCHMIDT Stefan 50, 282, 311, 318, 343, 382
SCHMIEGE Ulrike 67
SCHMIEGEL Thomas 313
SCHMITE Gérald 199
SCHMITT Christophe 51
SCHMITT Nicolas 51
SCHMITZ Kathrin 369
SCHMUCK Ragnar 311
SCHMUCKER Florian 269
SCHNABEL Michael 253
SCHNEIDER Susi 325
SCHNEIDER Wolf 108, 380
SCHNEIDER Wolfgang 71, 102, 170, 196, 220, 289
SCHNEIDERS Julian 46
SCHOEB Thomas 105, 261, 286
SCHOEFFLER Eric 149, 162, 168, 226, 230, 269, 324
SCHOLZ & FRIENDS INTERACTIVE, Hamburg 369
SCHOLZ & FRIENDS, Berlin 108, 146, 262, 302, 309, 380
SCHOLZ & FRIENDS, Hamburg 82, 92, 170, 325, 333
SCHOLZ Erik 282
SCHÖNHERR Peter 149, 301
SCHOONMAKER Thelma 381
SCHRADER Fabian 301
SCHRADER Sven 207, 219
SCHRAKE Maik 168
SCHRAMM Stephanie 375
SCHREGENBERGER Felix 105
SCHREIBAUER Susanna 303
SCHRENK Cordula 86
SCHREPFER Urs 133
SCHRÖDER Wolfgang 364
SCHROEDER Anna-Kristina 208
SCHROER Patrick 345
SCHUCHARDT Vera 280
SCHÜLLER Irina 116
SCHULTE Alexandra 152
SCHULTE Stefan 149, 171, 199, 204, 207, 219, 222, 290, 310, 320, 322, 338
SCHULTZ Micke 76, 279
SCHULZ Stefan 306
SCHUMACHER Jennifer 93, 154
SCHUMANN Ulrike 345
SCHUPP Jonathan 185
SCHÜRMANN Svenja 375
SCHUTTE Edsard 267
SCHWAB Florian 283
SCHWARZKOPF 168, 171
SCHWEDER Hendrik 311, 318, 343
SCHWEIGERT Irina 180
SCHWIEDRZIK Boris 170
SCHWINGELER Marie-Theres 39, 179
SCI-FI CHANNEL 232, 384
SCORSESE Martin 381
SCOTCH MAGIC TAPE 158
SCOTTEX 284
SCOTTING Harry 379
SCP, Gothenburg 252
SCRABBLE 249, 253, 337
SCRASE Bertie 304
SEAGULLS FLY, Rio de Janeiro 108
SEAT 209
SEGA 220
SEGRETO RESTAURANT 281
SEIDL CHOCOLATES 38
SELMORE, Amsterdam 44, 231
SELZER Toni 201
SENGERS Martijn 364
SENITSCHNIG Daniel 283
SENTRIX GLOBAL HEALTH COMMUNICATION, Milan 274
SEPPANEN Jouni 231
SEQUEIRA Susana 116, 213, 272
SERHATI Jehona 318
SEROUSSI Laurent 52
SETTESOLDI Giovanni 39, 159
SETZKORN Stefan 92, 170, 325, 333
SEUPEL Kathrin 143
SEWELL Andy 307
SHALMOR AVNON AMICHAY\Y&R INTERACTIVE, Tel Aviv 27, 72, 93, 299
SHAVIT Asi 171
SHEARER Paul 390
SHILO, New York 381
SHORE Ed 358
SHORTALL Greg 373
SHOTS 270
SHULDESHOV Jean 136
SHUMENSKO BEER 354
SIANI Stefania 184, 189
SIANO Luca 378
SIDHOM Saher 366
SIEBELT Christoph 306
SIEBENHAAR Dirk 102, 144
SIEGER Michael 209
SIEMENS 258, 333
SIERS Nicole 364
SIEVERS Martin 177
SIGL Florian 208
SIJMONS Tom 377
SILBER Joachim 119, 162, 344
SILBURN Paul 73, 157, 167, 232, 305, 342, 381
SILVA German 63, 77, 175, 226, 329
SILVER CROSS 352

SILVEY Scott 157, 342
SILZ Dirk 325
SIMION Lucian 299
SIMON Andreas 86
SIMON Philip 290
SINGSTOCK Elissa 184
SIPSAK Asu 244
SIRONI Laura 63, 329
SIRRY Shahir 204, 269
SISOMO, Copenhagen 321
SITJAR Xavi 202
SJÖDIN Anders 91
SJÖGREN Jens 108
SJÖVALL Jonas 285
SKAFF Philippe 233
SKÄRHEDEN Fredrik 359
SKARLAND Gunnar 76, 279
SKOG Johan 388
SKRABAL Philipp 235
SKY ITALY 233
SLIVKA Vlado 139
SLUIJTER Marco 293
SMART 210, 211, 280, 313
SMINT 36
SMITH Baker 66
SMITH Dave 58, 184
SMITH Xander 113
SMITS Jan-Willem 267
SMYTHE Rupert 110, 132, 172
SNCF 83
SNELDERS Daniel 101
SNELS Kristof 102, 291
SOARES Rui 213
SOCIAL CLUB, Stockholm 100
SÖDERLIND Felix 88
SÖDERLUND Steve 266
SÖDERQUIST Kalle 359
SÖDRA CELL 290
SOLAR Waldmann 144
SOLIDARITÉS 125
SOMMER Christian 176, 374
SONNEVELD Ruben 101, 286
SONNTAGS ZEITUNG 233, 235
SONNY, London 46, 109, 164, 166, 184, 233
SONY 132, 134, 136, 137, 140, 141, 264, 265
SOSSIDI Constantin 118, 203, 206, 207
SOTOMAYOR Alvaro 391
SPACE PATROL, Paris 109
SPAETGENS Matthias 108, 146, 262, 302, 309, 380
SPARKASSE 102
SPECSAVERS, Guernsey 172, 174
SPECTAB 390
SPEERS FILMS, Dublin 248
SPEERS Jonny 248
SPENGLER-AHRENS Dörte 196, 216, 298
SPILLMANN Martin 43, 321
SPILLMANN/FELSER/LEO BURNETT, Zurich 43, 321
SPINIFEX, Sydney 233
SPITALNY Alexandra 347
SPITZER Andy 275
SPRACHLABOR AUDIOPRODUKTIONEN, Düsseldorf 324
SPRUNG Frank 210
SQUIBB Vince 101, 111, 232, 381
SROKA Ryszard 390
SRV CONSTRUCTION 259
ST. CLAIR Bruce 208
ST. M. LEUX Emmanuel 208
STABEL Sverre 368
STADLER Charley 86
STADTMÜLLER David 375
STAKE Anders 182, 391
STALDER Andreas 293, 294, 303
STAMENKOVIC Jole 176
STANDEN Jamie 192
STANDKE Kathleen 376
STANEVIČIUS Rimantas 295
STANNERS Kate 73, 157, 167, 305, 342
STANZSKA Beatrice 290
STARCK Hans 262, 302, 350
STARK Landry 237
STARRING, Stockholm 373, 387
STAUDINGER Robert 33, 263
STAUSBERG Sven 310, 379
STEDMAN Poppy 353
STEFAN KRANEFELD IMAGING, Duesseldorf 59
STEFFEN Eike 324
STEFFENS Steffen 180, 193
STEGER Peter 306, 307
STEIMAN Rouven 332
STEIMATZKY BOOK STORES 93
STEIN Björn 111
STEINER Roman 114
STEINHILBER Jan 258
STEINKEMPER Markus 201, 210
STELLA 46
STELLER Sebastian 210
STEMMLE Eugen 76
STENBERG Henrik 100
STENBERG Mats 246
STENSRUD Eirik 66
STERN 312
STERR Gerhard 347
STEVENSON Mal 46, 48, 52
STEWART Clive 163
STIEGL 361
STIERL Annika 309, 369
STIGHÄLL Roger 371
STIHL 150, 151
STILLACCI Andrea 39, 90, 159
STILLER Mathias 71, 102, 170, 196, 220, 289
STINK, Berlin 154
STINK, London 48, 56, 101
STÖCKER Ramona 382

STOFFER Julia 278
STOLL Christian 226, 230
STOLZ Patricia 369
STORÅKERS McCANN, Stockholm 70, 155, 248, 369
STORATH Matthias 93, 154
STORGAARD Martin 49, 58, 191, 198
STORIES 356
STÖVER Birgit 118
STRADA 195
STRAUSS Oskar 196
STRAUSS Peter 253
STREICH Norbert 209
STREPSILS 175
STREULI Felix 105
STRICKER Christoph 202, 206
STRICKER Pablo 56, 76
STRIEGL Robert 114
STRINGER André 381
STRINNHED Mikael 149
STRUHAR Vladislav 101
STÜBANE Tim 149, 171, 204, 222, 301, 320
STUDIO AKA, London 48
STUDIO BEERLING 35
STUDIO BRUSSEL 300
STUDIO FUNK, Berlin 322
STUDIO FUNK, Hamburg 323
STUDIO INTERNATIONAL, Zagreb 341
STUDIO Ros 327
STUEBLER Dominic 162, 344
STUESSEL Therese 258
STULZ Martin 233, 235
STURGESS Sarah 157
STÜSSEL Therese 227, 247
STUTTERHEIM Alexander 387
STYLEWAR 101, 212
SUB MOVIE CHANNEL 231
SUETIN Julian 165
SUGAR POWER, Zurich 207
SULZBACH Martin 46, 382
SUNDBERG Carl 100
SUNDIN Mats 385
SUNDQVIST Marcus 108
SURFRIDER FOUNDATION 120, 349
SVENSSON Magnus 370
SVIRLOCH Matus 101
SWEDENBORG Jakob 365
SWEDISH INSTITUTE OF ASSISTIVE TECHNOLOGY 337
SWEDISH RAILWAYS 80, 81
SWEDISH STANDARDS INSTITUTE 337
SWEDISH TV LICENCE FEE 108
SWIFT MEGA COURIERS 286
SWISTOWSKI Joanna 278
SYDOW Pedro 170
SYSTEM INTERNATIONAL 66
SYZYGY, Bad Homburg 364
SZCZEPOCKI Adam 390
SZEPESI Melinda 69
SZTANSKA Beatrice 370
TABARES Esteban 137
TAILOR Tracey 233
TAIVAS, Helsinki 329
TALSO Micol 186, 189
TAMBOURGI Sally 192
TANG Patrick 377
TANGEN Jarle 67
TANK/Y&R, Stockholm 29
TANTRUM PRODUCTIONS, London 66
TARABILDA Rokas 295
TARIFA Moez 197
TAROUX Philippe 24, 160
TARPY Hugh 251, 319
TATE BRITAIN 251, 319
TATTOLI Williams 177
TÄUBNER Armin 105
TAVAN Christoph 367
TAVIDDE Joerg 180
TBWA\ESPAÑA, Madrid 136, 137, 141
TBWA\GERMANY, Berlin 46, 50, 282, 311, 318, 343, 382
TBWA\HONG KONG 328
TBWA\ISTANBUL 26, 227
TBWA\ITALIA, Milan 29
TBWA\MAP, Paris 52, 109, 127
TBWA\PARIS 24, 83, 88, 109, 113, 160, 161, 176, 366
TBWA\PHS, Helsinki 231, 248, 270
TBWA\VIENNA 263
TCM 242
TEAV Lang 363, 387
TEICHNER Fabien 144, 229
TELE2 68, 71, 324
TELEMAZ COMMERCIALS, Hamburg 76
TELENOR 370
TELIA 70
TELZIR 275
TÉMIN Frédéric 190, 234
TEMPELOU Eleni 247
TENNEMANN Kay 375
TEQUILA\London 358
TER HAAR Bart 388
TESA PACK 162, 344
TEULINGKX Jan 121, 178
TG4 248
THANDI Kulbir 217
THE DAILY TELEGRAPH 288
THE FAN CLUB, Malmö 168
THE GANG FILMS, Madrid 202
THE JUPITER DRAWING ROOM, Cape Town 256
THE PRODUCERS, Cairo 228
THE ROYAL SWEDISH OPERA 251
THE SYNDICATE, Athens 41
THEDENS Ina 124
THEIL Jens 231, 297, 332
THENENBACH Anno 180
THEROIN Magnus 100
THESE DAYS, Antwerp 365
THEY, Amsterdam 313

THIEDE Patrick 53, 255
THIEL Nina 374
THIEL Tim 255
THIELE Thomas 180, 193
THIES Viola 311
THIRACHE Sylvain 66, 144, 224, 229, 342
THITO Philippe 145
THOMAS Jeff 109
THOMAZ Lourenço 116, 213, 272
THOMPSON Carmel 277
THOMSEN Axel 185, 317, 345, 384
THORELIUS Jessica 370
THOROGOOD Julie 256
THORPE Ingrid 371
THUE Cecilie 40, 246, 247
THUY Michael 365
THWAITES Peter 46, 166
THYBAUD Denis 292
TIDE 294
TIETURI BUSINESS COURSES 266
TIJI TV 342
TILLMANNS, OGILVY & MATHER, Düsseldorf 340
TIMMERMANS Madelieve 365
TIMNEY John 275, 276
TINE MILK 40
TISCHER Axel 262, 290, 302
TITMARSH Sharon 48
TJOENG Dennis 211
T-MOBILE 67, 69, 73
TOADER Liviu 299
TOEPLITZ Franciszek 390
TOEPPER Markus 280
TOKIB, Paris 66
TOM Patrick 328
TOMCIC Daniel 38
TONCAFÉ STUDIOS 325
TORNÉRHIELM Linn 366
TORRES Fran 56, 76
TORVINEN Mikko 231, 248
TOSCANA Agostino 173, 177
TOTAL 220
TOWERS Dave 85, 327
TRABBOR 62
TRABOULSI Rami 121
TRACY Douglas 288
TRAKTOR 36
TRANSPORT FOR LONDON 110
TRAVIS Kevin 319
TREHMER STUDIO, Moscow 260
TRIANTAFYLLOU FILIMONAS 112
TRICOT Rémy 236
TRIDENT FRESH 36
TRIERVEILER Emiliano 311
TRIGGER HAPPY PRODUCTIONS, Berlin 154
TRITSCH Fabian 208
TROMBITAS Tanja 263
TROMM Friedrich 239
TROPICANA 63
TROTH Damon 110, 386
TRUMBACH Katharina 351, 355
TRY ADVERTISING AGENCY, Oslo 40, 246, 247
TRY Kjetil 40
TRYGG-HANSA 373
TSAKNAKIS Gregory 350
TSKHOVREBOVA Alina 165
TUCZEK Lena 211
TURGUL Kurtcebe 139
TURNER Dan 373
TURNER David 353, 357
TURNER DUCKWORTH, London & San Francisco 353, 357
TWIG Yariv 72, 299
UDDENBERG Magnus 29
UGGLA Lolo 388
UHU 152
UK DEPARTMENT FOR TRANSPORT 304, 323
ULICNY Rasto 101
ULLENIUS Andreas 87, 175, 285, 287, 331, 368
ULLOA Carlos 369
ULRICH Ferdinand 262, 302
U-MAN, Paris 109
UNCLE GREY, Aarhus 107, 314, 315
UNDÉHN Erik 99, 388
UNICEF 111, 306, 307, 384
UNO BREAD 26
UPSET, Athens 74, 247
US MEDIA, Amsterdam 389
UYTDENHOUWEN Bart 389
VACHEROT Sébastien 52, 109, 127, 366
VACULIK ADVERTISING, Bratislava 246
VALE LAURA May 163
VALENT Roman 246
VALENZUELA Sebastian 156
VALERI Massimo 221
VAN BAELEN Lieven 88
VAN BEECK Kris 63, 222
VAN BERKEL Carsten 284
VAN BERKEL Danielle 231
VAN DE KERCKHOVE Patricia 300
VAN DE LOO Jo 185
VAN DE VIJFEIJKEN Maarten 35
VAN DEN BROECK Joeri 300
VAN DEN VALENTYN Birgit 149, 171, 204, 222, 301, 320
VAN DER LANS Robert 101, 286
VAN DER MERWE Schalk 48
VAN DER PLAS Massimo 388
VAN DER SCHOOT Johan 370
VAN DER STRAATEN Violet 44
VAN DER VAEREN Manoëlle 52, 109, 127
VAN DER WERFF Mark 389
VAN DIJK Darre 103
VAN ELK Joris 35
VAN GOETHEM Bart 205
VAN KEMPEN Maarten 293
VAN OECKEL Johan 205

VAN PELT Poppe 44, 231
VAN PRAAG SIGAAR Joost 270
VAN VENROOIJ Frank 365
VAN ZWAM Jeroen 276, 377, 388
VANCE Tim 367
VANHELLE Arnaud 249, 337
VANHOOF Dieter 300
VANISH 163
VARETZ Ingrid 161
VARGHESE Jomy 37
VASSILIEV Artem 136
VÄSTRA VETINARY CLINIC 285
VATER Patrick 382
VAVAKIS Nikos 247
VCCP, London 111
VEAL Jay 200
VEDFELDT Klavs 147
VEGA OLMOS PONCE, Buenos Aires 166
VEGARS Albert 231
VEGESTORY 361
VELJKOVIC Ivana 263
VELOCITY FILMS, Cape Town 48, 98, 208, 256
VELOCITY FILMS, Johannesburg 144
VELUX 145
VENIKOV Dmitry 260
VENS Stephan 154
VERHEIJEN Erik-Jan 184
VERMAERKEN Caroline 389
VERMEYLEN Patrick 178
VERRONE Max 215
VERVROEGEN Erik 24, 83, 88, 109, 113, 160, 161, 176
VESCOVI Silvana 274
VETTER Gerhard 246
VETTURI Lorenzo 189
VICHY 170
VICINI Valentina 378
VIDELA Pablo 73
VIERA Sara 108, 380
VIGORELLI Gianpietro 259
VIKING 151
VILADRICH Alex 356
VILASECA Clara 77
VILLARD Rickard 125
VIRTUAL REPUBLIC, Düsseldorf 246
VISSER Anton 144
VITAMIN Well 357
VITKON Ariel 31
VITRUVIO LEO BURNETT, Madrid 242
VIZNER Scheffold 235
VOGEL Stephan 76, 115, 124
VOGTMANN Ilka 38
VOIGT Thorsten 152
VOITINSKY Alex 166
VOLKSWAGEN 200, 202, 203, 204, 205, 207, 208, 219, 221, 222, 223, 224, 310, 320, 364, 338
VOLTAREN 177
VOLVO 209, 305, 364, 390
VON BAEHR Ola 155, 369
VON CORSWANT Jacob 251
VON LIEBENSTEIN Johannes 46, 382
VON MÜHLENDAHL Paul 312
VON REIS Christoffer 32
VON SCHEVEN Burkhart 177, 310
VON SEHERR-THOß Julien 71
VON WERDER Malin 370
VON ZITZEWITZ Friedrich 317, 384
VONDERSTEIN Stefan 180, 181
VONTOBEL Nicolas 133
VRDOLJAK Andre 144, 330
VS ENERGY INTERNATIONAL UKRAINE 346
VUÇITËRNA Yll 318
VUIK Pim 206
VURAL Tunay 244
WAAIJENBERG Albert 84
WÄCHTER & WÄCHTER, Bremen 43, 163, 257, 275
WAERNESS Jens-Petter 309
WAGNER Reginald 351, 355
WAHL Nico 67
WAHL Viktor 289
WAHLGREN David 370
WAITROSE 353
WALDER Pascal 102
WALKER Adam 307
WALKER Pius 109, 377
WALKER, Zurich 109, 377
WALLIN Josephine 80, 81
WALLSTRÖM Daniel 371
WALTER Andreas 211
WAN-BAU Woof 194
WANDA, Paris 34, 64, 69, 212
WARD Helena 365
WARD-TAGGART Shirley 373
WARSOP Graham 256
WATERKAMP Hermann 145
WATERS Patrick 387
WATERSWIDGREN\TBWA, Stockholm 32, 357, 387
WCRS, London 110, 166
WEBER Knut 88
WEBER Marco 76, 115
WEBER Timm 82
WEBER Veronika 163
WEDDERBURN Ben 352
WEDL Karin 33
WEIGERTPIROUZWOLF, Hamburg 82
WEITZENBAUER Frank 227, 247, 258
WELLS Mike 134
WENDT Lennert 208
WENHOLD Philipp 298
WERNER Axinja 375
WERNER Martin 58, 209
WERRING OTNES Caroline 66
WERU WINDOWS 146
WESTERBEEK Fleur 389
WESTMORE Lucy 200, 218
WESTRA Niels 297

WETZEL Kathrin 380
WHEATER Kristian 288
WICKNERTZ Lotta 324
WIDGREN Kalle 32
WIDMAN Sofia 387
WIEDEMANN Joerg 309
WIEDEN+KENNEDY, Amsterdam 54, 58, 182, 184, 375, 380, 391
WIENDIECK Jan 145
WIENTZEK Marc 84
WIJKMARK Henning 370
WIKTOR LEO BURNETT, Bratislava 139
WILDE Johan 370
WILHELMI Anna 82
WILLEN David 43
WILLIAMS Christian 55
WILLIAMS Craig 391
WILLIAMS Jon 110, 386
WILLIAMS Lesley 166
WILLIAMS Rebecca 357
WILLIAMS Steve 216
WILLISON Dennis 73
WILLMOTT Howard 37
WILMERTS Eddy 129
WILSON Camilla 106
WINBERG Tomi 259, 266
WINBLADH Cilla 366
WINKLBAUER Thomas 86
WINKLER & NOAH 33
WINSCHEWSKI Anke 116, 214, 215
WINTHER Jerker 316, 368
WISSING Jocke 366, 369
WITTING Lennart 289
WOISCHKE Mareike 375
WOLANY Grit 89, 286
WOLCH Anthony 259, 266
WOLF Marilyn 230
WOLFE Daniel 307
WOLFF Benjamin 108
WOLFF Ricardo 199, 207, 219
WOLLRAB Maik 263
WONDERBOYS FILM, Munich 152
WONDERBRA 183, 186, 187
WONG Jeremy 135
WOOD Orlando 54
WOODFINE Helena 48, 208
WOOLER Simon 188, 321
WORLD AIDS DAY 112
WORLD VISION 379
WRANGLER 191
WRETBLAD Magnus 365
WÜBBE Stefan 269
WUESTHOF DREIZACKWERK 325
WWF 107, 119, 312
XENAKIS Yannis 350
XENICAL 277
XHAFERI Valon 318
XIBERRAS Stéphane 232, 236, 237, 292, 384
YAISH Fadi 32, 135, 157
YAKOBOWITCH Danny 156
YAKUSHEVA Tatiana 159
YAKUSHINA Maria 166, 260
YALGIN Levent 148
YAMMINE Georges 197
YAQU Pacha 374
YEDIDYA Matan 27
YELLOW PAGES 65, 299
YLITALO Kari 77
YOM Bill 116, 214, 215
YOUNES Samer 104
YOUNESS Tameem 228
YOUNG & RUBICAM, Frankfurt 325
YOUNG & RUBICAM, Madrid 220
YOUNG & RUBICAM, Paris 117, 120, 192, 334, 349
YOUNG & RUBICAM, Prague 255
YOUNG DIRECTOR AWARD 270
YPERLAAN Ernst 293
YURKO GUTSULYAK GRAPHIC DESIGN, Kiev 346
ZACKARI Brita 155
ZAMBALDI Paolo 186
ZANDVOORT Elsbeth 377
ZANINELLO Paolo 233
ZARAMPOUKAS Christos 376
ZATORSKI Darek 29
ZBIOK 337
ZBORALSKI Oliver 118, 203, 206, 207
ZEH Thorsten 294
ZEILER Andrea 347
ZELIKOVICH Asaf 45, 47
ZELL Fabian 216, 298
ZENELI Artan 318
ZETHNER Christian 49, 58, 68
ZETTERBERG Mikael 366
ZETTERHOLM Emma 360
ZHANG Jue 50, 382
ZIACO Letizia 259
ZILLIGEN Ralf 179, 210, 211, 280, 288, 313
ZINIC Nikola 348, 360
ZINK Anke Vera 115
ZINKE Gerrit 231, 297, 332
ZIPPER Tani 27
ZOETE Bouke 121, 178
ZOLL Dorothee 364
ZONNEN Michael 56
ZOTA Catalin 299
ZOUBEK Dan 196
ZOURAVLIOV Vania 196
ZUCKERMAN Craig 199
ZUELKE David 367
ZUENKELER Ulrich 268, 269
ZÜRICH CHAMBER ORCHESTRA 246
& CO., Copenhagen 49, 58, 147, 191, 198, 209, 341
.START, Munich 25, 323
123FLEUR.COM 90
13TH STREET 236, 237, 289
1861 UNITED, Milan 184, 186, 189, 233
2 AM, London 49